REGINALD W. BIBBY

holds the Board of Governors Research Chair in the Department of Sociology at the University of Lethbridge. Born and raised in Edmonton, he received his Ph.D. in sociology from Washington State University. He also has degrees in sociology from the

University of Alberta (B.A.) and the University of Calgary (M.A.), and a theology degree (B.D.) from Southern Seminary in Louisville. For more than three decades, he has been monitoring social trends in Canada through a series of well-known, *Project Canada* national surveys of adults and teenagers. These surveys are producing historic, unparalleled trend data, and have been described by colleagues and the media as "a national treasure."

Widely recognized as one of Canada's leading experts on religious and social trends, Professor Bibby has presented his findings in North America, Europe, Australia, and Japan, speaking at universities including UBC, Alberta, Manitoba, McMaster, Queen's, Toronto, Acadia, Oxford, Notre Dame, and Harvard.

His explicit commitment to taking his work beyond the academic community has resulted in his making a very large number of public appearances, having a high media profile, and writing twelve best-selling books that to date have sold more than 150,000 copies. In recognition of his outstanding contribution to the nation, the Governor General appointed him an Officer of the Order of Canada in 2006.

Also by Reginald W. Bibby

The Emerging Millennials, 2009

The Boomer Factor, 2006

Restless Churches, 2004

Restless Gods, 2002

Canada's Teens, 2001

The Bibby Report, 1995

There's Got to Be More!, 1995

Unknown Gods, 1993

Teen Trends (with Donald Posterski), 1992

Mosaic Madness, 1990

Fragmented Gods, 1987

The Emerging Generation (with Donald Posterski), 1985

Martia Moser

BEYOND THE GODS
&
BACK

*Religion's
Demise and Rise
and Why It Matters*

Reginald W. Bibby

Project Canada Books

Copyright © 2011 by Reginald W. Bibby

All rights reserved. No part of this publication may be
reproduced or transmitted in any form or by any means,
electronic or mechanical, including photocopying, recording, or
any information storage and retrieval system without permission
in writing from Project Canada Books,
www.projectcanadabooks.com.

A Project Canada Book
Lethbridge AB

Distributed by:

Project Canada Books
www.projectcanadabooks.com

Wood Lake Books
www.woodlakebooks.com

and

Novalis
www.novalis.ca

ISBN 978-0-98-106142-9

Canadian Cataloguing in Publication data available from
Library and Archives Canada

Design: Reginald W. Bibby

Editing and Index: Donna McCloskey

Printed and bound in Canada by
University of Lethbridge Printing Services

**To Doc Watts, Don Burke,
Armand Mauss, and Rodney Stark**

*Four exceptional people who
put their stamp on my work and life*

Contents

Takes on the Past, Present, and Future

"The present must have become the past
before one can win from it
points of vantage
from which to gauge the future."
-scientist Sigmund Freud

"The assumption that the future will be like the past
generally turns out to be wrong.
The trick is anticipating where things are moving,
not where they have been."
-journalist John L. Allen, Jr.

Preface

This is quite a different book from the first volume of what has evolved into a four-part series on religion in Canada. There are four main reasons why it is different.

First, the first book, *Fragmented Gods*, was written in 1987 – almost 25 years ago when the religious times were not the same. We were living in the immediate aftermath of a fairly long period where religion had been highly pervasive. Its shadow still could be seen in relatively high levels of service attendance, in greying but still very present men and women who had lived during more prosperous religious times. The attendance in many instances is now lower, those people no longer with us.

Second, I was in the early years of monitoring the religious and social situation in Canada. I had completed three "Project Canada" national adult surveys in 1975, 1980, and 1985, along with one national youth survey in 1984. We now have four additional adult survey data sets to draw on, bringing us to 2005 – and additional survey work of others that brings us to the present day. That first youth survey has been followed by others in 1992, 2000, and 2008. It now is possible to see with considerable clarity what has been taking place since the 1960s.

The third factor is highly personal but also is very important, since the way we put life together is significantly influenced by the personal. I have an eight-year-old daughter, Sahara, who has been a late addition to my life. She has been nothing less than a great gift, without question one of the most consistently happy and buoyant individuals I have ever known. She begins her days singing, smiles much of the day, sings in the bathtub before she goes to bed – and loves to laugh and tease. We have a wireless connection. But she has been slow to talk, and also has been a bit slow with some of her fine motor skills. The good news is that she is catching up. Her situation has given me, as a sociologist accustomed to explaining things in terms of social environment, a new appreciation for physical and neurological sources that influence who we are and what we can be.

And then there is the Internet – that wonderful resource that has made it possible to access unlimited information on a world-wide scale.

All four elements colour this book, along with my growing awareness of my own mortality.

The current times require a careful reading. With the help of the extensive trend data at my disposal, my appreciation for the importance of a wider range of possible sources of beliefs and behaviour, and the global information sources that can be accessed, I think you will find this book to be considerably richer than its three predecessors. It simply has had much more material, resources, and life experiences at its disposal.

Precisely because the resources are potentially so extensive, the book also has taken longer than the others to write. The explosion in the information at our fingertips means more people than ever before are competing to be read and heard. As a result, it is not easy to be adequately cognizant of all the important things that people have to say.

So as I frequently have reminded readers in the past, I have no illusions that this book says it all, but rather hope that it provides a contribution to the extensive conversations that are taking place about religion and spirituality, and why they matter.

I again thank my wife Lita for her support, and Sahara for her daily life-giving presence. I remain so very grateful to the University of Lethbridge for providing me with resources and tranquility now for close to four decades, along with the Lilly Endowment, the Louisville Institute, and Jim Lewis specifically for providing indispensable funding since 1990. I also have benefited greatly from the encouragement of a number of important friends, notably Jim Savoy, Stan Biggs, Trevor Harrison, Diane Clark, Ian MacLachlan, Grant Howell, Steve Kotch, Tim Callaway, and Mark Imbach – along with my three guys – Reggie, Dave, and Russ. Dave, in particular, has played a pivotal role in data collection and entry in recent years. I also want to thank James Penner for the major role he played in procuring the Project Teen Canada 2008 sample. Many thanks again to Donna McCloskey for both her valuable editorial contributions and her ongoing positive spirit.

Thanks to you, as well, for taking time to look at the book. Everyone gives contact opportunities these days, and I am no exception. Your comments and correctives are welcomed, primarily via the book website "www.beyondthegods.com."

Once more, my hope is that this book will stimulate thought and elevate life for all of us.

Reginald Bibby
Lethbridge, Alberta
January, 2011

Introduction

The person on the plane a short time back put the question to me: "So what's the situation with religion today?"

I wish I had been able to offer a quick and simple answer. After all, I wasn't sure that she wanted to go into much detail. I suspected that the question was asked out of an effort to be polite. I decided to take the easy way out. "It's a pretty tough question, and we only have about a four-hour flight," I said with a laugh.

But she surprised me by persisting. "No, I'm serious," she said. "I've actually been quite interested in religious developments in the country. I came out of a fairly religious home. My mother is still a pretty devout Anglican; my dad died a few years back. My husband and I attend once in a while. One of our three teens is involved with a church youth group that seems to be doing a lot of things, and she seems to enjoy it. Her grandma likes that," she added with a smile, as she took another sip of her wine.

"So what's up with religion in Canada?" she asked. Are many people still bothering with it? And do you know anything about what's going on with all the atheist talk that seems to be popping up a lot in the media? Some of those people like Dawkins and Hitchens seem to think we'd all be better off without religion," she added, showing that she obviously keeps an eye on the topic. "What do you make of all that?"

Tough questions, no quick and easy answers. But they are important questions these days both for people who value religion and those who do not. They are not just questions about religion. They are questions about life. If religion is slipping into the background in Canada – becoming something of a peripheral relic from the past, like other cultural memories such as old schools, old cars and old music – what, if anything, does it mean for Canadian life and Canadian lives?

These are the questions I want to address head-on.

The Trilogy Plus One

This is my fourth effort to assess the Canadian religious scene. The first appeared in the 1987 book, *Fragmented Gods*. At that time there seemed to be considerable support for the secularization thesis. With few exceptions, attendance and membership had declined steadily since the 1960s. People continued to identify with religious traditions. But most appeared to be pursuing religion in a fragmented, pick and choose, à la carte fashion.

In 1993, I updated the earlier analysis in *Unknown Gods*. The available data, I argued, pointed to ongoing participation problems for the country's dominant religious groups. However, I suggested that the situation was due not only to the selective consumption habits of individual Canadians but also to the failure of religious groups to respond well to widespread interests and needs.

The first two books were informed by and provided empirical support for the secularization thesis. Religion, by and large, I maintained, had suffered a significant loss in influence in Canada at the individual and institutional levels from the 1960s through the mid-1990s.

In 2002, a third book was released – *Restless Gods*. It carried the subtitle, *The Renaissance of Religion in Canada*. This book drew on extensive new data in maintaining there were signs of new religious life. Service attendance among teenagers and adults seemed to be plateauing across the country, with the exception of Quebec. To be sure, the new life was fairly modest, and I noted that it might turn out to be merely a minor blip on the secularization screen. The argument did not lack for critics both outside and inside the churches.[1]

To speak of "a renaissance" might have been to exaggerate developments a bit. Still, the available data did not support an ongoing, linear-like decline in participation similar to what occurred between about 1960 and 1990. My friend Roger O'Toole playfully suggested during an early "Author Meets Critics" session on the book that it might have been wise to put a question mark after the subtitle.

Still, some good theory developed by Rodney Stark, amended a bit to fit Canada, pointed to the very real possibility of a measure of revitalization taking place among the nation's long-standing, well-established groups.

This Latest Work

Life obviously is dynamic. New readings and new interpretations are always needed and should not be greeted with surprise. After all, social scientists are just that; we are not social psychics. With new data come new understandings of both the past and present.

Such is the case with this book.

In the course of seeing Canadian religious developments through secularization glasses, many of us thought the picture was fairly clear and the trends fairly obvious through most of the last century. Religion was in trouble, and things were going from bad to worse.

To the extent that our thinking was informed by prominent social scientists of the past, including Emile Durkheim, Karl Marx, and Sigmund Freud, along with contemporary thinkers such as Harvey Cox, Peter Berger, Bryan Wilson, and even "our own" Pierre Berton, what was unfolding was what was expected. Religion didn't really have much of a future in highly developed societies. Post-1960 patterns signalled the fact that what much of Europe had experienced was now being experienced in Canada. As academics, we were well-advised to give our attention to more lasting and uplifting topics.

However, the work of Stark and important new data opened my eyes to the possibility that a measure of religious revitalization was taking place around the turn of the new century.

As I write these words today, it is as if the current Canadian religious situation has come into focus – where a discernible reality is emerging that makes sense of the disparate information at hand.

It is the reality of religious polarization.

In much of my earlier work, I have made extensive use of my own Project Canada national surveys of adults and teens that span 1975 through 2008 (see Appendix A for details). These surveys, now eleven in all, provide considerable information on social and religious trends over a period of time that has been characterized by significant change in Canada. I will again make much use of that material.

But since approximately 2000, some fascinating survey work that spans the entire globe has been carried out by a number of organizations and research consortia. They include Gallup, the Pew Research Center, the World Values Survey, and the International Social Survey Programme.

What is invaluable about the information that is being generated is that, for the first time in history, we have data that allow us to look at religious developments in Canada in global perspective.

This book, I think, is easily my most informative, both because of the breadth of information it provides on Canada and because of the unprecedented view it provides of Canada in global perspective.

It consequently goes beyond anything that was possible in the first three books in "the gods series." It provides both good news and bad news for people who value faith and those who do not. As such, I have little doubt it will be received with the proverbial cheers and jeers.

But as the sports guy from yesteryear used to say, "I call it the way it is."

Let's be clear from the outset: the religious times have changed significantly over the past five decades. Some groups, led by the Roman Catholic Church outside Quebec, continue to flourish. Other groups, led by the United Church of Canada, may soon be on life-support. In the midst of such diverse experiences of prosperity and peril, the dominant story is the emergence of unprecedented polarization between those who are religious and those who are not, and what it means for personal and social life.

1 The Days of God's Dominion

"He shall have dominion also from sea to sea" – Psalm 72.8, KJV

TO view religion across Canada these days is like viewing devastation after some tragedy has hit. It's as if a secularization fire has devastated much of what, through the early 1960s, was a flourishing religious forest.

Around 1950, national service attendance, led by Quebec and the Atlantic region, was actually higher than that of the United States. Church-going – and for most Canadians it *really was church-going* – was relatively high pretty much everywhere.

To varying degrees, Protestant and Catholic groups had a significant place in Canadian life. One only has to think of leaders such as Cardinal Paul-Émile Léger in Quebec, Tommy Douglas in Saskatchewan, and E.C. Manning in Alberta; of the large number of people heading out to services on almost any given Sunday morning; of Sunday "Blue Laws"; of Christian radio stations and broadcasts; of the Lord's Prayer in schools....

Now, some 60 years later, that secularization blaze has destroyed much of religion's presence and influence. The collective devotion of the Atlantic region has been significantly reduced both by scandal and modernization. In Quebec, the Quiet Revolution of the early 1960s was accompanied by a

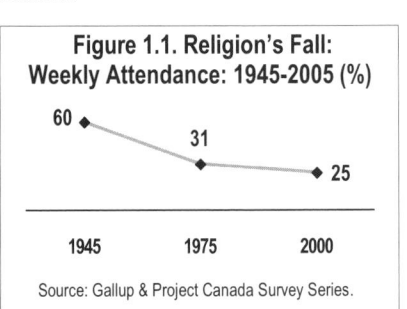

Figure 1.1. Religion's Fall: Weekly Attendance: 1945-2005 (%)

60

31

25

1945   1975   2000

Source: Gallup & Project Canada Survey Series.

The Days of God's Dominion   5

"quieter religious revolution" that decimated religious participation and authority. In Ontario, the west, and the north, the fire of secularization has torched Mainline Protestantism in particular.

However, as is often the case with devastating fires, secularization has not consumed everything. In some instances, there has been scorching rather than torching. Amidst the rubble, there are pockets of life – even vitality. Evangelical Protestant churches have been left largely untouched in many parts of the country, as have a large number of Roman Catholic dioceses and congregations and some Mainline Protestant groups.

And just when it seemed much of the Canadian religious forest was reduced to ruins, new seeds and new plants from other countries have begun to replenish parts of the forest. Growing numbers of Muslims, Hindus, Sikhs, and Buddhists have added new diversity and life to the old, fire-ravaged forest.

So it is that the Canadian religious situation today is characterized by

Table 1.1. Growth in Other Major World Faiths		
	1991	2001
TOTAL	3.8%	6.0%
Muslim	253,265	579,640
Jewish	318,185	329,995
Buddhist	163,415	300,345
Hindu	157,015	297,200
Sikh	147,440	278,415
Source: Statistics Canada.		

death and life, disintegration and reorganization, abandonment and participation, aging congregations and youthful congregations, disbelief and belief, the discarding and the embracing of religious rituals surrounding marriage, birth, and death.

The extensive variations are there for the viewing. What is far less clear is the overall picture that gives clarity to the seemingly disparate patterns.

This book offers such a picture. The evidence is illustrative and the argument is succinct. After all, this is not an overly long flight.

The Way We Were

Historians tell us that the new country of Canada that came into being on July 1, 1867 was, collectively, a highly religious country.

It was a time, wrote historian John Webster Grant, when membership in a particular group "ranked high as a badge of personal identity." To know a person's religious affiliation, he said, was to have an important clue about the individual's moral and political leanings, school system preferences, and even one's favourite newspaper.[1]

The founding Aboriginals had placed considerable importance on spirituality. To varying degrees, First Nations people across the country believed in a Creator who was seen as the source of everything that lived. Extensive beliefs and forms of worship and celebration existed. By 1867, missionary work had seen large numbers become at least nominally Christian.[2] In some instances, Christianity left room for elements of indigenous spirituality, resulting in syncretistic expressions of faith.

In Quebec – previously Canada East and, even earlier, Lower Canada – settlement from France dating back to the early seventeenth century had been accompanied by the arrival of Roman Catholicism. The Quebec Act of 1774 gave French-speaking habitants the right to practice the Catholic faith and French civil law. At the time of Confederation, the province was heavily Catholic – with observers claiming that much of the public and private life of Quebeckers was controlled by the Church.

In Ontario – previously Canada West and, earlier, Upper Canada – the arrival of large numbers of settlers from England resulted in Anglicanism being the numerically dominant religion in 1867. Presbyterians, Methodists, and Congregationalists were also prominent, in large part because of the magnitude of immigration from England and Scotland. Immigration also produced a significant Catholic presence: the Irish Famine of the 1840s, for example, resulted in the arrival of some 40,000 Irish Catholics.

The two other British colonies that were part of the new Confederation – Nova Scotia and New Brunswick – also knew a pronounced religious presence. Immigration from France brought Acadians to Nova Scotia, where they co-existed with Protestant immigrants from Britain. New Brunswick's creation in 1784 was due in large part to the arrival of significant numbers of United Empire Loyalists on the heels of the American Revolution.

The influx of large numbers of slaves from the United States via the Underground Railroad added further to the early religious mosaic as Black Baptists took up residence, particularly in Nova Scotia and southern Ontario.

As the young nation expanded to include further areas – Manitoba and the Northwest Territories (1870), British Columbia (1871), Prince Edward Island (1873), the Yukon (1898), Saskatchewan and Alberta (1905), along with Newfoundland (1949) – the number of people with religious ties also grew.

Table 1.2. Religious Identification: Early 1840s		
	Upper Canada 1842	Lower Canada 1844
Roman Catholic	13%	82
Church of England	22	6
Presbyterian	20	5
Methodist	17	2
Baptist	3	1
Jewish	<1	<1
Other denominations	8	1
No response	17	3

Source: Census of Canada, 1870-71, Vol. 4, Ottawa: 1876. Cited by Kalbach and McVey, 1976:223.

There is nothing surprising about the early Christian numerical monopoly. It was the direct result of the top-heavy emigration from France, Britain, and other western European countries where Christianity was pervasive – patterns documented thoroughly in two recent valuable works compiled by Paul Bramadat and David Seljak.[3]

Nationally-speaking, religion group numbers, as with the population as a whole, are primarily a function of net migration and natural increase – of net gains via immigration and birth, along with intergroup "switching." The early years favoured Christians.

So it was that immigration played a major role in Protestants and Catholics making up more than 95% of the national population from the time of the first census in 1871 through 1961. Over the 90-year period, the percentage of people claiming to have "no religion" never reached 1%.

Table 1.3. Religious Identification of Canadians: 1871-1961

	1871	1901	1931	1961
Roman Catholic	42%	42	41	47
Protestant	56	56	54	49
Eastern Orthodox	<1	<1	1	1
Other Faiths	2	2	3	2
No Religion	<1	<1	<1	<1

Source: Derived from Statistics Canada census data.

Participation

"Hard data" on actual involvement in religious groups, over against mere identification, are difficult to locate for the early years of Canada's existence.

Yet, in describing the religious situation just after Confederation, historian Grant wrote that "the morale of the churches was higher than ever. They were building larger edifices, devising more effective programs, and successfully shaping the moral values of the nation."[4]

More specifically, Peter Beyer of the University of Ottawa notes that things were looking numerically good for organized religion as Canada entered the twentieth century. Allowing for more than one service, says Beyer, churches had enough seating capacity in 1901 to accommodate more than the total Canadian population — "3,842,332 seats for a total population of 5,371,315." A survey carried out by Toronto newspapers in 1896 showed that 57% of the available seats in the Toronto area were occupied during any given service.[5]

But things seem to have gotten even better. The post-World War II years of the 1940s and 1950s appear to have been something of a golden age for church attendance and influence in Canada. According to the first known national attendance poll, conducted by the Gallup organization in 1945, 65% of Canadians over the age of twenty said that they had attended a religious service in a three-week period following Easter Sunday. A similar Gallup survey in the U.S. found that 58% of Americans had attended a service over a four-week period following Easter.

- Levels here were slightly higher for those 21-29 (69%) than others (64%) and for women (73%) than men (61%).
- In Quebec, where Catholics made up 95% of the population, 9 in 10 people said they had been to Mass during the three-week period.

The pollster noted that the levels were lower in "some western provinces" than elsewhere, and suggested it might have been related to "greater distances to travel." In footnote fashion, the release concluded with the statement, "The present survey compliments the one conducted by the Poll some months ago, in which ninety-five per cent of Canadians expressed their belief in God; and eighty-four per cent, their belief in a life after death."

CANADIAN INSTITUTE [▲] OF PUBLIC OPINION

PUBLIC OPINION NEWS SERVICE
RELEASE

Bullet 138-7

For RELEASE
SATURDAY, MAY 12, 1945 -- after 9 a.m.

GALLUP POLL OF CANADA

ABOUT ONE THIRD OF POPULATION

FOUND CHURCH ABSENTEES BY POLL.

Yet Canadian Record Better
Than That Found in U.S.

Such high levels of religious participation continued through the 1950s and '60s.

- Catholic attendance appears to have held steady at about 85% both in Quebec and in the rest of the country, while weekly Protestant attendance remained strong at around 45%. This was a time when Cardinal Léger would say of Montreal, "When I bow to say the evening rosary, all of Montreal bows with me."[6]
- Indicative of Protestant numerical prosperity, the membership of the United and Anglican churches peaked at over one million in 1965. During these heady days of the mid-40s to mid-60s, the United Church alone built some 1,500 new churches and church halls.[7]
- Other faith groups were growing as well. Between 1941 and the end of the 1960s, the number of Jews jumped from 169,000 to 275,000. During the same period, Jehovah's Witnesses experienced explosive growth, increasing from 7,000 to 170,000.

The religion business seemed to be booming.[8]

Table 1.4. Membership of Select Groups: 1871-1966 (l000s)*

YEAR	United	Anglican	Baptist	Pent	Lutheran	Presbytn	Roman Catholic	
1871	----	----	----	----	----	----	43%	1586
1881	170*	----	----	----	----	117	41	1773
1901	289*	368	----	----	----	214	42	2256
1921	401	690	----	----	----	351	39	3427
1931	671	794	132	----	----	181	39	4047
1941	717	836	134	----	----	174	42	4806
1951	834	1096	135	45	121	177	43	6069
1961	1037	1358	138	60	172	201	46	8343
1966	1062	1293	137	65	189	200	46	9160

Drawn from Bibby, 2002:11.

*--- Figures unavailable. Anglican figures = inclusive membership; in 1967, full Anglican membership = 657,000 vs. 1,060,000 for the United Church; United figures for 1881 and 1901 = Methodist; RC = % of Canadian population and approximate numbers; Baptist = Canadian Baptist Federation; Pentecostal = Pentecostal Assemblies of Canada; Lutheran = Evangelical Church of Canada, Lutheran Church in America, and Lutheran Church-Canada (Missouri Synod).

SOURCES: Yearbook of American and Canadian Churches, 1916-1966; United, Anglican, Baptist, Pentecostal, Lutheran, and Presbyterian yearbooks; McLeod 1982.

Influence

There is widespread consensus that religion once had an impact on Canadian lives and Canadian life. Writers tell us that religion was a central feature in the lives of our founding First Nations peoples. They have been described as "deeply committed to religious attitudes, beliefs and practices" which were grounded in "communion with nature and a connectedness with all of life."[9] Religion is also seen as having been an integral part of the earliest Roman Catholic and Protestant settlements.

Beyond pre-Confederation, religion appears to have had a major place during Canada's first century – from the 1860s to the 1960s. As one thinks of the past, it is difficult to envision Quebec without Roman Catholics, Ontario without Anglicans or Presbyterians, the Prairies with no evangelical Protestant presence, B.C. and the Atlantic region without the Church of England.

Religion's presence was fairly blatant in many of our institutions. By way of some broad illustrations...

- A large number of *hospitals and social service programs* across the country were initiated by religious groups.
- Individual *schools and entire school systems* were created by religious groups, notably Roman Catholics.
- *Universities* including McMaster, Queen's, Ryerson, Wilfred Laurier, Ottawa, Montréal, Laval, Acadia, Mount Allison, St. Mary's, Winnipeg, Brandon, and Regina were founded by religious organizations.
- Initiatives to establish fairness in *the workplace*, including supporting labour unions, were undertaken by many groups, including Roman Catholics in Quebec and social gospel-oriented Protestant denominations elsewhere, notably the United and Anglican churches.
- The influence of religious groups was also evident in the public sphere generally and the *political sphere* specifically. CBC footage of an event in Montreal in the 1960s reveals three prominent platform guests: Mayor Jean Drapeau, René Lévesque, and Cardinal Léger.[10]

One of the obvious reasons why religion was having significant input into Canadian institutions was because it also knew an important place in many individual lives.

At its best, religion is supposed to play itself out in everyday life. It therefore is not surprising that, to varying degrees, the personal faith of individual Canadians who were involved in religious groups was having an impact on them, beginning with their families.

But through individuals, along with the efforts of the groups themselves, religion's reach extended to the full range of institutional spheres in Canada – schools, the economy, government, the media, social services, sports and leisure, and so on. To the extent religion was important to individuals, it coloured life in Canada. Highly-regarded American historian Mark Noll goes so far as to say that, as of around 1950, Canada had a much stronger claim as a Christian nation than the United States.[11]

Today, in the early years of the twenty-first century, things have changed. Religion no longer occupies centre stage. Protestantism is not a pivotal feature of Anglo culture, while Catholicism is no longer at the heart of

Table 1.5. Frequency of Religious Instruction of Children: 1975-2005			
	1975	1990	2005
Regular	36%	28	19
Often	10	7	6
Sometimes	31	26	24
Never	23	39	51

*Item: adults with school age children: "How frequently – if at all – do your children attend Sunday School or classes of religious instruction which are not part of their regular school days?"

Québécois culture. Religion's importance for many other cultural groups has similarly declined as those groups have been increasingly integrated into mainstream Canadian life.

Religion obviously continues to have a presence. Old and new places of worship serve as reminders that it remains important for some people. We welcome visits by the Pope or the Dalai Lama, just as we welcome visits of the Queen or a President.

Yet, religion is expected to be both non-partisan and respectful of pluralism. Graduation invocations are no longer prayers; religious symbols have been decreed to have no place in public buildings. Even the Canadian Charter's declaration that "Canada is founded upon principles that recognize the supremacy of God and the rule of law" sounds somewhat anachronistic.

In the case of many Baby Boomers, the poetry of Kris Kristofferson still applies. The things that remind them of religion, such as a church bell or a Sunday School chorus, tend to take them back to something that they lost somehow, somewhere along the way.[12] For most Post-Boomers and emerging millennial youth, however, the bell is just a bell, the chorus just another kind of music.

The obvious question is, "What happened?"

Two factors appear to have been of central importance.

The first was a shift in *immigration patterns*. During the last few decades of the twentieth century, Mainline Protestants in particular saw their immigration pipelines largely dry up. Conversely, the Catholic Church was continuing to benefit from large numbers of arrivals from other countries, as were a number of other world faiths led by Islam. The Mainline Protestant immigration void was not made up via births. Something had to give, and it did.

Table 1.6. Religious Identification by Immigrant Status and Period of Immigration: 1951-2001					
	Foreign-Born			Immigration Period		
	1951	1971	2001	<1991	1991-00	1000s
NATIONALLY	**15%**	**15%**	**18%**	**12%**	**6%**	**1,830**
Roman Catholic	7	12	14	11	3	422
No Religion	---	---	19	11	8	391
Muslim	---	---	72	24	48	276
Orthodox	40	40	45	27	18	103
Baptist	12	11	16	11	5	36
Anglican	24	18	14	12	2	31
Jewish	44	38	31	24	7	22
United Church	12	8	5	5	<1	18
Presbyterian	24	23	18	15	3	12
Lutheran	37	34	21	20	1	9

Source: Statistics Canada census data.

The second key factor was the changing mindsets of Canadians – led by the *Baby Boomers*.

2 The Boomer Bust

"The age where religious leaders could appeal to obligation and duty to get people into the pews is over.""
—The Boomer Factor, 2006:71.

DEMOGRAPHICALLY, what happened was fairly straightforward. Canada's Great Religious Recession took place in large part because Protestant Mainline groups no longer knew the luxury of gushing immigration pipelines. To make matters worse, their birthrates were down and their policies and strategies for retaining their children were not always well-developed and well-executed. Their third and last numerical life-line – recruiting outsiders – was not really a viable solution, given the low priority that many assigned to evangelism.

The math was consequently pretty simple: by the 1970s the number of active members who were dying outnumbered the people who were taking their places.

Some social analysts at the time spoke of the inevitability of cultural forces eroding organized religion. Some theologians spoke of the death of Christendom. In retrospect, the demographer probably deserved the "A."

But immigration changes, declining birth rates, and limited "switching" only tell part of the national story and little of the story in Quebec.

Historian Noll has recently offered a provocative analysis of the marginalization of Christian groups as organizations in the post-1960s. He sketches the impact of rising nationalism on the Church in Quebec, governments' co-opting of personal welfare on the United Church, disestablishment on the Anglican Church, and isolation on evangelical groups.[1]

At the level of individuals, the decline in the importance of organized religion coincided with a number of significant social and cultural shifts in Quebec and the rest of Canada, the United States, and much of the western world. Occupying centre stage, due to both historical timing and their sheer size, were the Baby Boomers.

The Boomers and Religious Involvement

The post-World War II baby boom saw an annual average of 400,000 Canadian children born between the mid-1940s and mid-1960s. As onlookers such as David Foote of the University of Toronto remind us, Boomers were bound to have a dramatic impact on Canadian life, if for no other reason than that "there were so many of them."[2]

By 1966, the oldest members of the cohort were entering their 20s, while the youngest reached that age by 1986. From about 1980 to 2000, Boomers comprised more than 50% of all adults in the critically important and influential, 20-to-64-year-old cohort. Because of their size, they have been positioned to have a particularly significant impact on all spheres of Canadian life.

By 2015, they will make up only 30% of that strategic cohort, by 2020 just 20%. But since the 1960s, Baby Boomers have had an impact on everything they've touched – including, of course, religion.

Gallup polls found that, in 1956, 61% of Canadians claimed they had attended a service *"in the last seven days,"* a figure that is very similar to what we saw earlier for 1946. But, by 1965, that level dropped to 55%, and by 1975 to 41%.

The somewhat stricter measure used in our Project Canada national surveys, *"How often do you attend religious services?"* produced a lower, 31% figure for 1975.

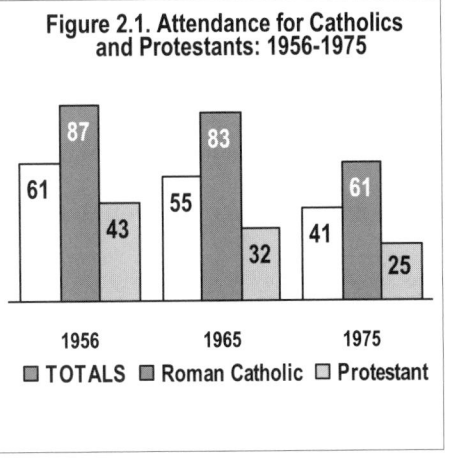

Figure 2.1. Attendance for Catholics and Protestants: 1956-1975

	1956	1965	1975
TOTALS	61	55	41
Roman Catholic	87	83	61
Protestant	43	32	25

This drop in attendance that began to show up in the mid-1960s was largely a Boomer phenomenon.

- The Project Canada surveys show that weekly service attendance among Pre-Boomers – people born before 1945 – remained a consistent 37% between 1975 and 2005.
- However, as early as 1975, the level of Boomer attendance was much lower (15%), and remained near that same level right through 2005 (18%).
- *In Quebec*, Pre-Boomer and Boomer differences were dramatic as early as 1975 (48% vs. 11%). Pre-Boomer attendance slipped somewhat (to 33%) while Boomer attendance, rather than showing signs of recovery, fell further (to 7%). In the apt line of journalist Konrad

Table 2.1. Weekly Attendance by Age Cohort: 1975 & 2005			
	CANADA	**Quebec**	**Else-where**
1975	**31%**	**35**	**29**
Pre-Boomers	37	48	33
Boomers	15	11	16
2005	**25**	**15**	**28**
Pre-Boomers	37	33	37
Boomers	18	7	22
Post-Boomers	24	13	28

Sources: Project Canada 1975 & Project Canada 2005.

Yakabuski, "church attendance in Quebec didn't so much collapse as vaporize – at least among those born after 1945."[3]

- *Elsewhere*, by 2005, there was a mild increase over time, but the Boomer level (22%) remained well below that of Pre-Boomers.
- In short, contrary to some highly-publicized rumours, Boomers never "returned to church" in sufficient numbers to offset earlier losses.
- The generation that has followed the Boomers – the "Post-Boomers" – has exhibited higher attendance levels than Boomers, but the cohort's participation level is still well below that of their Pre-Boomer grandparents.

These findings clearly show that "the religious recession" of the post-1960s was tied not only to changes in immigration patterns but also to the inclination of large numbers of Boomers to stay away from the churches. This leads us to again ask, "Why?"

Four Critical Shifts

The 1960s brought with them a number of key cultural and social trends. I have discussed ten in detail in *The Boomer Factor*. Four shifts appear to have been particularly significant in reshaping religion.

1. From Dominance to Diversity

Boomers were strongly influenced by the 1960s "rights revolutions" relating to civil rights, sexuality, women, and the posing of alternative, countercultural lifestyle possibilities. In Canada, many Boomers grew up with bilingualism, multiculturalism, and the Charter.

The net result has been what some writers have referred to as "the death of the monoculture" – the movement from sameness to diversity, accompanied by the explosion of choices in every sphere of life.

As I suggested two decades ago, Canada is a country with multiple mosaics that go well beyond intergroup relations. Pluralism at the group and individual levels has become part of the Canadian psyche. For some time now we have had not only a cultural mosaic but also a moral mosaic, a meaning system mosaic, a family structure mosaic, a sexual mosaic. And that's just the shortlist. Pluralism has come to pervade Canadian minds and Canadian institutions.[4]

The legitimation of choice can be seen as far back as the mid-70s. Our surveys show that young Boomers – in a remarkably short time – were breaking dramatically with their parents and grandparents in their views of such things as racial intermarriage, women being employed outside the home, sexual orientation, family life, and valid religions. Those portrayals of intergenerational conflict between Archie and "Meathead" in those *All in the Family* episodes in the 70s – remembered by at least a few of us – in retrospect were not an exaggeration. They summed up pervasive differences in outlook between Pre-Boomers and Boomers in both the U.S. and Canada.

Table 2.2. Approval: Boomers and Pre-Boomers: 1975		
	Boomers	**Pre-Boomers**
Whites & Blacks marrying	81%	46
Homosexual relations	43	21
Women being employed when their husbands can support them	84	58

Source: Project Canada 1975.

Such milieus in which options were emerging everywhere and truth was increasingly viewed in relativistic terms were hardly conducive to any religions that proclaimed absolutes and exhibited intolerance for things different. In fact, any religion that did not champion flexibility and freedom could expect to see its market share shrink.

Yet, ironically, religions that aligned themselves with social change ran the risk of becoming indistinguishable from culture, and – in the memorable words of Lutheran theologian William Hordern, failing "to tell the world something that the world [was] not already telling itself."[5]

2. From Obligation to Gratification

Many of us who lived back in the 1950s and 60s found those days very different from today with respect to some of the primary factors that seemed to motivate people.

To a fair extent, people seemed to be moved by loyalty, obligation, and duty – even, on some occasions, altruism. There was a sense that one should be loyal to one's country, old school, and maybe even a local grocery store or gas station. Some people felt it was their duty to get out of bed on a Sunday morning and attend church. It

Table 2.3. Church-Going as a Duty	
"My parents felt that they were supposed to go to church"	
Roman Catholics: Quebec	79%
Roman Catholics: Elsewhere	71
Christian *unspecified*	66
Conservative Protestant	61
Mainline Protestant	56
No Religion	48
Other Faith	41

Source: Project Canada 2005.

wasn't unusual to find someone who would spontaneously help out when needed. They'd change a stranger's flat tire, offer a couple of dollars if a person came up short at a check-out till, or lend a hand shovelling a neighbour's driveway – all with no expectation of return.

What's more, those themes of obligation and duty were drawn upon by organizations and companies, including sports teams. There was a sense that a parent should help out at the school, that a Catholic should attend mass, that a Canadian cultural icon like Eaton's should receive our support. In Regina, people were called on to save the Roughriders and in Calgary to save the Stamps, while in Winnipeg and Quebec City people were asked to get behind efforts to save the Jets and the Nordiques.

Why? Because, depending on the situation, it was our civic duty...or nationalistic duty...or religious duty.

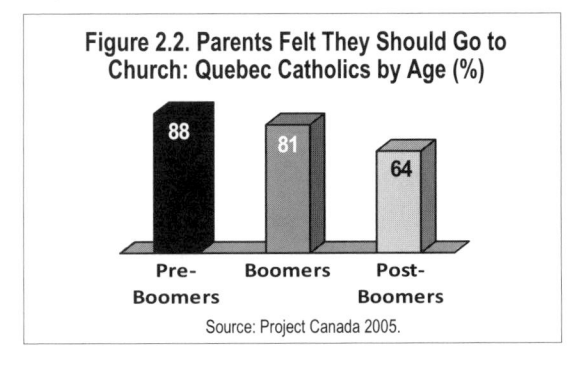

Figure 2.2. Parents Felt They Should Go to Church: Quebec Catholics by Age (%)

88 — Pre-Boomers
81 — Boomers
64 — Post-Boomers

Source: Project Canada 2005.

And then, of course, there was marriage. Ceremonies involved declarations that marriage was not to be entered into lightly – with couples solemnly swearing that they would remain faithful to each other, "for richer, for poorer, in sickness and in health, so long as [they] both shall live."

The Boomer era saw a major shift in motivational emphasis from obligation to gratification. Themes like duty and loyalty were replaced by a market model. That model stressed the importance of following the axiom of the marketing gurus: successful organizations determine needs and then meet them. In the process, they emphasize what's in it for us. What's more, they offer more – "value-added" features such as travel points or seasonal discounts or gift vouchers. We don't just get something we pay for; we get "more." By the new century, such an outlook had become pervasive, shared by Canadians of all ages.

So it is that, for some time now, the majority of us have been highly selective consumers in every area of life. Religion has not received an exemption.

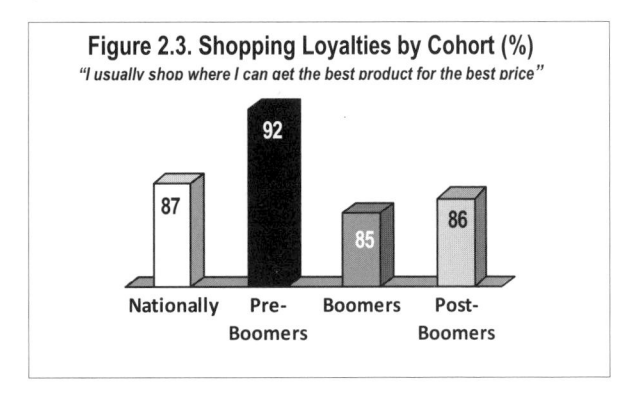

Figure 2.3. Shopping Loyalties by Cohort (%)
"I usually shop where I can get the best product for the best price"

To the extent that people consider the possibility of involvement in religious groups, they do so in highly pragmatic, consumer-like fashion. Large numbers of their parents may have considered that church-going was a duty – something becoming, for example, of "a good Catholic," with no questions asked.

But these days, the dominant sense of Canadians of all ages is that people should attend services not out of a sense of obligation but rather because they find it worthwhile.

Table 2.4. Views of Motivations for Church-Going (%)	NAT	Pre-Bs	BBs	Post-Bs
My parents felt that they were "supposed to go to church"	61%	69	63	54
People who attend religious services should go not because they feel they have to but because they find it to be worthwhile	87	90	87	85

Source: Project Canada 2005.

Lest religious leaders take such selective consumption personally, they only need to look at the way that Canadians, younger and older, approach relationships.[6]

"We want relationships to last forever.
But if they don't add very much to our lives
we follow the advice of the relationship guru
and discard them, 'turn the page,' and move on.
After all, if people don't enrich our lives
why should we bother with them?"

Of course there are people who continue to be motivated by duty, obligation, and loyalty. There still are people who act out of a concern for others. But they are in the minority.

If religious leaders still expect people to show up for services because that's what a good _____ does, my message is simple: "Good luck!"

3. From Deference to Discernment

For Canadians who lived in the 1950s and 1960s, a buzzword was "respect." People were expected to "respect" their elders and parents, their teachers and ministers, their doctors and the police, journalists and politicians – pretty much everyone who was an adult, and definitely anyone who had some credentials. There was also a high level of deference shown institutions, including schools, universities, governments, and churches. Acquiescence to the Church, for example, allegedly was particularly widespread among Roman Catholics in Quebec.

For Boomers, higher levels of individual freedom have included freedom of expression. Better educated, exposed to television and travel, and equipped in recent years with the Internet, Boomers have led the way in Canadians insisting that they have a voice in all realms of life.

They want input. They also are extremely demanding.

The result is that individuals and institutions are carefully scrutinized. They have to earn the right to be seen as authoritative and to be respected. We take it for granted that the critical evaluation of our leaders and experts is a positive thing.

Table 2.5. Attitudes Toward Authority

	NAT	Pre-Bs	BBs	Post-Bs
My parents taught me to respect people in authority	95%	96	95	94
I think that today people in authority have to earn our respect	86%	94	85	82
Critical thinking – whereby we evaluate our leaders and experts – is generally a good thing	95	96	95	94

- A doctor's diagnosis is checked and supplemented with information gleaned from the Web – giving new meaning to the old cliché about "getting a second opinion."
- A teacher or school counsellor's assessment of our children is evaluated in terms of what we ourselves know and further information we gain from "Googling" an assessment such as ADD or a learning disability or a speech delay.
- Individuals who serve as coaches and referees for our children find themselves having to contend with parents who are not lost for thoughts about abilities, playing time, and good and bad calls.

So it is that almost every business and every organization today offers us "contact" information. Every media outlet offers us "feedback" opportunity. Every big talent show offers viewer input. The emphasis on facilitating interaction is summed up in the fact that businesses and organizations, large or small, are on Facebook and Twitter, inviting us to enter into conversations.

It's not as if they have a choice. If they want to be successful, they have to be willing to hear us out.

But try as they might, virtually all of our primary institutional players have had difficulty in being the recipients of high levels of confidence – with the trends suggesting things will get worse before they get better.

- Only the police enjoy the confidence of a clear majority of Canadians.
- Schools, the media, the court system, religious leaders, politicians, and labour unions fare much worse.
- In general, confidence levels have declined since the 70s.

Table 2.6. Confidence in Leadership: 1975-2005

Have "A Great Deal" or "Quite a Bit" of Confidence

	1975	2005
The Police	75%	69
Schools	49	47
Newspapers	40	43
The Court System	49	42
Radio	***	40
Religious Groups	51	34
Television	44	33
Major Business	***	33
Your Provincial Govt	31	27
Labour unions	21	27
The Federal Govt	30	21

Sources: Project Canada 1975 and 2005.

The highly critical outlook that Canadians have also can be seen in survey results reported by Leger Marketing. In recent years, the polling company has found a decline in our trust of people in virtually every occupation.

Firefighters and nurses rank at the top of the trust rankings, while teachers, doctors and police officers also fare quite well. But there is trust slippage with bankers, church representatives, and – gasp – pollsters, along with lawyers and journalists. Trust in publicists has dropped significantly. Trust in politicians – well, let's just say it remains very low.

Table 2.7. Trust in Select Professions: 2002-2007

"Do you trust or distrust..."

	2002	2007
Fire fighters	98%	97
Nurses	96	94
Teachers	88*	89
Doctors	92	87
Police officers	88	84
Bankers	72	68
Church reps	73	61
Pollsters	70	59
Lawyers	54	52
Journalists	53	48
Publicists	47	31
Politicians	18	15

Source: Leger Marketing 2007. *2003

Indicative of "the death of deference," a national poll in the United States found that by the turn of the new century, younger Catholics were far less inclined than their older counterparts to blindly accept the teachings of the Church. Deferential obedience was giving way to critical discernment.

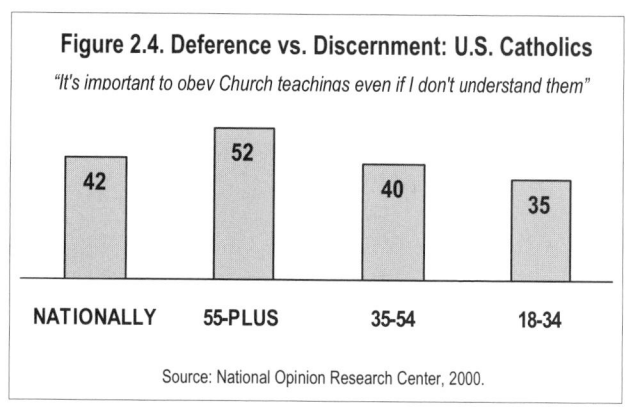

Figure 2.4. Deference vs. Discernment: U.S. Catholics

"It's important to obey Church teachings even if I don't understand them"

| 42 | 52 | 40 | 35 |
| NATIONALLY | 55-PLUS | 35-54 | 18-34 |

Source: National Opinion Research Center, 2000.

Another American research finding that would appear to be equally applicable to Canada: Catholic teenagers are now no more likely than other teens to express feelings of guilt. Christian Smith's research suggests Catholic young people often do not know enough about Church teachings to feel guilt; others are aware of teachings but disregard them rather than internalizing them.[7]

The shift from deference to discernment has put considerable pressure on religious groups to respond. People want opportunities for input. Yet groups have been put in a position of determining what is and what isn't negotiable. They also have had to cope with accelerated expectations.

They have not always been successful. Canadians who were not actively involved in religious groups in 2000 were asked if they would be receptive to greater involvement if they "found it to be worthwhile" for themselves or their families. Some 65% said either "yes" or "perhaps."

.

- Asked "what kinds of things would make it worthwhile?" 37% cited ministry factors – better meeting of spiritual, personal and relational needs.
- But another 30% said that organizational factors were an issue for them, such as wanting changes in style and outlook, as well as better leadership.
- Most of the remaining 33% indicated that the problem rested with factors related to themselves, such as work schedule, family indifference, and getting older.

Table 2.8. Worthwhile Involvement

Factors Cited by People Attending Less Than Monthly Who Say They Would Consider Being More Involved

Ministry Factors	**37%**
Organizational Factors	**30**
Changes in Style and Outlook	23
Better Leadership	3
Other	4
Respondent Factors	**30**
Other Factors	**3**

Source: From Bibby, *Restless Gods*, 2002:221.

These findings indicate that large numbers of people have strong feelings about what they expect from religious groups. The days of passive acquiescence are over.

Consistent with such thinking, renowned McGill philosopher Charles Taylor has written that, during the 1950s and 60s, the secularism mindset that dated back to the Enlightenment made a leap from intellectuals to the public sphere. One key component was a "coming of age narrative" where people felt they did not need to look beyond themselves for norms and values.[8] "Self-authorization," says Taylor, is "an axiomatic feature of modernity."[9] He maintains that such a sense of self-authorization has done more to advance secularism than scientific thinking.

4. From Homes to Careers

Between 1960 and 2000, the proportion of women employed outside the home doubled from some 30% to 60%. In 1930, the figure had been around 20%. A similar shift took place during the same period in the United States.

The extent of the social impact of this dramatic escalation in female employment during the Boomer era is difficult to overestimate. It affected family life, altering

both the age that
couples married and
the inclination to marry
or the necessity of
remaining married. It
affected the number of
children a couple could
have. It altered the
amount of time that
women and men could

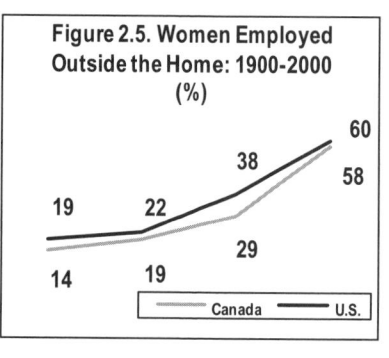

Figure 2.5. Women Employed
Outside the Home: 1900-2000
(%)

give to their children and to each other. It created new
pressures on time, adding a significant level of pragmatism
to time-use choices. In the process, it significantly affected
social and organizational involvement – including church-
going.

Highly respected sociologist Robert Putnam of
Harvard, in his best-selling book, *Bowling Alone*, released
in 2000, maintained that the increase in the number of
women in the labour force in the U.S. was "the most
portentous social change of the last half century."
Controlling for other factors, Putnam says, "full-time
employment appears to cut home entertaining by roughly
10 percent and church attendance by roughly 15 percent,
informal visiting with friends by 25 percent, and
volunteering by more than 50 percent. Moreover," he adds,
"husbands of women who work full-time are, like their
wives, less likely to attend church, volunteer, and entertain
at home."[10]

In short, something in the way of a revolution was
taking place in the way that personal life, family life, and
work life were being experienced. One of the most
prominent correlates was the widespread feeling of being
short on time. Of course couples had felt busy in the past.
But employment outside the home brought with it the loss
of control over schedule and location. It translated into
large numbers of people feeling that they were being pulled
in an array of directions and, overall, simply not having
enough time.

The data we have available suggest that it was not necessarily a case of dual-employed Canadians in the post-1950s becoming negative about religious involvement. A more accurate reading is that they frequently were feeling pressed for time. As a result, they were increasingly pragmatic about how they spent their time, and their resources more generally. They were open to things that added to their family life – why wouldn't they be?

If they could arrive at a church service and find that religious groups "were ready" for somewhat weary parents and their children, providing atmospheres that were relaxing, uplifting, and gratifying, then great!

However, there

Table 2.9. Time and Employment: Parents With School Age Children, 2003	
% Indicating "Never Seem to Have Enough Time"	
NATIONALLY	**47**
Employed married mothers	77
Employed cohabiting mothers	65
Employed married fathers	59
Employed divorced/separated mothers	58
Non-employed mothers	49
Source: Bibby, *The Boomer Factor*, 2006:82.	

is little evidence that religious groups – even those like the United Church who saw themselves as progressive and in touch with the times – "were ready" – that they understood something of the magnitude of the family and workplace transformation taking place.[11]

On the contrary, at a time when groups should have been adding resources that would result in improved ministry to babies, young children, teenagers, and tired moms and dads, quite the opposite often was taking place.

- Between the 1960s and 1990s, Mainline Protestant groups cut back on their number of Sunday Schools.
- Catholics, despite their official commitment to a "family, parish, and school" model of ministry, were not particularly strong in providing environments conducive to stressed-out parents…and children.
- Evangelical groups may have been an exception – not so much because they read the times better – but because "they lucked out": many already had good children and youth ministries in place, almost accidentally possessing the infrastructure to minister to the dual-employed.

As a result, rather than abandoning faith and their traditions, many pragmatically-minded Boomers gave churches the time they felt they warranted, in keeping with what they added to their lives and those of their families.

For many, that meant not dropping out altogether, but showing up on special occasions, notably Easter and Christmas, along with baptisms and christenings, weddings and funerals.

The Project Canada surveys since 1995 have shown that large numbers didn't rule out greater involvement. But they had to find that such participation enriched their lives and those of their family members.

In the light of such findings, one is hard-pressed to escape the conclusion that the problems of organized religion in the post-1960s, in large part, were tied to the fact Canada's groups too often did a poor job of responding to the changing family roles and needs of Boomers.

As a result, most continued to place a measure of importance on faith and retained their psychological and emotional ties with religious traditions. But, on weekends, sizable numbers found better things to do with their time.

The Aftermath

The net effect of the reluctance of Boomers to embrace organized religion is reflected in the finding that weekly attendance in Canada slipped from over 50% in 1960 to about 30% in 1980 and 25% by 2005.

However, except for Quebec Catholics, the cores of people actively involved in groups stabilized by 1980 – and have in fact increased since then in both the Conservative Protestant and Other Faith instances.

Table 2.10. Weekly Attendance: 1957 and 2005			
	1957	1980	2005
🍁	53%	28	25
Protestant	38	24	29
Conservative	51	53	64
Mainline	35	19	20
Roman Catholic	83	41	29
Outside Quebec	75	44	42
Quebec	88	38	14
Other Faiths	35	11	22

Sources: 1957: March Gallup poll; 2005; Project Canada 1980 & Project Canada 2005.

It is important to remember, however, that to base a percentage on who identifies with what group can be misleading if the size of the identification pools are shrinking. Such is the case with Mainline Protestants – the United, Anglican, Presbyterian, and Lutheran churches.

On the surface, their combined core of weekly attenders has remained steady at about 20% since about 1980. However, the percentage of Canadians identifying with the four groups dropped from 32% in 1981 to 20% by 2001. In light of their age structures as of the 2001 census, there is good reason to believe the combined total of the Mainline Protestant pool may now be no higher than around 15%.

Table 2.11. Catholic and Protestant Identification: 1931-2001									
% of the Canadian Population									
	RC	MLPROT	United	Ang	Pres	Luth	CPROT	Bap	Pent
1931	40	48%	20	16	8	4	8	4	<1
1961	46	41	20	13	4	4	8	3	<1
1981	46	32	16	10	3	3	8	3	1
2001	43	20	10	7	1	2	8	3	1
Source: Statistics Canada census data.									

This brings us back to the importance of immigration in determining group sizes. In analyzing the findings for the 2001 census, Statistics Canada noted that one reason for Roman Catholic growth has been immigration. Catholics accounted for nearly one-quarter of the 1.8 million people who came to Canada between 1991 and 2001. The pattern is not new: Roman Catholics "have remained the largest [single] religious denomination within each new wave of immigrants since the 1960s."[12]

As a result of what amounts to "a global circulation of the saints," Roman Catholics have continued to benefit from the arrival of Catholics from other parts of the world. In greater Toronto, for example, the Church has 1.7 million Catholics in 225 parishes, and celebrates Mass each week in 36 different ethnic and linguistic communities.[13]

Since the early 1960s, Protestants have not been anywhere as fortunate. Their share of "the immigrant market" has decreased steadily, first being surpassed by Catholics and then by new arrivals who either identified with other world faiths or said they had no religion.

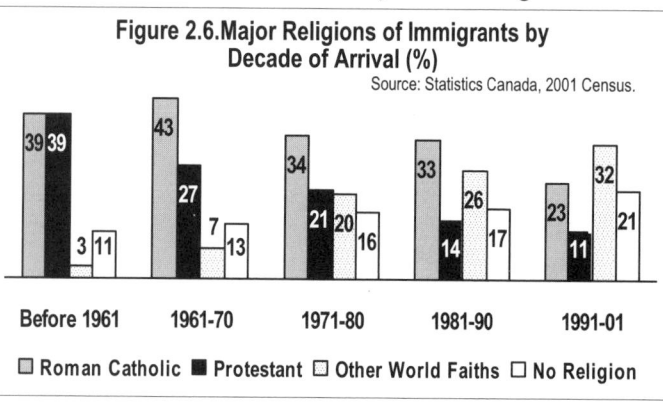

Figure 2.6.Major Religions of Immigrants by Decade of Arrival (%)

Source: Statistics Canada, 2001 Census.

☐ Roman Catholic ■ Protestant ☐ Other World Faiths ☐ No Religion

Apart from sheer numbers, with few exceptions, the primary countries of origin have been changing in favour of Catholics, Other World Faiths, and people with no religion.

Table 2.12. Those Changing Immigration Pipelines

Top 10 Ethnic Origins by Generation Status: 2006

	First Generation 6 million *Foreign-Born*		Second Generation 4 million *Canadian-Born, 1-2 Parents Born Elsewhere*		Third Generation-Plus 16 million *Self & Parents Canadian-Born*	
1.	Chinese	15%	English	26	Canadian	47
2.	East Indian	10	Scottish	16	English	24
3.	English	9	Canadian	15	French	23
4.	Italian	6	German	13	Scottish	18
5.	German	6	Irish	12	Irish	18
6.	Filipino	5	Italian	11	German	10
7.	Scottish	4	French	7	Aboriginal	5
8.	Irish	4	Netherlands	6	Ukrainian	4
9.	Polish	3	Ukrainian	5	Netherlands	2
10.	Portuguese	3	Polish	5	Polish	2

Population, 15 years of age and older; some respondents reported more than one ethnic origin.

Source: Statistics Canada, 2006 census, analysis series 97-562.

The Legacy

Young people obviously do not emerge out of a cultural vacuum. The key to understanding Canadian youth today is to look at their Boomer and Post-Boomer parents. Our most recent Project Teen Canada national survey of teenagers between the ages of 15 and 19 allows us to do just that. The survey, the latest in a series of surveys of teens conducted every eight years since 1984, had a sample of more than 5,500 young people, including a special oversampling of Aboriginals.[14]

It provides an intriguing snapshot of how the children and grandchildren of Boomers are looking in light of many of the explicit goals, efforts, and emphases of Boomers.

We know – thanks to the census – that the percentage of Canadians who said they had no religion jumped from 4% in 1971 to 16% by 2001. Their children and grand-children would be expected to follow suit. And they have.

Today's teens are reporting the highest level of "non-affiliation" in Canadian history. Some 32% say that they have "no religion" – up dramatically from 12% in 1984.

The declines and diminished pools in the case of Quebec Catholics and the United and Anglican churches are almost breathtaking.

Table 2.13. Religion Identification of Teens: 1984 & 2008			
	1984	2008	Census
Roman Catholic	50%	32	43
Outside Quebec	29	23	19
Quebec	21	9	24
Protestant	35	13	25
United	10	1	8
Anglican	8	2	5
Baptist	3	1	2
Lutheran	2	1	2
Pentecostal	2	1	1
Presbyterian	2	1	1
Other/Unspecified	8	6	6
Orthodox	--	2	2
Christian unspecified	--	3	3
Other Faiths	3	16	6
Islam	<1	5	2
Buddhism	<1	3	1
Judaism	1	2	1
Hinduism	<1	2	1
Sikhism	<1	2	1
Aboriginal Spirituality	<1	2	<1
Other/Unspecified	2	2	1
None	12	32	20

- Between 1984 and 2008, Quebec teens who said they were Roman Catholic dropped from 21% to 9%.
- During the same period, the percentage of teenagers across the country who identify with the United Church has fallen from 10% to 1%.
- The drop-off in the case of Anglican identification also has been sizable – from 8% to 2%.

A comparison of what teens say about their affiliation and what their parents told the 2001 census takers reveals considerable slippage: young people are typically less likely to say they identify with religions. The exception is Islam, where – perhaps reflecting a greater sense that one can be open – teens are *more likely* than adults to acknowledge their religion. The same pattern holds for a variety of additional faiths.

Millennial youth are also staying away from religious services in the largest numbers on record.

And if those headline findings on identification and attendance are not bad enough for religious groups, a further headline should be more than a shade unnerving:

God is slipping in the polls

The latest youth survey has found that the proportion of teens who say they are atheist is higher than anything we or any other pollsters have ever found.

Such findings undoubtedly lead observers to conclude we are seeing further evidence of rampant secularization. One prominent media commentator recently proclaimed, "If the future for institutional religion lies in the hearts and minds of the young, a dark night is sweeping down on the country's churches, synagogues, and temples."[15]

Actually, such a conclusion is a misreading of the times.

A synopsis of the new reality was provided by the highly publicized debate in Toronto between Christopher Hitchens and former British Prime Minister Tony Blair in December of 2010. In noting that it was the fastest selling show in the history of Roy Thomson Hall, journalist Lorna Dueck suggested the interest level was "a sign that religion is far from dead in the public imagination."[16]

The fact the two combatants had two different fan bases was also a tip-off on the current Canadian situation.

3 The New Polarization

*"Sure, lots of people are leaving,
but lots of people are also staying."*
–a beleaguered church leader

SECULARIZATION seemed to sum up the Canadian religious situation well as the 20th century came to a close. Proponents of the thesis, dating back to such luminaries as Comte, Durkheim, Marx, and Freud, all saw religion as giving way to science as civilization evolved. More recently the argument had been echoed and updated by prominent sociologists, including Bryan Wilson, Karel Dobbelaere, and Steve Bruce. Significantly, all of these individuals have been Europeans.

This "old story" about religion is still the story that the media typically tell. In December of 2010, Michael Valpy and Joe Friesen expressed things this way in the introduction to a five-part *Globe and Mail* series on the future of faith in Canada: "What we've seen is a sea of change in 40 years, a march toward secularization that mirrors what's happened in Europe."[1]

The Secularization Argument

Put simply, secularization refers to the decline in the influence of organized religion. While the line is not perfectly straight, it nonetheless is linear: secularization proceeds in a fairly relentless and non-reversible fashion.

Dobbelaere, the Belgian sociologist, offered an important clarification of the concept in pointing out that it has at least three major dimensions – institutional, personal, and organizational.[2] The spheres of life over which religion has authority decrease and its role becomes more and more specialized; religion has less and less of an impact on the daily lives of individuals – what Berger has referred to as "a secularization of consciousness"[3]; and religious organizations themselves are increasingly influenced by society and culture in the way they operate – their goals, their means, their content, and the way they measure success, for example.

By the 1980s and 90s, all three dimensions of secularization were generally recognized to characterize at least much of Protestant Europe, as well as Canada.

The United States, as one of the world's most advanced societies, appeared to be an important exception to the secularization rule. Such apparent anomaly, however, was readily explained away by many prominent observers, including Peter Berger and Thomas Luckmann.[4]

They argued back in the early 1960s that, despite high levels of religious participation in America, secularization was already rampant. Their explanation was that secularization was taking the form of "secularization from within" rather than "secularization from without." On the surface religion was flourishing; but if one looked more closely, they said, the structures and content of religion in the U.S. were being ravished by secularism. By way of one memorable illustration, Berger wrote that, when it came to values, "American Christians [held] the same values as anyone else – only with more emphatic solemnity."[5]

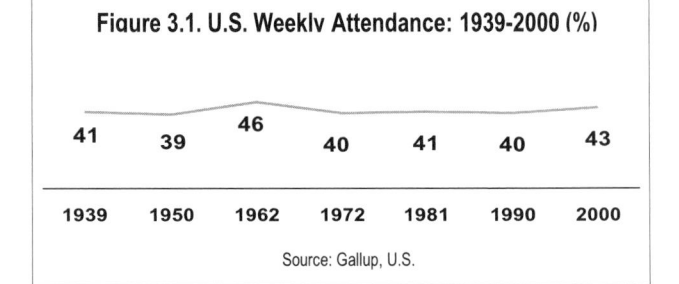

Figure 3.1. U.S. Weekly Attendance: 1939-2000 (%)

41	39	46	40	41	40	43
1939	1950	1962	1972	1981	1990	2000

Source: Gallup, U.S.

The American religious situation aside, the secularization thesis was assumed to be applicable to Canada. I certainly concurred, providing considerable documentation in support of the argument in *Fragmented Gods* (1987) and *Unknown Gods* (1993). There didn't seem to be much more to say. Things appeared to be bad and getting worse for organized religion "up here."

The Revitalization Argument

What makes life interesting, of course, is when the unexpected occurs. In 2000, a surprising finding emerged from the national youth survey.

A Cause for Pause Finding

In 1984, we had found that some 23% of teenagers claimed to be attending services on approximately a weekly basis. In 1992, that figure dropped to 18%. When we did the 2000 youth survey, I expected that the teen attendance level would probably drop another five percentage points or so – to around 13%. It didn't happen.

Instead, we found that the percentage of weekly attending teenagers rose to 21% – reaching essentially the same level as in 1984. Increases took place across all major religious groupings – Catholicism, Protestantism, and other world faiths, with the single exception of Roman Catholicism in Quebec, where attendance continued to drop off.

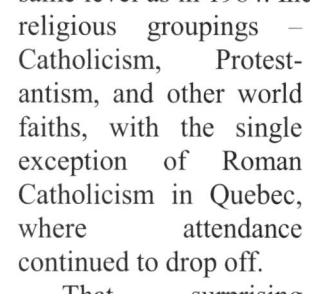

Figure 3.2. Teenage Weekly Attendance: 1984-2000 (%)

23   18   21

1984   1992   2000

Source: Project Teen Canada Survey Series.

That surprising national finding resulted in my reflecting on a fairly radical possibility – that a modest resurgence in religious participation might be taking place in Canada. After all, people like Harvey Cox and Peter Berger were acknowledging they had made an error in buying into secularization thinking, and underestimating religion's resiliency.[6] Maybe I had too.

Later in 2000, we completed the Project Canada adult national survey, providing an opportunity to obtain a new reading of adult attendance. What that new survey revealed was that attendance had slipped very modestly from 1995 – the weekly level from 24% to 21%, the monthly levels from 34% to 30%. However, upon closer examination, I discovered that the apparent decline was camouflaging some signs of life that were corroborated using Statistics Canada data.[7]

- Among *Conservative Protestant groups*, an increase in attendance levels had taken place since 1990.
- In the case of *Mainline Protestants* – the United, Anglican, Lutheran, and Presbyterian denominations – the collective numerical haemorrhaging stopped in the 90s.
- As for *Roman Catholics*, attendance declines during the decade had slowed significantly both inside and outside Quebec – although levels in Quebec remained very low.
- *Other major faith groups*, despite facing problems of sustaining growth, together had experienced a heightened profile and, to varying degrees, added quantitative and qualitative vitality to the Canadian religious scene.

Table 3.1. Weekly Service Attenders in Canada: 1957-2000				
	1957	1975	1990	2000
NATIONAL	53%	31	24	21
Protestant	38	27	22	25
Conservative	51	41	49	58
Mainline	35	23	14	15
Roman Catholic	83	45	33	26
Outside Quebec	75	48	37	32
Quebec	88	42	28	20
Other Faiths	35	17	12	7

Sources: 1957: March Gallup poll; 1975, 1990, 2000: Bibby, Project Canada Survey Series.

In presenting these data in *Restless Gods*,[8] I concluded, "These overall findings about the churches suggest that some important new developments are taking place – that there is something of a renaissance of organized religion in

Canada."[9] Whether or not it continued seemed to be highly dependent on how the dominant existing religious groups responded to readily apparent consumer demand. Here my thinking was influenced considerably by Rodney Stark.

Stark's Challenging of Secularization

I had met Stark in 1972 when I was a graduate student at Washington State University and he was a newly arrived professor at Seattle's University of Washington on the other side of the state. A decade or so earlier, he had been a graduate school student at Berkeley with my primary WSU mentor, Armand Mauss. Originally from North Dakota, he started out as a journalist; he also played briefly for the Winnipeg Blue Bombers.

Stark took chances with flair. In the early 1980s he took on the secularization school of thought by posing a fairly simple but creative and compelling argument – the kind of argument which, after the fact, left many of us wondering, "Why didn't we think of that?" His provocative argument, now well-known, has been variously described as a market model and as rational choice theory.

Put very succinctly, Stark – in collaboration with key associates William Bainbridge, Roger Finke, and Laurence Iannacone[10] – maintained that there are some needs "that only the gods can provide."[11] They pertain particularly to death, along with purpose and meaning – including the meaning of life and the meaning of events in life.

Using a market analogy, Stark argued that the persistence of such questions means that, in any setting, there is a fairly constant market demand for religious responses. What varies is the supply-side. In societies where the religious economy has been "deregulated," groups or "firms" that have difficulties will lose "market share" to groups that are more vigorous and less worldly.

Consequently, for Stark, secularization does not lead to the end of religion; on the contrary, secularization stimulates innovation. He gave particular attention to the emergence of sects (breakaway groups from existing religious bodies) and cults (new religious traditions).[12]

So it is, said Stark, that "In an endless cycle, faith is revived and new faiths born to take the places of those withered denominations that lost their sense of the supernatural."[13]

As for which groups tend to win and which ones tend to lose, the key is costs and benefits. The higher the costs of membership, the greater the material, social, and religious benefits of membership. "People tend to value religion according to how much it costs," wrote Finke and Stark, and "because 'reasonable' and 'sociable' religion costs little, it is not valued greatly."[14] Individuals consequently make "a rational choice" to belong and participate.[15] Conversely, as religious bodies ask less of their members, their ability to reward them declines. In short, the more mainline a denomination becomes, the lower the value of belonging to it, resulting eventually in widespread defection.

Stark and his associates claim extensive historical and contemporary support for their general thesis, as a result of their research in the United States, Canada, and Europe. They found a consistent positive correlation between the existence of cult centres and people having no religion.[16]

A Canadian Adaptation of Stark

There is an important practical problem with trying to apply Stark's stimulating thinking to religious developments in Canada: things don't fit – at least without some important alterations.

As I pointed out in some detail in *Restless Gods*,[17] census data on religious identification over time reveals two distinct patterns: the stable dominance of established Christian groups and the difficulty new entries have had in cracking that monopoly.

Table 3.2. Religious Composition of Canada: 1891-1991			
	1891	1941	1991
Catholic	42	44	47
Protestant	56	52	36
Other	2	3	5
No Religion	<1	<1	12

Source: Canadian census data.

- Between 1891 and 1991, the Catholic share of the population grew while the Protestant share declined. The drop for Protestants, however, was not due to new groups expanding.
- The decrease in the size of their market share instead coincided with a rise in the proportion of Canadians who said they had "no religion" – an increase due in large part to the methodological fact that "no religion" only became an acceptable census option in 1971.[18]
- During the 1951-2001 period when "the market" seemingly was ripe for newer entries to make inroads, groups such as Jehovah's Witnesses and Latter Day Saints made tiny gains.

Table 3.3. Population Percentages of Select Groups: 1951 and 2001		
	1951	2001
Baha'i	**	.1
Jehovah's Witnesses	.2	.5
Latter Day Saints	.2	.3
Unitarians	.1	.1

Source: Statistics Canada Census Data.

- Further, as of the beginning of the 21st century – by which time the country's well-established groups had been in numerical decline for some three decades, the actual numbers for would-be competitors were extremely small. For all the media hype about disenchanted and disaffiliating Canadians turning to new options, relatively few in reality seized the opportunity.
- In a nation of some 30 million people, less than 25,000 identified with such highly publicized alternatives as Pagan (including Wicca), with the figures for New Age and Scientology under 2,000. The New Age total in allegedly receptive British Columbia was 690, with the numbers for Ontario and Quebec only 380 and 25 respectively.

Table 3.4. Sizes of Select Religious Groups: 2001	
Pagan	21,080
Baha'i	18,020
New Thought*	4,000
Humanist**	2,105
New Age	1,530
Scientology	1,525
Gnostic	1,160
Rastafarian	1,135
Satanist	850

*Includes Unity, New Thought, Pantheist
**Technically not a religious group.

Source: Statistics Canada 2001 Census.

These data point to the fact that we have an extremely tight "religious market" in Canada, dominated by Catholic and Protestant "companies." New entries find the going very tough.

A more plausible argument that is compatible with Stark's thesis is that secularization may stimulate not only the birth of new groups but also the rejuvenation of older ones. [19]

Throughout his work, Stark stresses that religious economies will be stimulated by religious pluralism resulting from "deregulation." Presumably some of the older companies would go back to the drawing boards in the light of changing times and a more competitive marketplace.   In fact, in the last chapter of Stark's third major work on the topic, he and Roger Finke acknowledged such a possibility, whereby "the sect to Church cycle" reverses itself. They commented that the literature provided few hints of such a possibility, despite the historical example of something as blatant as the Counter Reformation of the seventeenth century.

They saw a key component of such possible resurgence to be new, highly committed clergy, who in turn call their congregations to commitment and emphasize traditional religious content. Only people like this, they maintained, will be motivated to be involved in declining groups where secular rewards are low. Growth, they theorized, will take place initially at the congregational level, and they provide preliminary data on a number of U.S. groups that are consistent with their argument.[20]

Long-standing major corporations and other organizations realize that in order to survive and thrive they have to be in an ongoing mode of change. The primary players who occupy the Canadian religious scene are no exception.

As I reminded readers a decade ago,[21] denominations such as Anglicans, the United Church, Presbyterians, and Lutherans, along with the Roman Catholics in Quebec and elsewhere, are no fly-by-night operations. They have long histories and recuperative powers. They don't just roll over and die. Many are part of durable multinational corporations with headquarters in places like Rome and Canterbury. Such well-established religious groups don't readily perish. They retreat, retrench, revamp, and resurface.[22]

To sum up: participation declines are neither inevitable nor irreversible. On the contrary,

1. if people continue to identify, and
2. if they are reluctant to turn elsewhere, and
3. if they have interests and needs, and
4. if their identification groups respond,

it will be only a matter of time before the established groups experience numerical revitalization.

Theoretically, it all seemed to make perfect sense.

~

So, which is it? Secularization or revitalization? Is religion in Canada in a downward spiral that dates back to the 1960s? Or are there signs of new life as the country's dominant religious groups respond to ongoing interests and needs?

Actually, the answer is that both patterns are facets of the dominant pattern that makes sense of everything: polarization.

The Canadian Religious Reality

To the extent that many of us bought into the secularization thesis, one of the key sources of data was the steady decline in religious participation in the post-1960s.

Yes, that oft-cited summary chart, corroborated by other sources, that pegged weekly attendance at around 60% in 1945, 31% in 1975, and 25% by 2005 was pretty convincing. The reason is that the trends resonated with what most people had been experiencing.

The attendance figures in turn appeared to be fairly highly correlated with the membership numbers for major Protestant groups, and a general sense of Roman Catholic participation trends, particularly in Quebec. Moreover, it was widely acknowledged that religious influence in the lives of individuals and the life of the nation had known a corresponding decline over the charted period.

Still further, following Dobbelaere, Luckmann, and Berger, there was ample evidence that secularization had not stopped at church steps, but had invaded many congregations and denominations. Secularization was widely visible "within."

In short, I found that few people ever challenged the general attendance slide trajectory. The numbers documented experience. As such, many religious leaders, for example, were almost relieved to be given some data that confirmed what they felt had been taking place.

The fact that the decline in religious participation did not continue unabated – as seen in the increase in regular teenage attendance and the levelling off of adult attendance in the 1990s – was what led to speculation about religion experiencing something of a comeback. Even a respected public opinion pulse reader like Allan Gregg mused about the possibility.[23]

But the speculation was hardly limited to survey research findings. The theorizing of Stark provided a reputable and credible academic explanation for the unexpected resurgence that seemed to be showing up in national surveys.

Blame It On the Pollsters

The primary reason for much of the confusion in reading the Canadian religious situation is that we typically have been looking at only part of the picture. It's been like taking a family photo and leaving out dad or a couple of the kids.

We have been focusing our attention on the proportion of people actively involved in religious groups. As the proportion went down, we saw evidence of secularization. As the proportion levelled off and even went up, we saw evidence of revitalization.

For example, typical Gallup polls over the years focused on the percentage of Canadians who had attended a religious service "in the past seven days." I myself have zeroed in on people who say they attend at least weekly or monthly. In the U.S., Gallup's regular reports on service attendance continue do the same thing.

Here's a quick, two-question test:

1. Approximately what percentage of Canadians attend services every week?
2. Approximately what percentage of Canadians *never* attend services?

Now, if you are following polls reasonably closely, chances are you would say, in response to the first question, "between 20 and 25%." As for the second question, you – like just about everyone else – would draw a big blank.

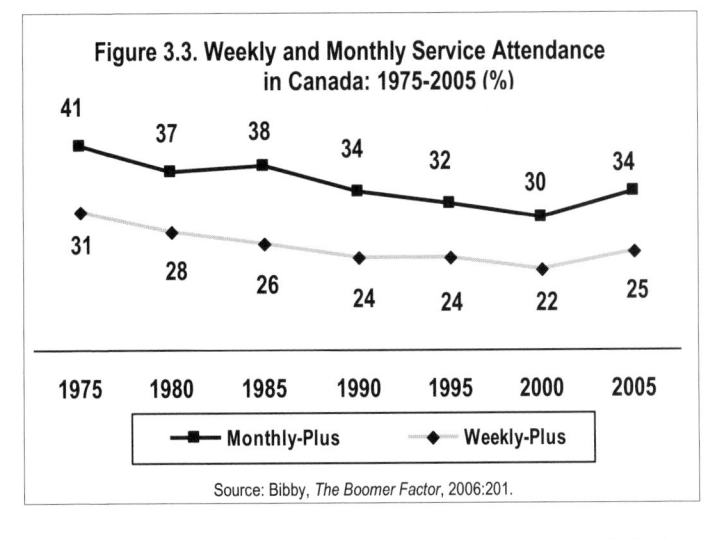

Figure 3.3. Weekly and Monthly Service Attendance in Canada: 1975-2005 (%)

Source: Bibby, *The Boomer Factor*, 2006:201.

In probing participation trends, what we have failed to do is keep a close eye on everyone – not only the religiously active but also those who are not particularly active or not active at all.

As a result, the photos we have been using to splice together the religion story have been incomplete. Important information that could help us understand the total situation has been left out.

This first became apparent to me when I was analyzing the Project Teen Canada findings on attendance spanning 1984 through 2008. If one only looks at what amounts to weekly or monthly-plus attendance, the religious situation appears to be remarkably stable.

- As noted earlier, some 23% of young people were attending services on a regular basis in 1984, with the figure for 2008 a very similar 21%.

- A typical and seemingly obvious interpretation would be that things haven't changed very much. Right?

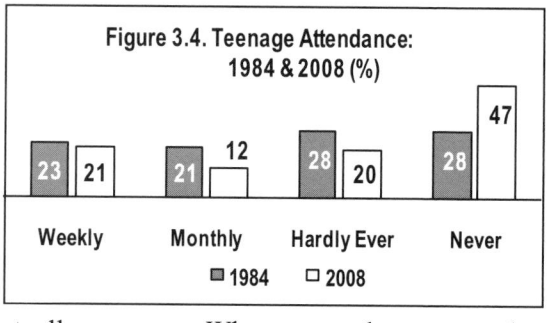

Figure 3.4. Teenage Attendance: 1984 & 2008 (%)

Weekly   Monthly   Hardly Ever   Never
■ 1984   □ 2008

Actually, wrong. When we take a snapshot that includes everyone by looking at other responses to the attendance item, what we find is that the percentage of teenagers who say they "never" attend services has almost doubled since the 1980s, from about 25% to 50%. The middle of the attendance continuum has been shrinking.

This, everybody, is an example of growing religious polarization.

Such evidence suggests that religion in Canada is far from a thing of the past. But in recent decades, there has been an important momentum shift away from religion. Non-religion's market share has been increasing. Growing numbers of people are living life "beyond the gods." That trend is what has led many of us to think in terms of *secularization*.

However, during the same period, a significant segment of Canadians has continued to value religion. The size of that proportion of pro-religious people has remained fairly constant. To the extent it has shown signs of increasing, some of us have raised the possibility that *revitalization* is taking place.

When we look at the trend data for everyone – the involved and non-involved alike – what we see is a pattern of growing *polarization.*

The polarization can be seen through the eyes of a number of measures of religiousness or what some refer to as "religiosity." Three of these are service attendance, identification, and belief in God.

Attendance: Weeklys and Nevers

We have just seen that Canadian youth have become increasingly polarized with respect to attendance. A solid core of close to 1 in 4 are attending religious services at least once a week. However, almost 2 in 4 say they "never" attend services.

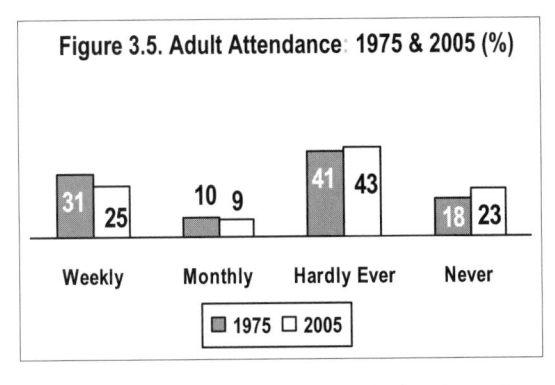

Figure 3.5. Adult Attendance: 1975 & 2005 (%)

31	10	41	
25	9	43	18 23

Weekly   Monthly   Hardly Ever   Never

■ 1975 □ 2005

Among adults, attendance polarization has been increasing since the mid-1970s. Weekly worship-going decreased from 31% to 25%, while the percentage of those never attending increased from 18% to 23%.

Obviously, if the youth pattern persists as teens move into their 20s, 30s, and beyond, the adult distribution will be characterized by greater polarization.

Identification: Affiliates & Non-Affiliates

Since the 1960s, an increasing number of Canadians have been indicating that they have "no religion." At first the percentages were fairly small – only 4% in 1971 when the response became an acceptable category for the census-takers for the first time.

However, with each census since, the figures have increased, reaching 16% by 2001. That doesn't look like a pronounced dichotomy between "religion" and "no religion." But two related findings are worth noting.

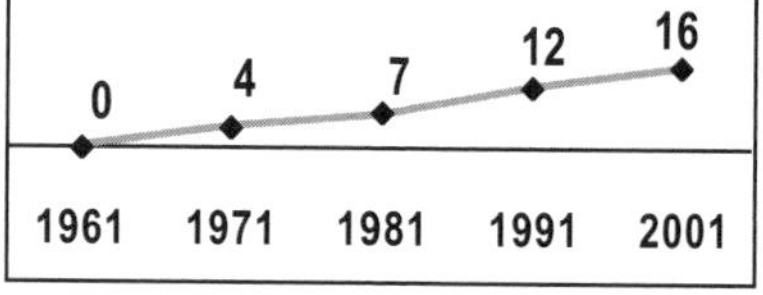

First, the number of adults in the "no religion" category is second only to Catholics. They also tend to be young. As such they constitute a significant bloc of people. In theory, to the extent they have some common characteristics, they could wield a fair amount of influence in public affairs.

Figure 3.6. No Religion: 1961-2001 (%)

1961	1971	1981	1991	2001
0	4	7	12	16

Second, the "no religion" sector has been growing at a fairly fast rate. As we saw earlier, the 2008 Project Teen Canada survey findings reveal Boomers and Post-Boomers, including immigrants, have been producing a generation of young people with the highest percentage of "no religion" on record.

Table 3.5. Canada's 10 Largest Groupings

	Numbers	%	Median Age
1. Roman Catholic	12,793,125	44%	37.8
2. No Religion	4,796,325	16	31.1
3. United Church	2,839,125	12	44.1
4. Anglican	2,035,500	8	43.8
5. Christian (unspecified)	780,450	3	30.2
6. Baptist	729,475	3	39.3
7. Eastern Orthodox	606,620	2	40.1
8. Lutheran	606,590	2	43.3
9. Muslim	579,640	2	28.1
10. Protestant (unspecified)	549,205	2	40.4

Source: Statistics Canada, 2001 Census.

- In 1984, 12% of teenagers said they had "no religion."
- In 2008, that level jumped to 32%.

Currently, the proportion of teens who say they have "no religion" is neck-and-neck with those who say that they are Roman Catholic.

Table 3.6. Religion Identification of Teenagers: 2008

Roman Catholic	**32%**
No Religion	**32**
Other Major Faiths	16
Protestant	13
Christian *unspecified*	3
Orthodox	2
Other/Unspecified	2

Source: Project Teen Canada 2008.

Belief: Theists & Atheists

There has been a lot of talk in recent years about the rise of atheism in Canada, particularly in the light of the popularity of books by the so-called atheist writers – notably Richard Dawkins, Christopher Hitchens, and Sam Harris.[24]

Such assumptions have been short on hard data. We've been monitoring thoughts about God since the inception of the Project Canada surveys in 1975. What we have found is that there has been very little change in the percentage of Canadians who say that they definitely do not believe in God. In 1975, the figure was 6%; in 2005, it was 7%.

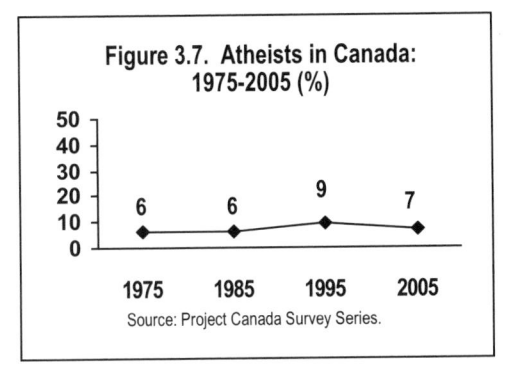

Figure 3.7. Atheists in Canada: 1975-2005 (%)

Source: Project Canada Survey Series.

But as with the monitoring of service attendance, it's important to include everyone, rather than prematurely cropping the photo.

A closer look at "the God data" shows that some important shifts in thinking have been taking place over the past few decades.

- While the percentage of outright atheists has remained fairly stable, there has been a significant *decrease* in the proportion of Canadians who say they "definitely" believe in God.

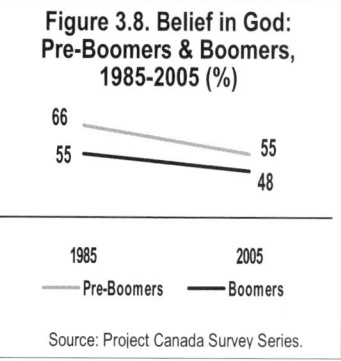

Figure 3.8. Belief in God: Pre-Boomers & Boomers, 1985-2005 (%)

Source: Project Canada Survey Series.

- The ambivalence was showing with Boomers and Pre-Boomers, undoubtedly reflecting in part the deference to discernment shift.
- In turn, that ambivalence and critical attitude have been passed on to their millennial children and grandchildren.

The latest cohort of emerging teens is considerably less likely to assert "definite" belief in God or a higher power, and far more inclined to say either that they "don't think" they believe in God or to say they "definitely do not" hold such a belief.

A striking and significant finding? To the best of my knowledge, the 16% total for atheism among teens today is the highest level of atheism ever recorded for any age group in Canada.

Table 3.7. Belief in God or a Higher Power*: Adults & Teenagers, 1980s & Now (%)

	ADULTS		TEENS	
	1985	2005	1984	2008
Yes, I definitely do	61	49	54	37
Yes, I think so	23	32	31	31
No, I don't think so	10	11	9	17
No, I definitely do not	6	7	6	16

*1984 & 1985: "God exists"; in 2005 & 2008: "God or a higher power"
Source: Project Canada Survey Series.

At this point in time, unequivocal theists – at around 50% – readily outdistance unequivocal atheists – at just under 10%. But another 40% of the population are sitting in the middle of "the God continuum," undecided on belief versus non-belief. These adults will soon be joined by "the new breed" of God-thinkers – the emerging millennials.

Belief in God represents a third area of religious polarization in Canada.

-a grade 1 student in Victoria

Obviously these three measures – attendance, identification, and belief – are interrelated. However, while the correlations between them are fairly high, they are far from perfect. Now, don't get dizzy with numbers and miss the point of the following.

- Some 95% of *weekly attending teens* identify with a religious group, and 75% are unwavering theists. However, 45% of those who *never attend* services identify with a religion, and only 29% are outright atheists.
- Just 30% of teens *who identify* with a religion are weekly attenders, but about 50% are ardent theists.
- And among teens who *definitely believe in God*, only 44% are weekly attenders and 20% never attend – even though 93% of them identify with a religion. That said, 26% of atheists identify with a religion, even though a mere 15% ever attend a service.

If all that sounds a bit bewildering, it should. The reason is that there are lots of complexities to these three religion variables. Fortunately, they are summed up fairly concisely in the correlation matrix table below (1.000 = a perfect relationship, .300 and higher is generally seen as an appreciable association).

It's precisely because of their less than perfect relationship to each other that I want to draw on all three in looking at some of the characteristics of people who are religious and those who are not.

Table 3.8. Correlation Matrix for Attendance, Identification, and Belief: Adults and Teenagers			
		Identification	Belief
ADULTS	Attendance	.418	.496
	Identification	---	.477
TEENS	Attendance	.442	.508
	Identification	---	.528

Polarization in Summary

This examination of attendance, identification, and belief reveals that Canada is not a country characterized by either pervasive secularization or revitalization.

Rather, the findings show that solid cores of people are either involved or not involved in religious groups, either identify with traditions or do not identify with any, and are either theists or atheists.

According to these data, religion remains important for a fairly stable segment of the population. However, since the 1960s, what has changed is the proportion of people who are ambivalent about religion.

Table 3.9. Polarization Over Time				
	Adults		Teenagers	
	1975	2005	1984	2008
Attendance				
Weeklys	31%	25	23	21
Nevers	18	23	28	47
Identification				
Yes	91	85	88	68
No	9	15	12	32
Belief in God				
Theists	61	49	54	37
Atheists	6	7	6	16

Source: Project Canada Survey Series.

As some Canadians in the "ambivalent middle" have moved toward religion, observers – including myself – have suggested that a measure of "renaissance" and "revitalization" might be taking place.

As others in the "ambivalent middle" have moved away from religion, we have suggested that we are witnessing the latest manifestations of secularization.

More accurately, what has been emerging is polarization – two dominant postures toward religion.

Polarization is almost equally common among *women* and *men*.

Table 3.10. Polarization and Gender: Adults & Teenagers					
	ATTENDANCE		IDENTIFICATION		BELIEF
	Weekly	Never	Yes	No	Theist	Atheist
ADULTS						
Females	25%	21	86	14	54	4
Males	25	25	85	15	45	10
TEENAGERS						
Females	21	47	70	30	38	14
Males	21	47	67	33	35	18

Sources: Project Canada 2005 and Project Teen Canada 2008.

However, there are some notable variations by place of birth, regions of the country, and religious "families."

Young people born outside Canada, along with those born here but with at least one foreign-born parent, tend to be slightly more religious than their Canadian-parent counterparts. Immigration in recent years has added vitality as well as numbers to the Canadian religious scene

Table 3.11. Polarization by Geographical Background: Teens					
	ATTENDANCE		IDENTIFICATION		BELIEF
	Weekly	Never	Yes	No	Theist	Atheist
Foreign-born	28%	37	76	24	51	10
Parents foreign-born	26	43	72	28	40	13
Canadian parents	17	52	64	36	32	20

Sources: Project Teen Canada 2008.

- Religiousness is most pronounced in the *Atlantic* region, along with *Saskatchewan* and *Manitoba.*
- *Ontario* and *Alberta* are characterized by similar levels of attendance and belief, with identification slightly higher in Ontario than Alberta.
- *Quebec* and *British Columbia* are characterized by similar low levels of weekly attenders. But Quebeckers are much more inclined than people in B.C. to show up at least occasionally, and are far more likely to identify with a religion, notably, of course, Roman Catholicism. At minimum, a cultural attachment to faith remains strong.
- *Polarization* is most pronounced in *British Columbia.*

Table 3.12. Polarization and Region: Adults					
	ATTENDANCE		IDENTIFICATION		BELIEF
	Weekly	Never	Yes	No	Theist	Atheist
Atlantic	39%	16	92	8	63	4
Sask-Manitoba	36	13	83	17	61	4
Ontario	28	21	84	16	53	7
Alberta	27	27	77	23	54	8
Quebec	15	21	94	6	40	8
British Columbia	17	38	65	35	36	11

Sources: Attendance, belief - Project Canada 2005; identification - Statistics Canada 2001.

These findings challenge some long-standing stereotypes about religion in Canada. The infamous Bible Belt that has been ascribed to Alberta dating back to Premier "Bible Bill" Aberhart in the 1930s and 40s hasn't really known much empirical support for quite some time; sociologist Harry Hiller argued back in the 1970s that the depiction never knew actual empirical support.[25] Now we see that Alberta has equal proportions of weekly and never attenders. Religiously and non-religiously, the province is closer to Ontario than Saskatchewn and Manitoba. For some time now, Canada's "real" Bible Belt has been found in the Atlantic region.

"Beautiful B.C." is without question the most secular province in the country. Yet it continues to have significant numbers of people who attend, identify, and believe.

One needs to be careful in assuming that polarization is not very common among people who identify with religious groups.

Can an Anglican be an atheist? Can a Baptist never attend church? Of course; our correlation matrix documents such common realities. The empirical question is how prevalent are these patterns?

- Polarization, as measured by attendance or belief, is least pronounced among *Conservative Protestants*, followed by *Catholics outside Quebec*. That said, 1 in 3 Conservatives are not weekly attenders, and 1 in 3 Catholics outside Quebec do not express unequivocal believe in God.

- Polarization is more pronounced among *Mainline Protestants*, *Other Faith* groups, and *Quebec Catholics*.

- However, it's also important to note that the percentages of people who occasionally attend or are ambivalent believers constitute majorities or near-majorities in the case of all three of these latter groups. At this point they are not lost to the groups. But they could go either way.

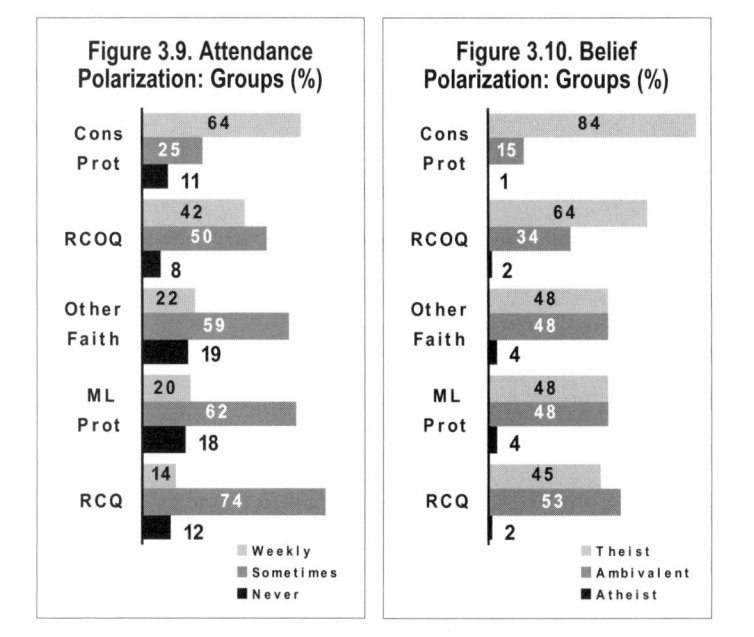

Figure 3.9. Attendance Polarization: Groups (%)

Figure 3.10. Belief Polarization: Groups (%)

The extensive data from the Project Teen Canada survey in 2008 serve as a reminder that one needs to be cognizant of the tremendous variations that exist within the very broad and heterogeneous "Other Faith" category.

- The survey shows that religiosity levels are particularly high among Sikh, Muslim, and Hindu young people.
- Patterns for teens identifying with Christian groups are similar to what we have just seen for adults. Conservative Protestant youth exhibit high levels of religiousness, followed in turn by Roman Catholics outside Quebec, Mainline Protestants, and Quebec Catholic teenagers.

Teenage Polarization in the Mosaic
Service Attendance & Belief in God or a Higher Power

	Monthly+	Never	Theist	Atheist
NATIONALLY	33%	47	37	16
Roman Catholicism	37	35	41	5
Outside Quebec	47	28	49	3
Quebec	16	51	27	13
Protestantism	68	18	66	4
Conservative	91	5	91	5
Mainline	44	29	44	29
Orthodox	43	24	63	1
Christian *unspecified*	69	15	78	2
Other World Faiths	46	30	66	7
Sikhism	82	7	57	2
Hinduism	61	12	52	4
Islam	56	22	83	2
Judaism	41	26	41	9
Aboriginal Spirituality	25	45	45	7
Buddhism	19	59	27	17
No Religion	7	79	9	38

The Project Teen Canada 2008 national survey of more than 5,500 young people – including a special oversample of 500 Aboriginals attending band-run schools – makes it possible to look at teenagers by their religious and non-religious identifications. Such illustrations follow throughout the book.

These findings on differences by region and religious groups document the fact that the national polarization pattern clearly has some important variations.

What's more, because life is dynamic and ever-changing, movement in both directions of "the polarization continuum" has been taking place and will continue to take place.

But overall, nationally-speaking, the two positions have become increasingly entrenched. Neither will disappear in the foreseeable future. What is at issue is the extent to which both will ebb and flow – grow or not grow.

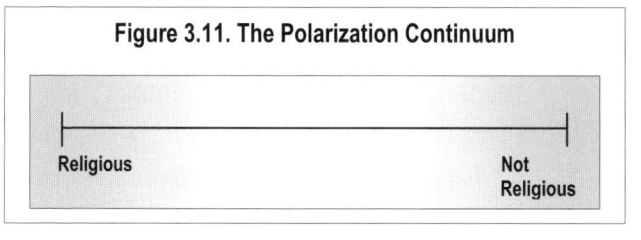

Figure 3.11. The Polarization Continuum

Religious

Not Religious

The Global Situation

How unique is the Canadian polarization situation? The question is straightforward. The answer is not. It requires a global examination of religion – obviously a mammoth undertaking.

Fortunately, a number of invaluable poll resources for pursuing such a task have emerged recently.

- Among them is the World Values Survey, produced by a cooperative network of social scientists. It dates back to 1984 and has been repeated about every ten years. It now includes some 100 societies and 90% of the world's population.[26]
- Since 2005, Gallup has conducted worldwide polls that have included more than 140 countries.[27]
- Global data have been generated through the International Social Survey Programme, whereby researchers from some 50 countries have included topical sections in their national surveys dating back to the mid-1980s.
- The Pew Research Center in the United States has carried out international surveys since 2001.[28]

I again have to express my deepest appreciation to the Gallup organization, the World Values Survey researchers, the Pew Research Centre and the International Social Survey Programme for providing the rich and priceless data that make the following summaries, analyses, and conclusions possible.

Recently, an invaluable synthesis of the global survey work to date was produced by Tom W. Smith, the highly regarded survey director and prolific author at the National Opinion Research Centre in Chicago.[29] His comprehensive report for the Templeton Foundation was released in late 2009. It is entitled, *Religious Change around the World.*[30] The Centre describes Smith's report as "the most comprehensive analysis to date of global religious trends."

Looking at data for the United States, Europe, Asia, Latin America, and Muslim countries, Smith concludes, "No simple generalization adequately captures the complexity and nuance of the religious change that has been occurring."[31] He offers a number of key points in his summary.[32]

1. On balance, the evidence indicates that the world, including the United States, has been moving in a secular direction. Modernization and education are associated with a tendency for religious beliefs and behaviour to decline. However, these correlations are neither overly strong nor uniform. They do not add up to simple confirmation of the secularization theory.

2. The patterns of religious decline are characterized by variation and diversity. In Europe, for example, secularization has continued. But overall changes are modest and less striking than differences between nations. In Eastern Europe, the collapse of Communist rule has seen religion rebound in some places but not in others. There is no uniform post-Communist pattern.

3. In many settings, there are clear elements of transformation in addition to decline. Still, on average, there has been "a secular tilt to religious change."

4. All that said, secularization is not inevitable. Religion exhibits resilience and the ability to rebound.

The three indicators of religiousness we have used to gauge polarization in Canada are also helpful in examining the prevalence of polarization around the globe. Of particular importance, an international reading enables us explore some of the correlates of polarization worldwide.

It is easy to drown in all the numbers that can be presented. I consequently want to remind readers of something I invariably emphasize in presentations: I myself am not particularly interested in numbers; I am interested in ideas.

As a result, I want to present just enough numbers to allow us to get a good reading on religiousness around the world. Every country will not be included. However, I will provide information on my sources so that the statistics for many other countries of interest can be pursued.

Some Quick Bottom Lines

The three measures of religion – attendance, identification, and belief – provide an initial reading of the range in religiosity around the planet. *Salience* – religion being a part of one's daily life – is also a valuable measure in making comparisons across groups. Worship attendance, for example, may not be equally valued. While cutting points are far from absolute, some general patterns are fairly clear.

- *Extremely high* levels of religiosity are found in settings such as Thailand, Nigeria, the Philippines, and India.
- A *second tier* of high religiousness is found in countries like Brazil, Iraq, Iran, and El Salvador.
- A *third tier* includes Mexico, Italy, Poland, and the U.S.
- With the *four tier* – Israel, Spain, Canada, Germany, Russia, and Australia – polarization is more pronounced.
- In the *fifth tier*, religiosity is low. Countries include France, Britain, Hong Kong, the Czech Republic, Sweden, and China.

Some countries such as the Philippines, Pakistan, Greece, and the Ukraine are enigmatic, knowing high levels of salience, identification, and belief, yet relatively low levels of attendance. Japan is characterized by salience and identification levels that fall below belief and attendance.

Table 3.13. Salience, Attendance, Identification, and Belief: Select Countries*

	Salience	ID	Belief	Attend
Thailand	97%	99	98	80
Nigeria	96	99	99	89
Philippines	96	99	99	64
Saudi Arabia	94	99	99	68
Pakistan	92	99	99	56
Ethiopia	90	99	99	78
India	90	99	99	73
Dominican Republic	87	99	97	53
Brazil	87	93	97	49
Iraq	86	99	99	53
South Africa	85	84	99	57
Iran	83	99	99	45
El Salvador	83	83	98	68
Mexico	73	83	97	60
Italy	72	83	82	49
Greece	71	97	96*	29
Poland	69	92	96	62
United States	65	84**	88	43
Ireland	54	94	96	56
Israel	51	96	95	39
Spain	49	84*	92	39
Ukraine	46	58*	85	23
Korea, Republic of	43	63*	98	35
CANADA	**41**	**84****	**85**	**26**
Germany	40	75*	77	30
Cuba	34	90**	75	20
Russia	34	52*	91	15
New Zealand	33	74	79	27
Netherlands	33	58	74	26
Australia	32	81	83	23
France	30	57*	80	20
Finland	29	85	91	12
United Kingdom	27	77	86	20
Hong Kong	24	85**	56	19
Japan	24	48*	87	38
Czech Republic	24	41	57	15
Sweden	17	75*	70	17
China	---	7**	60	9

*The items: "Have you attended a place of worship or religious service in the past 7 days?"; % identifying with a religion; % neither agnostic nor atheist; religion is an important part of one's daily life.

Sources:
Attendance, salience - Gallup WorldView 2010; ID - World Factbook, CIA 2010; *Dentsu 2006, **varied sources (e.g., attendance for China = WVS, ID for Canada = 2001 census); Belief: computed from the World Religion Database in Smith 2009:284-287.

Overall, global variations in religiousness are readily evident. I leave it to readers to draw their own specific cut-off points depending on the importance one gives to each of the four religiosity measures.

Generally speaking, religion is viewed as personally important by higher percentages of women than men in many national instances, including Canada. The gender differences are predictably smaller in settings where levels of religiousness are very high, such as Nigeria, Pakistan, and Indonesia.

That said, it is not quite so readily evident as to why pronounced gender differences in the importance accorded religion are found in a fairly large and diverse number of settings. Among them are places where religious identification is high – Honduras, Peru, Brazil, and Poland, but also settings where identification is much lower, including the Ukraine and Russia.

Come to think of it, we still haven't really answered the gender difference question well with respect to the U.S. and Canada. Maybe it's nurture, maybe nature – maybe neither.

Table 3.14. Identification and Religion's Personal Importance by Gender: Select Countries			
	ID	Women	Men
Nigeria	99%	92	92
Pakistan	99	91	91
Honduras	99	81	63
Turkey	99	69	60
Peru	97	76	63
Indonesia	96	95	95
Brazil	93	82	69
Poland	92	46	24
United States	84	66	52
Mexico	84	66	46
CANADA	**84**	**37**	**23**
Italy	82	37	17
United Kingdom	77	35	30
Germany	75	25	17
Ukraine	58	42	26
France	57	12	9
Russia	52	21	6

Source: "Global gender gaps," Pew Research Center 2004.

Assessment

Canada is experiencing a growing level of religious polarization. As such, we stand in contrast to settings that are characterized by both religious and secular monopolies. We most closely resemble countries such as the Ukraine, Germany, and Australia.

Some of Canada's long-established groups, led by the United Church, Anglican Church, and the Roman Catholic Church in Quebec, have been losing significant ground. The sizes of the two Protestant groups have been shrinking due to declining immigration additions that have not been offset by the retention of their children. Adding to such problems is the fact that they are characterized by considerable polarization re: involvement and belief.   In Quebec, Catholic identification remains strong. But, like their Mainline counterparts, Quebec Catholics are highly polarized when it comes to both participation and belief.

Given their aging demographics, it is no exaggeration to say that the United and Anglican denominations are in the midst of serious numerical crunches that are having daunting human and financial resource implications.[33] The former is said to be closing one church a week, and has "shuttered" 400 in the past decade.[34] It makes old ministries difficult to sustain, new ministries difficult to implement.

As for the Catholic Church in Quebec, it knows the luxury of people who continue to think they are Catholics. However, greater involvement and greater commitment to the Church and faith remain highly elusive.[35]

The importance of documenting the reality of religious polarization in Canada and elsewhere does not end with simply getting a clearer understanding of what is happening to religion here and in the rest of the world.

The far more significant question that potentially is of interest to just about everyone is the question of consequences – the implications for the quality of personal and collective life, starting with the ability of people who are religious, and those who are not, to co-exist.

To these important questions we now want to turn.

4 Polarization & Pluralism

"Our image is of a land of people with many differences...
but a single desire to live in harmony."
-Pierre Elliott Trudeau

OUR Canadian mosaic is supposed to encompass pretty much everything imaginable. What started out as a cultural mosaic with Pierre Trudeau's unveiling of the federal government's multiculturalism policy in the House of Commons in 1971 has given birth to a multi-everything psyche in Canada.

As discussed earlier, the multiculturalism infant left its racial and cultural group cradle soon after it was born. In the course of growing up over the past several decades, it travelled across the country, visiting our moral, religious, family, educational, and political spheres. Pluralism is enshrined in our minds and institutions. We now have multiple mosaics in virtually every area of Canadian life.[1]

Pluralism's familiar emphases consist of tolerance, respect, appreciation for diversity, and the insistence that individuals be free to think and behave according to their consciences. Ours is a society in which just about everything within the limits of the law and civility is possible.[2]

Great principles. What's more, they have been increasingly realized in Canada since the 1960s.

However, having faced some monumental challenges to pluralism in areas such as language, race and ethnicity, gender, Aboriginal issues, sexual orientation, disabilities, and age, one of the biggest challenges has been emerging in recent years – religion.

In fact, concern about the difficulties in accommodating different religions – notably Islam – prompted the *Globe and Mail* to revisit the merits of multiculturalism as a whole in a series of articles in late

2010. The headline of an October editorial declared that the time has come to "Strike multiculturalism from the national vocabulary." The editorial called for replacing the term multiculturalism with pluralism, and refocusing the debate on the concept of citizenship with responsibilities.[3]

Then there's the question of whether there is an alleged "religious right" emerging that could impose theocratic government in Canada – according to Marci McDonald.[4] The argument is provocative but precarious: just 44% of evangelicals identify with the Conservative Party; so do 32% of Mainline Protestants, 23% of Catholics outside Quebec, and 20% of people who identify with other faiths.

Two decades ago, in my book, *Mosaic Madness: Pluralism Without a Cause*, I questioned the value of a visionless coexistence that emphasized the virtues of differences over commonalities. "If what we have in common is our diversity," I asked, "do we really have anything in common at all?"[5] I argued that we needed to transcend our mindless relativism, interact with each other and determine what is better and best from our rich body of cultural options. In that way, I maintained, we could realize Pierre Trudeau's goal of creating "a richer life for us all."

For the record, the book was a bestseller. But in practice, few people seemed to listen. With religion, rather than race or ethnicity the key issue, they are listening now.

Debates about things like marriage commissioners and same-sex marriages, Christmas stories and preschool settings,[6] serve as reminders – says journalist Susan Martinuk – that "there are only so many rights to go around. Giving more rights to one group inevitably means taking rights from another."[7] As Rex Murphy wryly notes, that can translate into something like the crucifix being ruled out and global warming beliefs being ruled in.[8]

The Tension of Coexistence

Social scientists have long documented various patterns of interaction. Almost a century ago, two very influential sociologists at the University of Chicago, Robert Park and Ernest Burgess, drew attention to what they called "the four great types of interaction" – competition, conflict, accommodation, and assimilation.[9]

They maintained that as groups relate to each other, the dominant forms of interaction pass through these four stages. Those stages have been readily evident in Canada.

Construction of the Mosaic

One of the hallmarks of Canada has been the historical effort to create and sustain a flourishing nation built on diversity.

In the beginning, the country's central cultural-group dilemma was how to create one nation comprised of descendants from Britain and France.[10] A subplot was how to incorporate increasing numbers of people arriving from other parts of the world. The Aboriginal host population that was forced to share the land with all these uninvited newcomers initially was not given a major part in the unfolding national drama.

One by one, the country's diverse parts – like varied mosaic tiles – have been assembled in the mosaic art piece.

Quebec. As late as the 1950s, Anglophones and Francophones existed as "two solitudes" occupying separate geographical and cultural turfs. They shared no common vision and no consciousness of kind – two traits that are indispensable to the existence of group life.[11]

Therefore one of the first major tasks in nation-building began to take place as the Royal Commission on Bilingualism and Biculturalism released its seven-volume report between 1965 and 1972. That task was resolving the fundamental question of how Quebec and the rest of Canada could exist as a nation.[12]

The Commission reported that Canada was in the throes of a major crisis that called for convincing Quebeckers that they could experience equality and mutual respect with the rest of the country. Francophones in that province were experiencing considerable linguistic, economic, and occupational inequities in both the public and private sectors.[13]

As a consequence of "The B & B Report," it was decreed that Canada had two founding peoples – the British and the French. The Official Languages Act of 1969 declared that Canadians were free to live out life in either of the two official languages – English or French. Federal and provincial initiatives were escalated to transform life in Quebec.

Such efforts hardly put an end to division between Quebec and the rest of the country. But they were an important start in breaking down the two solitudes.

Ethnicity and Race. Ethnicity was once a very divisive variable. In large part it was related to the widespread belief in British cultural superiority. It also was the consequence of nationalistic rivalries in Europe that were further fuelled by two major World Wars prior to 1950. Some Canadians felt sufficiently stigmatized that they changed first names and surnames in Anglo directions, such as "Martinuk" becoming "Martin" and "Jozefa" becoming "Jo."

For some time now, tensions between ethnic groups have subsided, first in the form of accommodation stimulated by official multiculturalism, and in recent decades taking the form of considerable assimilation.

Racial divisions persisted much longer. Tolerance that would contribute to full participation in Canadian life – rather than acceptance – seems to have been the short-term goal of Canada's multiculturalism policy.

Racial discrimination has had a long history in Canada. In the late nineteenth and early twentieth centuries English-speaking Canadians, as with many people throughout the Western world, shared the belief that Anglo-Saxons represented the forefront of biological evolution. The most desirable immigrants were British and American, followed by Western and northern Europeans, then other Europeans. Near the bottom of the pecking order were the pacifist religious sects – Hutterites, Mennonites, and Doukhobors. Last were Blacks and Asians.[14]

The result was that people in the latter categories experienced severe discrimination in gaining entrance to Canada and finding jobs and equitable pay. In some jurisdictions, they were not allowed to join unions, be elected to public office, or vote. World War II saw some 22,000 Japanese Canadians removed from the Pacific coast and relocated to the B.C. interior and other provinces. As for Jews, historian Howard Palmer summed up a national tragedy with this poignant line: "Canada closed its doors to Jewish immigrants at the time when they desperately needed refuge from Nazi persecution in Europe."[15]

In the last three decades or so, partly as a result of multiculturalism ideals and initiatives, racial barriers have been coming down. One tangible indicator is the large increase in the acceptance and incidence of interracial marriages.

The marginalizing of Aboriginals that was so obvious in the B & B's statement about the country's "founding peoples" has by now been widely recognized. There have been lots of apologies, lots of programs, and considerable amounts of money invested in improving the lives of First Nations peoples. Their long-standing experiences with severe poverty, poor health, inadequate education, and a wide range of additional severe personal and social problems – notably crime, violence, alcoholism, drug abuse and suicide – no longer are escaping national notice.[16]

What still is required are effective responses that can elevate life for larger numbers of Aboriginals. There seems to be a particular lack of clarity with respect to what it is that the majority of First Nations peoples want – beyond the meeting of vital immediate needs. What is their vision or visions? Life on reserves? Life off reserves? Involvement in the broader regional, national, and global economies?

But the desire for positive coexistence clearly is in place.

Gender. Adjustments also needed to be made to ensure that women could participate fully in Canadian life. Competition and conflict stages have been apparent.

Between the 1860s and 1960s, women contributed generously to Canada's social life. For their efforts they were rewarded by being treated first as noncitizens and later as second-class citizens.[17]

At different points in time women were not allowed to retain property or control their own finances. They couldn't vote in any province before 1916 or vote federally until 1918. It took until 1929 for women to be declared "persons" and therefore eligible as full citizens to hold any public office. Quebec, nonetheless, withheld the provincial vote from women until 1940. Comparatively, women received voting privileges in the United States in 1920, in Britain in 1928, and in Japan in 1945.[18] It took until 1957 for a woman (Ellen Fairclough) to be appointed to the federal cabinet and 1989 for a woman to become the head of a major national party (the NDP's Audrey McLaughlin). In 1993, Kim Campbell became the first female Prime Minister – albeit on an interim basis; due to summer and election timing, she never sat in Parliament as PM.

Occupationally, women were expected to marry and stay home, with employment for women restricted primarily to those who were single or financially disadvantaged. They typically were hired last, fired first, and paid less.[19] Education for women was geared primarily to preparing them for marriage and family life, and did little to contribute to vocational flexibility. By 1960, only about one in four university students were women, with most enrolled in nursing, home economics, and education programs.[20]

Women also were excluded from a variety of roles in organizations, and even from the organizations themselves. So-called "women's tasks" and even blatant "No Women" signs summed up the common organizational story.

In response to significant lobbying by women's groups, a Royal Commission on the Status of Women in Canada was established in 1967. In late 1970 its findings were tabled in the House of Commons. Issues included equal pay for work of equal value, family law, educational opportunities, access to managerial positions, birth control, maternity leave, and daycare.

Today considerable progress toward gender equality has been made. There also has been a significant shift in public attitudes. As early as the mid-1980s, sociologist Monica Boyd could write, "Although vestiges of traditional attitudes persist, Canadians are becoming more egalitarian in their attitudes and opinions about women and women's issues."[21] Our Project Canada surveys show that the equality of women is now a given for the vast majority of people across the country. What is at issue is the extent of its realization.

Some Other Mosaic Pieces. As attention has been drawn to other people who are facing barriers to full participation in Canadian life, the mood and inclination of governments and the public have moved towards inclusion.

For example, legislation and tangible initiatives have been put in place to respond to the needs of Canadians with varied disabilities. Children who have learning difficulties, individuals with physical limitations – including people who are blind, deaf, and disabled – have been identified as requiring assistance that will enable them to share in life as fully as possible.

Age discrimination has been given increasing attention in recent years. One specific issue that has been addressed is mandatory retirement. The practice has been eliminated in many jurisdictions and job situations. More and more Canadians have the option of continuing to be employed as long as they literally are willing and able to hold down jobs. As more and more people remain productively employed past sixty-five, the new retirement norm may become seventy – maybe even seventy-five.

Despite the fears of some observers that people working past sixty-five would work past their prime productive years and block the occupational gates for younger people, the early data suggest that there are few downsides to opting for a system of voluntary retirement.

Those who opt for retirement frequently are the least productive or least enthralled with their jobs. They are happy to move on. Those who stay longer seldom continue to work beyond the age of 70. With mortality apparent, many express the desire to do other things while they can.

A Mosaic With Limits?

Resistance to people participating fully in Canadian society because of their race or ethnicity, their gender, disabilities, or age have all been seen as discrimination. The reason is that such characteristics are variables over which individuals have no control. As such, discrimination has been a justice issue that has called for corrective responses.

However, this is not to say that, in the minds of the populace, everything goes.

Sexual orientation, for example, is an issue that has often received a fairly negative response from a large number of people. As gays and lesbians have attempted to pursue careers, employment, parenthood, positions of ministry, and marriage, they have known considerable support, but also considerable opposition.

At this point in Canadian history, a number of adjustments – legal and otherwise – have been made to bring about a measure of accommodation. But full assimilation into Canadian life in the sense of full integration and acceptance is still very much the proverbial "work in progress." This tile still doesn't quite fit in.

One of the major reasons for the resistance, of course, is that many Canadians do not view homosexuality as *an involuntary attribute* like race or gender, but rather as *a voluntary moral decision*. One is obliged to accept attributes. But one is not obliged to accept moral choices.

Consequently, it's predictable that some of the most vociferous opposition to gay equality has come from the primary "morality makers" – religious groups.

As such, the pitch of the debate has often escalated, emotions have run high, and the mood has not always been particularly civil or compassionate. After all, for many, this is not just a debate about lifestyles. It is a debate about what is and what is not of God.

The debate has underlined the difficulty that any society has in sustaining unity while at the same time satisfying highly diverse segments of the population.

The goal expressed by Pierre Trudeau – "of a land of people with many differences but a single desire to live in harmony"[22] – is severely tested when the players involved are identified, not by their ethnicity or gender or age, but by their religion.

When a specific issue arises that involves highly divergent moral interpretations – in this case homosexuality – clearly the only resolution lies with accommodation. In the case of gay marriage, for example, federal legislation was passed that made it legal. However, religious communities are not obliged to carry out gay marriage ceremonies.

The bigger question goes beyond specific moral issues such as same-sex marriage or abortion. In a Canada that is characterized by growing polarization along religious lines, the question is how to achieve harmony between those who are religious and those who are not.

But things get even more complicated when religious groups assert teachings that fly in the face of pervasive norms and even laws. When the numbers of people involved with those groups are relatively small – such has been the case with groups like Doukobors or Jehovah's Witnesses – they can be labelled deviant, dismissed as "sects" and "cults," and have minimal impact on society as a whole.

However, when their numbers are sizable, such as is the case with Muslims in Canada, the potential for conflict with everyone else – including conflict with those of other religious persuasions – is very high.

So it is that the range and the elasticity of Canada's mosaic is being severely tested in the case of religion.

- One issue is polarization involving those who are religious and those who are not.
- A second critical issue is the polarization between some groups – notably Muslims but also other groups that sometimes take on culture, such as evangelicals – and everyone else.

It all adds up to tension within the hallowed mosaic.

The tension can also be expected to be accompanied by a fair amount of passion. On the religious side of things, when one believes that he or she has "seen" or "heard" the gods, such a sense of revelation carries with it a measure of authority and urgency.

Conversely, the non-religious onlooker can respond to faith claims with scepticism, cynicism, and derision.

When the person with faith – complete with conviction, earnestness, and a missionary spirit – meets the person with no faith, the end result is seldom conversion. It may be martyrdom. Conversely, the person with no faith who belittles and ridicules the person with faith runs the risk of finding that such a devotee does not necessarily subscribe to the guideline of "turning the other cheek."

Religious polarization may well test Canada's mosaic limits.

A Canadian Reading

In early 2009, ads approved by the Toronto Transit Commission ran on buses and trains declaring, *"There's Probably No God."* The ads were sponsored by the Freethought Association of Canada, and had debuted in Britain a few months before. The lead  ad line was followed with a second in smaller print: *"Now Stop Worrying and Enjoy Your Life."*

About two weeks earlier, in the wake of the British campaign, the United Church of Canada had got into the act with a national print and online ad campaign of its own that included a prominent ad in the *Globe and Mail*. The original atheist ad lines were cited, with two new lines added, resulting in a choice-like format: *"There's Probably A God"* followed by the same, *"Now Stop Worrying and Enjoy Your Life"* second line. People were invited to "Join the discussion at wondercafe.ca," a United Church website.

The denomination's moderator at the time, David Giuliano, explained that the ad was "directed not at ourselves, but rather at people who might be questioning the reality of God. Our intention," he said, "is to invite people who are questioning to join us in conversation about their beliefs. Hence the tagline, 'Join the discussion at wondercafe.ca.'"[23]

Keith Howard, the executive director of the campaign known as *Emerging Spirit*, commented, "God has been co-opted by many causes, from football to starting wars, and I think it is time we had a really good discussion about what we mean by God, what God's priorities might be and how that impacts how we live our lives."[24]

For his part, Freethought Association president Justin Trottier said that he welcomed what he called the "cheeky" United Church counter-ads, adding, "That's what this is all about: dialogue."[25]

The "war of ads" was greeted with enthusiasm by the media and given extensive exposure across the country. The dialogue between spokespeople for the two sides was friendly, positive, and polite. Appearing together on the CTV national news, for example, Howard and Trottier were both buoyant and congenial. It seemed apparent that theists and atheists could easily co-exist – even become the closest of friends.

Not everyone was enthralled. In Calgary, colourful and controversial Roman Catholic Bishop Fred Henry commented, "If the benchmark is that [ads] should be non-offensive, I'm offended." He suggested the ideal date to launch such a campaign would be April Fool's Day.[26] Don Hutchinson of the Evangelical Fellowship of Canada said that the posting of such ads meant "religion is welcome in the public square, and this is really good news."[27]

If such a public display of pleasantries between religious and non-religious people could be normative, we could be optimistic about the accommodation of religion and non-religion in Canada. We would be looking at mutual respect, courtesy, and calm. Atheists could be part of broader interfaith…err, intersomething dialogue.

As one of my favourite comedians used to put it, "If life were only like that."

The ping-pong game was evident in the eastern U.S. as Christmas approached in 2010. A billboard outside the Lincoln tunnel sponsored by the Catholic League for Religious and Civil Rights read, "You Know It's Real: This Season Celebrate Jesus." An American Atheists-sponsored billboard on the New Jersey side of the tunnel read, "You know it's a myth. This season, celebrate reason!"[28] Hmmm.

In January of 2011, a second atheist-promoted ad began to be distributed across Canada. This time the slogan read, "Extraordinary Claims Require Extraordinary Evidence." This ad was obviously more provocative, in that it went on to explicitly list "ALLAH, BIGFOOT, UFOs, HOMEOPATHY, ZEUS, PSYCHICS, CHRIST." A longer version contained a far more detailed list of claimants.

Justin Trottier, now the national executive director of the sponsoring Centre for Inquiry, commented that the ads were not designed to offend religious Canadians but rather to "generate debate" about so-called extraordinary claims.

Trottier added, "We are not here to mock people who believe in these claims."[29] The website for the Canadian branch of the Centre for Inquiry notes that the Centre "promotes and advances reason, science, secularism, and freedom of inquiry in all areas of human endeavour."[30]

Needless to say, one could anticipate that some of the responses would be a shade less cordial and light-hearted than the Trottier-Howard exchanges.

A Lutheran theologian based at the Graduate Theological Union at Berkeley, Ted Peters, has noted, "It used to be that atheists didn't bother anybody. They simply stayed home from church on Sunday and avoided praying. The social impact was minimal. But now," he says, a new breed of atheists is zealously crusading to liberate the world from the chains of religion.[31] John Allemang of the *Globe and Mail* recently summed things up this way: "Proponents of atheism have found their comfort zone in the modern Western world, where penalties for infidelity are few but the residual sense of outrage is still strong enough to propel their attacks on a no-longer vengeful God to the top of the bestseller lists.[32]

The "new atheists" are passionate. And they are being widely read, seen, and heard.

Latent and Overt Conflict

The incident is well-known. In the spring of 2010, American commentator and author Ann Coulter, well-known for her conservative and controversial opinions, was scheduled to speak at three Canadian universities – Western, Ottawa, and Calgary. However, the Ottawa presentation was cancelled by organizers who felt there was a risk of physical violence.

Coulter is well-known for inflammatory comments against Muslims, liberals, and gays. Prior to her arrival in Ottawa, she had been warned by the university's academic vice-president, "Promoting hatred against any identifiable group would not only be considered inappropriate, but could in fact lead to criminal charges."[33]

OK. If we are going to go after everyone who appears to be promoting hatred or hostility toward *any* identifiable group, fair enough. But we don't.

Listen to these diatribes...

- Author A has described the Roman Catholic Church as a "profiteering, woman-fearing, guilt-gorging, truth-hating, child-raping institution."[34]
- Author B has written that "all religious belief is sinister and infantile," and that "religion multiplies suspicion and hatred." He goes so far as to say that "religion poisons everything."[35] Further, in 2006 he told a Toronto audience that he is in favour of decriminalizing hate speech – that free speech must include hate speech.[36]
- *The Sunday Times* in London reported that these same two authors were part of a movement to see Pope Benedict XVI arrested for international crimes against humanity when he arrived in England for a September 2010 visit. Author A denied that he wanted to slap the cuffs on the pontiff personally, but credited the idea of the arrest to his "fellow deity slayer," Author B. [37]

Now, I'm not particularly thin-skinned, but the things these two authors have said about religion generally and the Catholic Church specifically are a tad hateful. A cursory peek at what someone like Sam Harris has to say about religion shows their animosity is far from unique.

Note that both of these authors have been treated as superstar celebrities in Canada – a notch above rock stars. The media have enthusiastically promoted their ideas. They are invited to our campuses. They are asked to speak to our organizations. Even debate former Prime Ministers. They are, of course, Richard Dawkins and Christopher Hitchens.

The fact that few people seem to either notice or care about what they have to say about religion – and usually Christianity more specifically – points to the reality of religious polarization in Canada. If either Dawkins or Hitchens said such things about just about any other category – Aboriginals, Asians, gays, or women – or were as direct in demeaning Jews, Muslims or, heaven forbid, atheists, there would be a major uproar.

But there is scarcely a detectable whimper. Even the religiously devout in Canada are incredibly blasé. Connie denBok, a United Church minister in Toronto, has summed things up this way: "There is a pathological politeness among Canadian church people," who tend to keep silent in the face of attacks against belief in God.[38] I would add, "as well as attacks on themselves."

Such hostile critiques, rather than immediately making people wince – like a distasteful racist or sexist joke at a banquet – seem to be welcomed by a sizable number of people who are not religious and are not sympathetic with organized religion.

The very different responses to Ann Coulter and the two celebrity atheists are not aberrations. They are consistent with our survey findings.

What Canadians Have to Say

The idea that racial and cultural diversity is good for Canada is scarcely in doubt at this point in our history. Large majorities of people who both value and do not value religion endorse the idea. The principle of diversity being a virtue is not in doubt.

Table 4.1. Views of Diversity by Religion

"Racial and cultural diversity is a good thing for Canada" (Agree)

	🇨🇦	ATTENDANCE		IDENTIFICATION		BELIEF	
		Weekly	Never	Yes	No	Theist	Atheist
Adults	94%	85	79	81	86	83	78
Teens	94%	81	76	80	79	82	72

Source: Project Canada 2005.

What's more, if we ask people if they are willing to at least tolerate how others choose to live their live, almost everyone indicates that they are. Canadians may not be excited about what other people do and think. But at least they are willing to be accommodating, in the Park and Burgess sense.

So far so good. Things just might work.

However, when we pin people down on specifics, we find that a few cracks begin to appear in the mosaic.

Table 4.2. Tolerance: Adults

"Generally-speaking, I am willing to at least tolerate how people choose to live their lives"

	ATTENDANCE		IDENTIFICATION		BELIEF	
	Weekly	Never	Yes	No	Theist	Atheist
94%	95	94	94	97	95	98

Source: Project Canada 2005.

Religion's Contribution. In asking Canadians for their assessment of religion's impact in Canada and in the world as a whole, we would expect that their responses would vary by their religious inclinations. No surprise there.

However, what is interesting to note is the magnitude of the differences.

- Just over 6 in 10 teenagers feel that *"organized religion's overall impact on life in Canada is positive."* They are not quite as upbeat when they look elsewhere: some 5 in 10 offer a positive assessment of religion's influence on the *rest of the world.*
- The assessments of religion both nationally and globally differ fairly dramatically by all three religiosity measures. In the case of belief, for example, only about 3 in 10 teens who are atheists feel religion is having a positive impact in Canada, with the figure dipping to 2 in 10 for what's happening globally.

Table 4.3. Attitudes Toward Religion: Teenagers

		ATTENDANCE		I.D.		BELIEF	
		Weekly	Never	Yes	No	Theist	Atheist
Organized religion's overall impact on life in Canada is positive	63%	82	48	71	45	78	29
Organized religion's overall impact on the world as a whole is positive	48	69	35	56	30	65	21

Sources: Project Teen Canada 2008.

In the case of adults, on the surface it appears that Canadians are pretty much split 50-50 on whether or not the decline in religious participation has had a negative impact on the quality of life in the country. They also seem to be almost equally divided on whether or not our society would be better off if people attended services more often.

Table 4.4. Attitudes Toward Religion: Adults						
▮✦▮	ATTENDANCE Weekly	Never	I.D. Yes	No	BELIEF Theist	Atheist
The decline in participation in org. religion has had a significant negative impact on life in Canada	50	81	30	57	15	58	17
Our society would be better off if people attended religious services more often	44	86	12	51	4	65	5

Sources: Project Canada 2005.

It's almost as if the attitude of many never attenders is that something has been lost, but what's done is done. The past is the past. There's no turning back. There may even be a feeling that it's simply too late, summed up by the line in the old love song: *"It makes no difference now."*

- A closer look by religiosity reveals that adults who are religious are much more likely than others to think the participation decline has had a negative effect on Canada.
- What perhaps is surprising is that 30% of those who never attend services share the perception of life being adversely affected by the attendance drop.

It is worth noting that, while some people who are not religious think the decline in participation has been detrimental, very few of them maintain that we'd be better off as a society if people attended services more often.

They include only 12% of people in the "never attend" category – far below the 30% who think our quality of life has suffered.

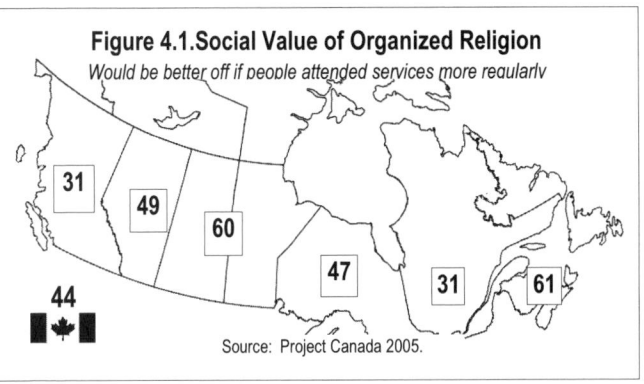

Figure 4.1.Social Value of Organized Religion

Would be better off if people attended services more regularly

Source: Project Canada 2005.

Religion's Place. Canadians who are religious and those who are not differ considerably in their perceptions as to the appropriate place of religion in life, especially by attendance. When asked to respond to the question, *"Ministers should stick to religion and not concern themselves with social, economic, and political issues,"* only about 2 to 10 weekly attenders agree, versus 6 in 10 people who never attend services.

People also differ a great deal in their perceptions of the power that religious groups have in Canadian life. Some 6 in 10 of those who are not religious by any of our three measures think groups have "too much power." In contrast, only 1 in 10 weekly attenders and about 2 in 10 people who identify with a tradition or believe in God hold such a view.

Confidence in Groups. Predictably, Canadians also differ considerably by involvement in the confidence they express toward religious group leaders. Seven in 10 weekly attenders indicate they have high levels of confidence, with that level dropping to 1 in 10 for adults and 2 in 10 for teens who never attend services. Differences are smaller by belief and identification.

Table 4.5. Attitudes Toward Leaders & Power by Religiosity

	ATTEND		I.D.		BELIEF	
	Week	Never	Yes	No	Theist	Atheist
ADULTS						
Ministers should stick to religion and not concern themselves with social, economic, and political issues	47%	23	61	45	61	35	69
Religious groups have too much power in our nation's affairs	29	10	55	23	59	19	68
Have "great deal" or "quite a bit" of confidence in religious orgs	34	70	9	38	6	52	8
TEENS: confidence religious orgs	39	75	19	50	16	65	10

Sources: Project Canada 2005 & Project Teen Canada 2008.

In recent decades, considerable attention has been drawn to the issue of clergy abuse, particularly involving Roman Catholic clergy.[39]

Just before Easter in 2010, the criticisms of the Catholic Church escalated on what seemed to be a worldwide level. The furor began with a report in the *New York Times* on March 12th headlined, "Abuse scandal in Germany edges closer to Pope." The story linked the 1980 reassignment of a priest accused of molesting boys to the current Pope when he was in charge of the Munich archdiocese – an accusation denied by the archdiocese.

The story was given extensive news coverage. Moreover, it was seized on by anti-religion commentators such as Christopher Hitchens. He wrote a column for *Slate* in which he accused the Pope of "obstructing justice on a global scale" and said his "whole career has the stench of evil." Respected Catholic commentator John Allen called for "true friends of the Pope" to press for full disclosure.

On March 24, the *New York Times* published a second article, accusing top Vatican officials – including the future Pope – of not defrocking a priest in the Archdiocese of Milwaukee who had molested as many as 200 deaf boys.

Understandably, the report created another global media firestorm. Additional stories, such as an Associated Press release linking the Pope to a mid-80s abuse case in the Diocese of Oakland, further fuelled the furor.[40]

Some of the responses emanating from Rome and elsewhere did little to contribute to calm. In a Good Friday homily, the Pope's personal preacher likened the tide of allegations about cover-ups to the "more shameful aspects of anti-Semitism."[41] The same day, Quebec City Archbishop Marc Ouellet, primate of the Roman Catholic Church in Canada, accused media members of having "ulterior motives" in linking the Pope to the scandals.[42]

Not everyone was defensive. That same Good Friday, the head of German's Catholic bishops issued a statement, denouncing past failures in the Church's handling of abuse cases.[43] Thomas Reese, a priest and Vatican expert based at Washington's Georgetown University, commented, "You know, you wish that people in the Vatican had at least some idea of how what they say will be perceived by an audience outside of the Vatican clergy."[44]

On April 8th, eight days after Easter, the Vatican posted a new guide on its website that for the first time made public an explicit policy regarding reporting abuse to law enforcement authorities. Canadian bishops have been obligated to report child sexual abuse since 1992, when the Canadian Council of Catholic Bishops published the booklet, *From Pain to Hope*. The booklet states, "Everyone has a duty to report sexual abuse."[45]

However, the very next day, the *Globe and Mail* released a story accusing the Vatican and Canadian Catholic officials of trying to keep secret a sex scandal in the mid-90s involving a priest in the Ottawa area.[46] The writer of the story, Tu Thanh Ha, noted that the situation was in direct conflict with the Church's sexual abuse policy.

The Canadian Conference of Catholic Bishops issued a statement the same day, saying it was unable to comment on correspondence dating back to 1993. It did, however, reaffirm its policy of disclosure, adding that it remains "even more determined than ever to provide children with a safe environment."[47]

When Pope Benedict made his fall 2010 four-day visit to England and Scotland amidst highly-publicized opposition and speculation that he would be greeted with considerable hostility and even violence, the trip went off without serious incident.[48] Protesters were readily outnumbered by supporters, and the visit was declared "an overwhelming success" by the government's organizer. Catholic officials not only were pleased, but were speaking of the possibility of a "Benedict bounce" – a subsequent positive effect on the Church.[49]

In view of the extensive attention that has been given to scandals that in Canada included the 1989 disclosure of the Mount Cashel orphanage travesties and the negative information about residential schools that has involved the indictment of a number of Protestant groups as well as Catholics, the obvious question is what impact has all this had on Canadians' confidence in religious groups?

The initial answer is: a lot. While confidence in Canadian religious leaders slipped somewhat from the mid-1970s to the mid-80s, it dropped significantly specifically between 1985 and 1990.

However, despite the ongoing publicity given to scandals of various kinds, confidence in religious leaders has remained about the same since 1990.

Figure 4.2. Confidence in Religious Leaders: 1974-2005
% Indicating Have "A Great Deal" or "Quite a Bit" of Confidence

1974	1979	1985	1990	1995	2000	2005
58	60	51	37	36	33	34

Sources: 1974, 1979: Gallup Canada; 1985-2005 Project Canada Survey Series.

What about participation? Are people staying away as a result of their waning confidence?" The short answer appears to be: "Not much."

An analysis of attendance patterns between the crucial 1985-90 period when confidence in leaders crashed reveals a surprising result: attendance levels remained remarkably stable, even in the Atlantic region. Many Canadians, led by Catholics, were upset with their leaders and, to varying degrees were disillusioned and demoralized.

Table 4.6. Confidence & Attendance: 1985-90*

	1985		1990	
	Confid	Attend	Confid	Attend
🇨🇦	51%	26	37	23
BC	40	19	30	22
Prairies	51	23	33	22
Ontario	46	23	32	21
Quebec	54	27	48	23
Atlantic	74	42	40	41

*Confidence: "A Great Deal" or "Quite A Bit"; Attendance: Weekly
Sources: Project Canada 1985 and Project Canada 1990.

But there were no signs that they were making a massive move toward church exits. The modest attendance decreases in no way matched the confidence level declines.

Despite all that happened, the prevalent thinking seemed to have been, "Some of the leaders have been messing up badly. But my faith and church are still important to me."[50]

The situation in the United States may be informative. By the mid-1990s, Catholic obedience to the Church's weekly mass attendance requirement had faded to Protestant levels of about 45%.[51] But in 2002-03, when attention peaked regarding sexual abuse in the Church, Gallup found that by February of 2003, Catholic attendance dipped to the lowest level the pollster had ever found.

However, in assessing the situation as of April 2009, the Gallup organization reported that Catholic attendance was essentially unchanged from 1995. "That's an extremely important finding," the pollster noted, "given the upheaval caused by the sexual abuse scandals." While polling in 2002 and 2003 documented a decline, "attendance rebounded by the end of 2003 and has since remained on par with its pre-scandal level of about 45%."[52]

Table 4.7. U.S. Attendance: 1955-2005

Have attended a service "in the last seven days"

	Catholics	Protestants
1955	75%	42
1975	54	40
1985	50	40
1995	46	43
2005	45	45

Sources: The Gallup Poll, January 6, 2004 & April 9, 2009.

Dec 2001	46%
Dec 2002	41
Feb 2003	35
Nov 2003	45

The resiliency and outlook were verbalized recently by *Toronto Star* Sunday columnist Angelo Persichilli:

> *I am a Catholic. Even though, I must confess, I'm not a good one. ...Pedophilia is a crime, and those responsible for that crime must be punished. But at the same time, I cannot approve of the politically motivated posturing over these crimes and the denigration of the entire institution of the Catholic Church. The Catholic Church will eradicate pedophiles from its ranks.*
> *...And today, I'll go to mass.*[53]

Comfort Levels. A standard item that I have used since the inception of the Project Canada surveys asks people how comfortable they think they would feel around a wide range of individuals.[54] They have been asked to put themselves in a situation where they encounter a person, and the only thing they know about the individual is a trait such as their race, religion, sexual orientation, or the fact they are an ex-convict or a person with AIDS. The question that has been put to them is, *"What do you think your immediate reaction would be?"* with the response options *"At Ease," "A Bit Uneasy,"* or *"Very Uneasy."*

- The most recent survey Project Canada survey found that some 85% of Canadians admitted they would feel uneasy around an *ex-convict*, with the figure coming in at approximately 50% for a person with *AIDS* and 25% for a *homosexual* – whether male or female. Anticipated uneasiness was consistently higher in each instance for religious people.

- In the case of the unknown individual being *a born-again Christian*, some 30% expressed uneasiness – with the levels around 50% for those who were not religious, and 20% for those religious by our three measures. The finding is reminiscent of the results of a U.S. national survey in 2007 where 44% of Americans reported that "Christians get on my nerves."[55]

- Around 20% of Canadians said they would feel uneasy in the presence of *a Muslim*, 5% if the person was *a Jew*. In both cases, differences by religiousness were small.

Table 4.8. Rapport and Religiosity

"Please put yourself in the situation of just having met a person and the ONLY thing you know about them is ONE of the following. What do you think your IMMEDIATE reaction would be?"

% Indicating Would Feel "A Bit Uneasy" or "Very Uneasy"

	■♦■	ATTENDANCE		IDENTIF		BELIEF	
		Weekly	Never	Yes	No	Theist	Atheist
An ex-convict	86%	86	82	87	82	86	81
A person with AIDS	49	52	42	53	30	52	37
A male homosexual	27	43	20	30	11	34	18
A born-again Christian	31	21	44	28	50	22	54
A Muslim	18	18	21	19	13	17	18
A Jew	5	4	6	5	4	5	8

Shading: difference of 10 percentage points or more

Source: Project Canada 2005.

Obviously, things don't just run one-way. In 2006, a national poll carried out as part of the global World Values Survey asked Canadians how they felt about an atheist holding public office. The wording was harsh: *"Politicians who don't believe in God are unfit for public office."*

One in 4 (24%) people agreed, including 33% of weekly attenders and 6% of those who never attend services. The level was the same as it was in 2000.

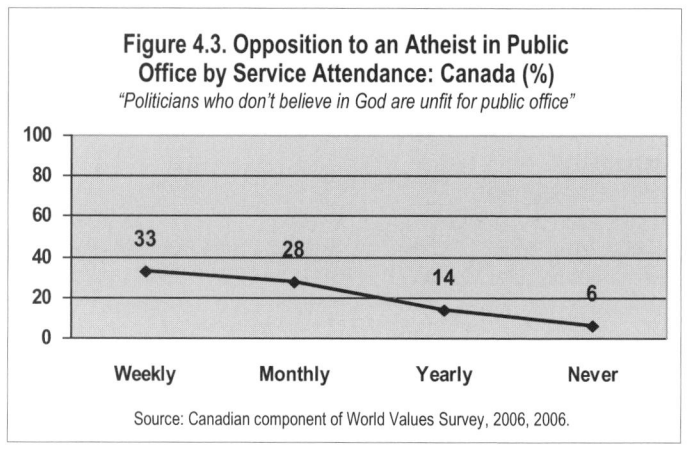

Figure 4.3. Opposition to an Atheist in Public Office by Service Attendance: Canada (%)

"Politicians who don't believe in God are unfit for public office"

Source: Canadian component of World Values Survey, 2006, 2006.

Comparable data for earlier times are difficult to locate. But there is little doubt views toward atheists holding down public positions of various kinds have softened with time. For example, our 1985 Project Canada survey found that 57% of Canadians felt atheists should be allowed to *publish* their views, but only 14% thought they should be allowed to *teach* their views. Homosexuals, incidentally, did not fare much better, at 54% and 14% respectively. Today, of course, such overt opposition would be a violation of human rights.

Speaking of homosexuals, as we have just seen, the majority of people who are religious, along with even larger majorities of people who are not religious, claim they would feel comfortable in their presence. A majority of Canadians, religious and otherwise, also say homosexuals are entitled to the same rights as everyone else.

That said, only a minority of weekly attenders say they approve of or even accept the idea of same-sex marriage. Attitudes are somewhat softer by identification and belief.

Table 4.9. Homosexuality and Religiosity: Adults & Teens

	🇨🇦	ATTENDANCE		IDENTIF		BELIEF	
AGREE		Weekly	Never	Yes	No	Theist	Atheist
Homosexuals are entitled to the same rights as other Canadians	81%	63	90	78	95	73	93
SAME-SEX MARRIAGE							
Approve & accept	48	17	69	42	80	32	70
Disapprove but accept	22	21	16	24	13	24	16
Disapprove & do not accept	30	62	15	34	7	44	14
TEENAGERS							
SAME-SEX MARRIAGE							
Approve & accept	47	23	57	40	62	29	61
Disapprove but accept	26	26	25	28	22	28	21
Disapprove & do not accept	27	51	18	32	16	43	18

Sources: Project Canada 2005 and Project Teen Canada 2008.

The posture on same-sex marriage among teenagers is fairly similar to adults – with the exception of weekly attenders being slightly more positive, and non-religious youth being somewhat more negative. The latter finding may be a tip-off on the fact that sizable numbers of non-religious teens have been recent arrivals in the "never, none, and not" categories of attendance, identification, and belief.

Significantly, teens with immigrant roots are more inclined than others to experience and endorse conventional family and sexual expressions.[56] As Valpy and Friesen recently noted, "On matters such as homosexuality, the role of women, sex education and religious instruction, immigrant religious groups are embracing debates that pit them against the majority public opinion." They suggest that the result could be growing division, where "faith groups may find more common ground with one another than with secular institutions." They add, there is a "growth of a kind of militant secularism among non-believers...that treats the religious as unenlightened or backward."[57]

*Canadian Youth Provide Some Preliminary Data
on Where Polarization is Most Acute.*

- Belief that religion's impact on the world is positive is highest among Conservative Protestants, Orthodox Christians, unspecified "Christians," Catholics outside Quebec, Hindus, Muslims and Sikhs.
- Conservative Protestant and Muslim teens are far less likely than others to approve of same-sex marriage.
- A slight majority of teens endorse the idea that all world religions are equally valid, led by Hindus and Buddhists. Conservative Protestants are disinclined to hold such a view.

Teenage Polarization in the Mosaic
Religion & Morality

	Religion's World Impact Is Positive	Approve of/ Accept Same-Sex Marriage	All World Religions Equally Valid
NATIONALLY	48%	73	60
Roman Catholicism	55	75	68
Outside Quebec	63	72	68
Quebec	37	79	68
Protestantism	62	51	40
Conservative	70	31	22
Mainline	50	75	61
Orthodox	67	54	68
Christian *unspecified*	72	52	41
Other World Faiths	57	67	67
Hinduism	72	72	89
Islam	64	45	59
Sikhism	63	61	70
Judaism	49	87	57
Buddhism	44	83	78
Aboriginal Spirituality	35	92	57
No Religion	30	84	60

The Global Situation

When we look at religious pluralism in worldwide context, some basic general patterns seem apparent in the midst of considerable complexity.

- Global data on religious identification, attendance, belief, and salience point to the fact that some countries such as Nigeria and Pakistan know the dominance of Islam and Christianity, and have very high levels of religiousness. In such settings, religion knows a *monopoly*.
- Countries including Canada and the United States know higher levels of *religious diversity*, as well as lower levels of practice and belief.
- In still other settings, such as Britain, Sweden, and France, religious identification, practices, and belief slip further. In these countries, indifference to religion and/or secularization is extensive, to the extent that, for purposes of categorization, we might think of them as being characterized by *secular monopolies*.
- Generally speaking, as countries move from religious monopolies to polarization to secular monopolies, the personal importance of religion decreases.

Table 4.10. Identification, Belief & Salience: Select Countries

	ID	Salience	Ctn	Muslim	Other	Indigenous
Religious Monopoly						
Pakistan	99%	92	<5	95	<5	<5
Philippines	99	96	90	5	<5	5
Nigeria	99	96	40	50	<5	10
Polarization						
United States	84	65	80	<5	<5	<5
Spain	84	49	80	<5	<5	<5
CANADA	**84**	**42**	**80**	**<5**	**<5**	**<5**
Secular Monopoly						
United Kingdom	77	27	70	<5	<5	<5
Sweden	75	17	70	<5	<5	<5
France	57	30	50	5	<5	<5

Sources: ID and salience, see Table 9.1; breakdowns derived from Factbook, CIA 2010.

As would be expected, in those settings where religious monopolies exist, people are more likely than their counterparts in other countries to feel that "most faiths" make a positive contribution to their societies.

That said, the differences in views concerning the positive contribution of religions tend to be fairly small between countries characterized by religious and non-religious polarization and those where secularity is dominant.

Table 4.11. Salience and Positive View of Religion's Role: Select Countries

Most Faiths Make a Positive Contribution to Society
(Scale of 5-1, Agree to Disagree)

	Salience	Contribution
Religious Monopoly		
Senegal	98%	4.5
Pakistan	98	3.6
Ethiopia	91	4.2
Malaysia	95	4.2
India	79	4.1
Polarization		
South Africa	82	4.3
Italy	72	3.6
United States	67	3.9
Israel	50	2.8
CANADA	**45**	**3.6**
Germany	44	3.3
Belgium	37	3.3
Netherlands	33	2.9
Secular Monopoly		
United Kingdom	29	3.5
France	25	3.3
Norway	20	3.0

Sources: Computed from Gallup Coexist Index 2009:11-15.

Relative to people in other countries, Canadians are positive about what religious groups bring to national life – not quite as positive as people in the U.S. or India or Africa, but not as negative as many people in a number of European settings.

What stands out about people in countries characterized by religious monopolies is not just their views about religion's contribution, but also their views about truth versus relativity.

- In settings characterized by a *religious monopoly*, the inclination is for people to see "one true religion" existing.
- As countries experience greater *religious diversity*, including having greater proportions of people with no religion – such as in Canada – the populace has a greater inclination to think of there being "many true religions."
- In settings where *secular monopolies* exist, such as Sweden, there is a decrease in the belief in any one true religion, and a tendency either to relativize or dismiss religious truth altogether.

Table 4.12. Views of Religious Truth by Polarization

	One True Religion	Many True Religions	No True Religions	Totals
Religious Monopoly				
Pakistan	91%	9	0	100
Philippines	74	18	8	100
Nigeria	71	28	1	100
Polarization				
Spain	38	38	24	100
United States	22	73	5	100
CANADA	**17**	**69**	**14**	**100**
Secular Monopoly				
United Kingdom	13	68	19	100
Sweden	10	67	23	100
France	9	70	21	100

Source: Computed from Gallup International Millennium Survey 2001 as found in Smith 2009:278-279.

Again I would emphasize that I am talking about general patterns and broad strokes. When one is trying to synthesize global patterns, variations and exceptions seem to be everywhere.

Against the framework I have just offered, it is intriguing to examine some views that people in North American, Europe, and Asia have, for example, of Christians, Jews, and Muslims. The data were collected by the Pew Global Attitudes Project and released in 2005.

- In countries where Islamic *monopolies* exist, attitudes toward Muslims predictably are positive. Those sentiments are somewhat more restrained toward Christians, with the exception of Lebanon. Attitudes toward Jews are extremely negative. In India, the dominance of Hinduism is associated with fairly positive opinions of Christians, somewhat less positive views of Muslims, and very negative attitudes toward Jews.

- In European and North American settings characterized by *polarization*, including Canada, there is a tendency for positive views of all three groups to be quite a bit higher than elsewhere.

- In those countries where *secular monopolies exist,* following years of Christian dominance, something of a "shadow effect" seems to contribute to very positive attitudes not only toward Christians, but also toward Jews and Muslims as well. In China, where all three groups have known a limited presence historically, favourable attitudes are low in each instance.

Table 4.13. Views of Christians, Jews, and Muslims: Select Countries

% Indicating They Have "Very" or "Somewhat" Favourable Opinions of Each Group

	Christians	Jews	Muslims
Religious Monopoly			
Indonesia	58	13	99
Jordan	58	0	99
Morocco	33	8	97
Pakistan	22	5	94
Lebanon	91	0	92
Turkey	21	18	83
India	61	28	46
Polarization			
United States	87	77	57
Poland	86	54	46
Germany	83	67	40
CANADA	**83**	**78**	**60**
Netherlands	83	85	45
Spain	80	58	46
Secular Monopoly			
Russia	92	63	55
United Kingdom	85	78	72
France	84	82	64
China	26	28	20

Source: Computed from Pew Global Attitudes Project 2005.

In commenting on their findings, the Pew Research Center notes that in most of Europe and North America, "pluralities judge some religions as more prone to violence than others, and those that do, mostly have Islam in mind," while in "predominantly Muslim countries...most have Judaism in mind."[58] But what is particularly noteworthy is that unfavourable attitudes tend to be lower in countries that do not have religious monopolies.

These findings suggest an important possible correlate of polarization: the accommodation necessary for co-existence is extended to diverse religious groups.

Atheists. What about the case with people who are not religious, such as atheists?

Somewhat surprisingly, atheists have not fared very well in a polarized setting such as the United States. Since 1958, Gallup has been asking Americans if they would be willing to vote for a well-qualified person for president who happened to be an atheist.[59]

In 1958, 18% said they would. Twenty years later in 1978, the figure had increased to 40%. But Gallup's probe three decades later in 2007 found the figure had only increased to 45%.[60]

In fact, Gallup reported that being an atheist was the most detrimental trait for a possible 2008 candidate – well ahead of religion, race, gender, marital status, age, and sexual orientation (so much for the 72-year-old's anonymity!).

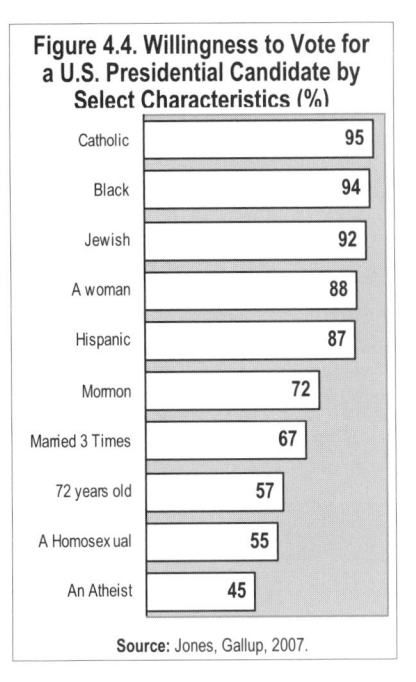

Figure 4.4. Willingness to Vote for a U.S. Presidential Candidate by Select Characteristics (%)

Catholic	95
Black	94
Jewish	92
A woman	88
Hispanic	87
Mormon	72
Married 3 Times	67
72 years old	57
A Homosexual	55
An Atheist	45

Source: Jones, Gallup, 2007.

Canadians do not seem to have anywhere near the same trepidation as Americans about atheists in a political office.

- In the 2006 World Values survey just noted, only 17% were opposed to atheists in office.
- Differences between women and men were fairly small.
- Opposition was higher for people 55 and older than others; that said, close to 80% of Canadians in that older age group were *not* opposed to atheists occupying public offices.

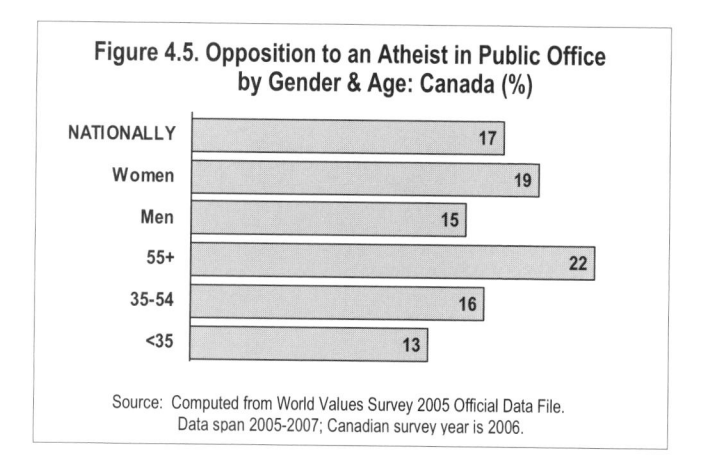

Figure 4.5. Opposition to an Atheist in Public Office by Gender & Age: Canada (%)

Source: Computed from World Values Survey 2005 Official Data File. Data span 2005-2007; Canadian survey year is 2006.

When we look at attitudes around the world toward an atheist in public office, we once again see that acceptance of different worldviews – in this case atheism – increases as we move from settings where a religious monopoly exists to places where polarization is more typical.

As would be expected, in countries where secular monopolies exist, there is very little consternation about atheists holding public office. If anything, what would be more interesting to know is the extent to which people in such places are open to *religious* people holding office.

There is an opportunity to take just such a look. The same World Values Survey also asked respondents to respond to the item, *"It would be better if there were more people with strong religious beliefs in public office."*

- Predictably, agreement is highest where religious monopolies exist, such as Iran.
- Yet, people in such countries sometimes are not quite as convinced – notably India and Iraq.
- In far more polarized settings, the pro-religious sentiment is much lower – 42% in the United States and only 23% here in Canada.
- However, the levels of agreement drop to just 12% in Finland, 6% in Norway, and 5% in Sweden.
- People in these latter three Scandinavian countries are not telling the pollsters that religious types are unfit for public office. But they are saying that their presence would not necessarily elevate life for everyone.

Table 4.14. Views of Atheists, Religious People in Public Office, and Atheist Populations: Select Countries (%'s)

	Atheists Unfit	Religious: Better Off	% Pop Atheists
Religion Monopoly			
Iraq	87	52	3
Iran	75	68	<1
Malaysia	64	58	2
Thailand	64	57	<1
Zambia	55	60	<1
Morocco	53	61	<1
Ethiopia	49	47	<1
India	49	38	2
Turkey	48	48	2
Polarization			
South Africa	49	59	1
Brazil	49	48	1
Ukraine	44	42	3
United States	32	42	4
Argentina	29	26	2
Mexico	26	37	3
Chile	26	36	3
CANADA	**18**	**23**	**6**
Viet Nam	18	25	24
Poland	17	29	1
Australia	13	14	10
Italy	12	18	3
Korea, Republic of	12	18	29
Germany	11	21	19
Spain	11	13	7
New Zealand	8	16	7
Secular Monopoly			
Finland	10	12	3
Sweden	3	5	17
Norway	4	6	7

Source: World Values Survey, 2005. Atheists in public office item: "Politicians who dont' believe in God are unfit for public office." - % in table disagreeing.

Assessment

There is little doubt that Canadians are divided when it comes to their views of religion's impact on the country and the world. Confidence in leaders and comfort levels with individuals also vary considerably. Conversely, the perceptions that religious Canadians have of people like homosexuals and atheists are not always positive.

Media readings of public opinion show that there currently is a fairly high level of tension between at least some segments of the population and others. If people who are not religious were once feeling the wrath of those who valued religion, these days the situation has swung 180 degrees. Led by their "stars," atheists have never had such a collectively high profile. The aggressiveness of their attack on religion is as disconcerting in a pluralistic Canada as any attack on the non-religious in recent memory.

My cursory math at the extensive number of reader responses to the "future of religion" series in the *Globe and Mail* in December of 2010 led me to conclude that more than 95% were negative about religion, with comments frequently and even typically hostile and, yes, commonly hateful. An exaggeration?

Charles Lewis of the *National Post* wrote a blog in early December of 2010 on the heels of the Christopher Hitchens-Tony Blair debate in Toronto entitled, "Dear atheists: most of us don't care what you think."[61] In it, he pulled no punches in pointing out that Blair essentially was "wasting a lot of words on a pompous ass whose main intellectual arsenal is sneering and using sarcasm" in joining Dawkins and others in being "out to prove how stupid religious people are." The debate between atheists and the religious, wrote Lewis, has no end in sight, and "seems to sell tickets." For certain types of intellectuals "it is like watching boxing without the blood." He concluded the piece by saying that the debate is useless "for one simple reason: most atheists do not have a clue what religion is about. Real faith is like real love. Faith is not up for debate."

Not the kind of passivity that riles Connie denBok.

Two weeks later, Lewis informed readers that nothing he ever has written in his three decades as a journalist "came close to the kind of negative reaction that this piece called forth." He added, "Most of the 800 or so responses on the blog were either incredulous or hostile."

In a response to Lewis, the Communications Officer for the Canadian Secular Alliance, Gary Reid had this to say: "Love may not be debateable, but it is also acknowledged to be blind. If Hitchens says or implies that people of faith are stupid, then he is wrong to do so and Mr. Lewis is justified in being offended. They may simply be blind."[62]

Such is the mood of the times.

Into the late December 2010 fray waded Irshad Manji, the articulate and outspoken, self-described borderline Muslim. She proposed, "in this, the season of giving." that "we give novelty a chance" by moving the debate "beyond the stale polemics that insult everybody's intelligence. She challenged atheists to make the effort to "honour" her thoughts as "a person of faith" and to allow her to reciprocate and engage in "a robust and respectful conversation."[63]

Hopefully we will find that the Canadian mosaic can handle such "robust and respectful" dialogue.

For all the consternation about conflict between those who are religious and those who are not, our survey findings actually point to a surprisingly positive conclusion.

Despite the variations in religiousness and non-religiousness, co-existence and acceptance – officially at least – seem to be the prevalent norms.[64]

The all-Canadian approach to dealing with diversity, whereby we at least tolerate differences even when we do not necessarily approve of things different, is widespread.

In the immediate future, religious polarization appears to be something that can be subsumed under our pluralism umbrella. In fact, somewhat ironically, there is reason to believe that the religious polarization we are experiencing actually may be "a pluralism plus." The very fact that Canada is characterized by neither a religious monopoly nor a secular monopoly may be contributing to an enhanced capacity to handle religious and non-religious diversity in a way that is fairly unique in the world.

Balance may be best.

There is also hope that on a worldwide basis, religion can bring people together, rather than drive them apart.

In recent years, one of the more articulate, influential, and strident spokespersons for religion's potential to contribute to good has been the renowned religion scholar Karen Armstrong. A former nun and self-proclaimed "freelance monotheist," she has maintained that Christianity, Islam, and Judaism share a common basic bottom line that can be summed up in the proverbial Golden Rule – treating others the way we would want them to treat us. With the help of the TED Foundation, she unveiled a "Charter of Compassion" in November of 2009 that attempts to inspire "worldwide community-based acts of compassion."[65] As to what will evoke such compassion, she said in a March 2009 interview with journalist Bill Moyer, "Basically a sense of urgent need."[66]

Another high-profile advocate of religion's potential to bring the world together is former British Prime Minister Tony Blair. He has established a faith foundation that is working to bring about greater respect and understanding between world faiths. In a November 2010 interview with the *Globe and Mail*'s John Geiger, Blair had this to say: "I think the place of faith in the era of globalization is the single biggest issue of the 21st century. In terms of how we minimize the prospects of conflict and maximize the prospects of peace, the place of religion is essential." Blair added, "I think religious could be a civilizing force."[67]

In Canada, the reality of growing religious polarization raises significant questions beyond sheer co-existence. What are the implications for individual Canadian lives and for Canadian life as a whole? As Valpy and Friesen have put it, the shift raises "profound questions about our social values."[68]

To those important questions we now want to turn.

5 Polarization & Personal Well-Being

*"The mind is the source of
happiness and unhappiness."*
–Buddha

THE debate is age-old. Does religion contribute to the elevation of life, or do individuals and societies function equally well – or even better – without it?

Virtually everyone has an opinion. Some of the wise men of old, such as Marx and Freud, felt that religion was an illusion that helped people cope with life and death. But it needed to be replaced with real-life solutions – such as altering social conditions in the case of Marx, and rational responses to the quest for happiness and desire for immortality in the case of Freud. People who have valued religious faith have been just as vocal in asserting that religion and spirituality have the potential to elevate life for individuals and collectivities – families, communities, nations, and the world.

These days the old questions about religion and well-being continue to be raised. Only the faces have changed.

So it is that critics such as Richard Dawkins, Christopher Hitchens, and Sam Harris emphatically have decried what religion does to individuals and societies. Dawkins has written that faith isn't "just harmless nonsense" but can be lethal nonsense.[1] Hitchens is similarly hostile in asserting that all religious belief is sinister and infantile, going so far as to say that "religion poisons everything."[2] And Harris has declared that "religious faith remains a perpetual source of human conflict" and that "our enemy is nothing other than faith itself."[3]

Pretty strong claims.

Not to be outdone, people who are pro-faith are not exactly speechless. For decades, prominent American evangelist Billy Graham emphasized that if people wanted to experience true and lasting peace and joy, they needed "to find Christ." The former head of the Anglican Church of Canada, Michael Peers, said in a 1996 interview during his time as Primate, "I think that if we were not around, the level of meanness would go way, way up."[5] The Archbishop for the Toronto Roman Catholic Archdiocese, Thomas Collins, told worshippers in his 2010 Easter homily, "It is the experience of the risen Lord down through the ages that has made the Church a beacon in a world of darkness, and does so to this day"[6]

If this were a public forum and at this point we moved away from the panelists and asked the audience to wade in, I suspect that the line-ups at the microphones would be huge.

Those speaking invariably would appeal primarily to personal experience, history, the biographies of others in making their cases for and against religion contributing to well-being.

Beyond personal and subjective observations, it is extremely important that we also have some solid research findings that help us to understand some of the correlates of polarization.

What I want to do is to draw on our extensive Project Canada national surveys of adults and teenagers to offer a uniquely Canadian reading on things that can contribute to the debate.

Those surveys provide us with the opportunity of hearing from more than 20,000 people, both older and younger, who have been conversing with us dating back to the mid-70s.

Of particular importance, the extensive information our participants have provided makes it possible for us to look at their thoughts, values, beliefs, and experiences from the standpoint of whether or not they personally value religion.

It also allows us to explore the important question of the impact of religious polarization on Canadians and Canada.

Obviously, the question of religion's impact on life and lives is a very broad one. What I want to do is focus on *four fairly basic areas* that I think provide a good introduction to a conversation about religion's possible influence.

I have no doubt that these findings and thoughts will be greeted with intense and passionate responses. I also have no doubt that readers will readily cite other important areas of life where religion's role needs to be explored. Hopefully, future research will be undertaken in response to the latter call.

The four areas? *Personal life, spirituality, interpersonal life*, and *life after death*.

The Universal Goal

The reality hardly requires research: everyone wants to be happy. The question, of course, is how to find happiness.

Sources of Happiness

Ask ten people and the ten answers will invariably revolve around sources such as relationships, family, money, health, careers, and leisure activities. One or two might mention religion. Those of us who like to try to synthesize things might maintain that it comes down to social, economic, physical, achievement, and spiritual factors, and the relative importance we place on each.

While all of us are walking data and, as such, are entitled to our own personal take on what brings us happiness, there have always been people who packaged themselves as enlightened experts who (a) know what happiness is and (b) know how it can be attained.

Religious and spiritual gurus have been and continue to be among the most prominent of such self-appointed and self-anointed experts. But in recent decades they have been joined by a surprising number of academics who include psychologists, economists, and jurists. Their specialty? "Happiness Research."

Chris Barrington-Leigh, an economist at the University of British Columbia, notes that the research dates back to the 1970s and an interest in understanding the relationship between national wealth and individual happiness. In a recent interview with the *National Post*, he pointed out that the purpose of the research is to "learn everything we can and pursue policies" that maximize life. "Measuring progress solely by growth in GDP," he says, "is an outmoded idea because we have better ways to measure our social objectives."

Barrington-Leigh suggests that the primary sources of happiness for Canadians include social factors – notably interaction with family, friends, and institutions.[7]

Some of the more popular recent works in the burgeoning field include *Stumbling on Happiness* (2006) by Harvard psychology professor Daniel Gilbert, *The Politics of Happiness* by former Harvard President and law professor Derek Bok, *Happiness Around the World: The Paradox of Happy Peasants and Miserable Millionaires* (2010) by University of Maryland professor Carol Graham, and *The Happiness Equation* (2010) by Singapore economist Nattavudh Powdthavee.[8]

All four books document the precarious relationship between money and other alleged paths to happiness. To varying degrees, the authors explore policy implications.

Much publicity has been given to the fact that a commission appointed by French President, Nicolas Sarkozy, issued a report in late 2009, calling for new statistical tools to be developed to measure quality of life, including subjective and objective well-being.[9] The report came about as a result of a growing sense that there are other elements to happiness than a country's gross domestic product.[10] In 2010 the British government followed suit, with Prime Minister David Cameron announcing the country will start measuring people's psychological and environmental well-being.[11] Pressure is being placed on other countries, including Canada, to introduce similar measures.

Religion and Happiness

People of faith obviously feel that personal happiness – and, for that matter, marital happiness, and family and relational happiness more generally – is enhanced by religion, even if many increasingly distance themselves from that overt term. To varying degrees, religions call on people to give of themselves. There are costs involved that are sometimes substantial.

But in the end, one of the most basic rewards that religions promise is happiness. Apart from beliefs, a key component often appears to be social networks within congregations – an idea substantiated in an article by Robert Putnam and colleague Chaeyoon Lim published in late 2010 in the prestigious *American Sociological Review*.[12]

That said, religion obviously is not without competitors for attaining happiness. In the spring of 2010, for example, Pat O'Brien, the president of Humanist Canada at the time, stated on the association's website, "We want people to know that belief in god is not necessary to live a full, moral, and happy life." O'Brien's thinking is obviously widespread. It is a viewpoint that is endorsed not only by large numbers of people who are not religious but also by many who are.

In the minds of some individuals, religion plays a unique role in the realization of happiness. For others, it is one pathway, but not the only one.

For a third category of observers, religion is not a source of personal happiness but in fact may contribute to strain and pain. An example that could be cited would be the guilt-ridden young woman I have mentioned in the past who exclaimed to a counsellor, "My problems began the day I became a Christian."[13]

In a fourth category are people who see religion as an illusory source of happiness. They would include individuals like Marx, who concedes that religion, like a drug, soothes symptoms but doesn't deal with underlying causes.

A Canadian Reading

The recent controversies involving the efforts of academics and politicians to measure happiness remind us that it is an extremely elusive concept to tap. What is particularly problematic is the common finding that a precarious relationship exists between objective and subjective indicators. People who should be unhappy often are happy; people who should be happy are not necessarily happy.

Much of the problem lies with the complexity of how people arrive at a state of happiness. To date, at least, objective measures are not exactly known, in methodological parlance, for high levels of either validity or reliability – tapping the concept and doing so with precision. *Globe and Mail* writer Sarah Hampson has aptly described such attempts as similar to "performing surgery with a shovel."[14]

This side of simply acknowledging that the measures are "tapping" different things, one – in the end – has to go with the subjective measures, and allow for all kinds of relativity with respect to how people get there.

Ultimately, one is happy because one *thinks* she or he is happy – not because the individual meets some kind of external criteria. We have to go with what people say. Far be it from me as a researcher to inform people who tell me they are "Very happy" with life or "Not very happy" with their marriages that my objective measures tell me the opposite!

That's my way of saying that personal happiness and personal well-being are best determined by asking people for their own personal assessments in environments in which they can be as honest with themselves and me as possible. The objective correlates raise other questions.

We have done that in our national surveys, asking adults to complete questionnaires where and when they are comfortable. Teenagers have filled out questionnaires in classroom settings, with every effort made to ensure anonymity and confidentiality.

Outlook. Some 93% of Canadians maintain that they are "very happy" or "pretty happy." And while everyone knows that marriages and comparable relationships are not always perfect, people are remarkably positive about their experiences at any single point in time when they are in them. About 9 in 10 further say that they are highly satisfied with the quality of their lives.

In view of those very high levels reported, we would not expect there would be much difference between people who place a high level of importance on religion and those who do not. That's the case.

- The differences between people who *attend* weekly and those who never attend are very small.
- The same is true when we compare people who *identify* with a group and those who do not.
- The happiness and satisfaction levels of *theists and atheists* are also virtually the same.

Table 5.1. Outlook by Religiosity: Adults						
🍁	**ATTENDANCE**		**I.D.**		**BELIEF**	
	Weekly	**Never**	**Yes**	**No**	**Theist**	**Atheist**
Happiness:						
"Very" or "Pretty"	93%	96	91	93	91	95	92
Marriage/Relationship						
"Very" / "Pretty" Happy"	95	97	94	96	93	95	93
Quality of your life:						
"Very" / "Fairly Satisfied"	89	91	89	89	90	90	90

Source: Project Canada 2005 National Survey.

There clearly are any number of variables or characteristics that can influence the outcomes by attendance, identification, and belief. We might, for example, anticipate variations with each category by such things as age, gender, education, and income – and we could readily control for any of them.

What I am saying is that, regardless of such variations, collectively, taken as aggregates, there are no noteworthy differences between people who are religious – using these three measures – and those who are not.

Self-Esteem. It is treated as virtually self-evident that good self-esteem – positive self-worth – is a fundamental component of positive and productive living.

It therefore would be expected that religions that believe in optimum living for individuals would also give considerable attention to instilling good self-esteem.

To be sure, religions such as Christianity do so, but not without introducing a measure of tension. On the one hand, Christianity teaches individuals that they should love themselves precisely because they have worth, having been created by God and being loved by God. At the same time, it calls for individuals to downplay an emphasis on themselves in favour of God and others.

If this were a phone-in show, you and I can imagine that this topic would also generate more than a few calls and considerable emotion.

There are some Canadians who would claim that religion has made a significant contribution to their sense of worth. There are others who would say just the opposite – undoubtedly pointing to the experiences they and others have had with condemnation, guilt, and maybe even abuse.

Regardless of the role religions play, Canadian culture more generally officially places considerable value on cultivating positive self-esteem. It is viewed as an important and essential component of healthy living. Parents and schools, programs and activities are all expected to play roles in instilling and sustaining good self-esteem in children. In the case of adults, it is taken for granted that healthy relationships and environments contribute to positive self-esteem.

So what is the relationship between religion and self-worth?

The Project Teen Canada surveys have been exploring self-esteem for some time. The latest – the 2008 survey – included a number of items probing how teenagers view themselves. Three statements were aimed at examining (1) virtuousness, (2) competence, and (3) appearance – all three key components of one's self-image:

1. I am a good person.
2. I can do most things very well.
3. I am good looking.

Overall, the good news in the findings is that the vast majority of Canadian young people express highly positive views of themselves. Differences between females and males tend to be fairly small.[15]

With respect to religion, here as with outlook, differences tend to be very small by attendance, identification, and belief.

- Teenagers who are weekly service attenders and those who never attend look much the same.
- There are slight differences between teens who identify with a religion and those who do not, as well as modest differences between theist and atheist youth.

But in general, religious young people and other young people exhibit very similar self-image response levels.

Table 5.2. Self-Image by Religiosity: Teenagers						
🍁	ATTENDANCE		ID		BELIEF	
	Weekly	Never	Yes	No	Theist	Atheist
I am a good person	94%	95	94	95	94	95	91
I can do most things very well	80	80	78	81	77	82	76
I am good-looking	77	79	76	78	74	79	73

Source: Project Teen Canada 2008.

Personal Concerns. We all are well aware of the fact that we can be very happy with life overall, but that is not to say for a moment that we do not have concerns. Some, of course, are more readily resolved than others.

In the case of adults, the Project Canada surveys over time have documented what we all know well – that their primary concerns tend to pertain to time, finances, and health.[16] In the case of teens, the youth surveys have found that, for some time, the no. 1 personal concern has been the pressure to do well at school, followed by what they are going to do when they finish school. Money and time are also among their foremost concerns.[17]

Two problems that appear to be relatively common are loneliness and depression. They also are issues that religion presumably might be able to address, given the emphasis that many faiths give to the importance of community, as well as hope in the face of perplexion and despair.

An examination of loneliness and depression by religiosity among both adults and younger people offers some insightful findings.

- First, concern about both loneliness and depression is considerably higher among teenagers than adults. This, in the age of Facebook, where the percentage of teens claiming they have four or more close friends has skyrocketed from 49% in 1984 to 72% in 2008.[18] Back in those distant 80s before the Internet was born, 35% of young people said they were troubled by loneliness. A cause for pause is that the figure today, in the midst of social networking and friends that allegedly number in the hundreds, is 33%. Something's not quite right.
- Second, there are very few appreciable differences in loneliness and depression by religiosity – as measured by attendance, identification, and belief – in the case of either adults or teenagers.

What is somewhat disconcerting is that a noteworthy number of teens and adults are experiencing loneliness and depression, with or without religion.

Table 5.3. Personal Concerns by Religiosity: Adults and Teens
Concerned "A Great Deal" or "Quite a Bit" About…

	![🍁]	ATTENDANCE		ID		BELIEF	
		Weekly	Never	Yes	No	Theist	Atheist
ADULTS							
Loneliness	20%	19	20	20	20	20	16
Depression	18	11	17	18	16	16	21
TEENAGERS							
Loneliness	33%	34	32	32	31	33	31
Depression	35	35	36	34	36	37	37

Source: Project Canada 2005 and Project Teen Canada 2008 national surveys.

A Preliminary Bottom Line. These findings are consistent in pointing to no significant differences between Canadians who are religious and those who are not when it comes to personal well-being.

Such "no difference" findings do not mean that religion is not a significant source of well-being for some people. Faith is unquestionably an important source of happiness and positive self-esteem for many.

For example, the Project Canada 2005 survey asked the 1 in 3 Canadians who attend services at least once a month, *"What is the main thing your religious involvement adds to your life?"* Responses were open-ended.

Personal enrichment was the dominant characteristic cited by individuals in all groups – most noticeably Catholics outside Quebec and adherents to faiths other than Christianity. *People* are of particular importance to Mainline Protestants, *God and spirituality* to Quebec Catholics and Conservative Protestants. Incidentally, in the U.S., Gallup has found Protestants are inclined to cite people factors, Catholics to cite faith factors.[19]

Table 5.4. What Involvement Brings by Group, Age, and Gender					
"What is the main thing your religious involvement adds to your life?"					
	Personal Enrichment	The People	God & Spirituality	Nothing	Total
ALL	**56%**	**22**	**21**	**1**	**100**
RCOQ	63	16	21	<1	100
RCQ	48	21	26	5	100
ML Protestants	49	31	19	1	100
Cons Protestants	52	23	25	<1	100
Other Faiths	70	23	7	<1	100
18-34	59	27	14	<1	100
35-54	49	22	28	1	100
55+	59	19	21	1	100
Women	55	24	20	1	100
Men	57	20	22	1	100
Source: Project Canada 2005 and Bibby 2006b.					

Younger and older adults were somewhat more likely than middle-aged adults to cite the importance of personal enrichment, and slightly less inclined to mention God and spirituality. Differences by gender are minor, as are variations by congregational size.

In short, for the 1 in 3 Canadians who attend services monthly or more, the number one "return" across all of these demographic categories is personal enrichment.

What the Actively Involved Say Their Involvement Adds to Their Lives

Personal Enrichment
...A sense of purpose and strengthening and hope...a place to regroup my inner-self and handle everyday events...contentment, happiness, strength...peace and serenity that make life easier...

The People
...Companionship in my spiritual journey...help and fellowship...a sense of belonging and common experience...connection and support...friends and spiritual enrichment...I'm 86 years old and the minister comes to my home every month...belonging...a sense of a special community of people...

God & Spirituality
... A connection to God...a place to be safe and grow...it strengthens my spirit which in turn strengthens my relationship with God...an opportunity to collect my thoughts and give thanks for everything I have....it sustains my relationship with God... spiritual comfort and support...

Source: Derived from Bibby 2006b.

That said, religion is not a unique source of personal well-being. Our findings indicate that Canadians who never attend services are just as likely to report high levels of personal well-being.

What is centrally important in all this is that frequent attenders and never attenders find different means of reaching the same personal well-being ends.

Canadian Youth and Variations in Personal Well-being

- The self-report that one is either "very happy" or "pretty happy" differs little by religious group, and by having "no religion."
- The inclination to report that depression is something that concerns one "a great deal" or "quite a bit" is slightly lower for Protestants and Jews than other teens.
- Depression is slightly higher for "Christian unspecified," Sikh, Buddhist, and teens who value Aboriginal spirituality than it is for others.

Polarization in the Mosaic
Happiness and Depression

	Happy	Depression A Concern
NATIONALLY	90%	35
Roman Catholic	92	34
Outside Quebec	93	34
Quebec	92	32
Protestant	93	26
Conservative	95	25
Mainline	89	27
Orthodox	95	31
Christian *unspecified*	89	45
Other Faiths	89	38
Judaism	93	22
Sikhism	93	47
Buddhism	89	44
Hinduism	89	30
Islam	87	39
Aboriginal Spirituality	85	46
No Religion	88	36

The Global Situation

Large numbers of people in many countries around the world acknowledge that their lives are enhanced by religion.

They range from almost everyone in religious monopolies such as Saudi Arabia, Iraq, and Iran through 65% majorities in the Ukraine and Canada, to 35% minorities in Britain, Japan, and Sweden.

In a release in late October of 2010, the Gallup organization reported that its analysis of more than 500,000 interviews with Americans over the previous two years had found that those who are the most religious also have the highest levels of well-being.

Religiosity was based on both salience and attendance measures, with well-being probed using subjective and objective indicators.

Gallup reported that the relationship held after controlling for numerous demographic variables.[20]

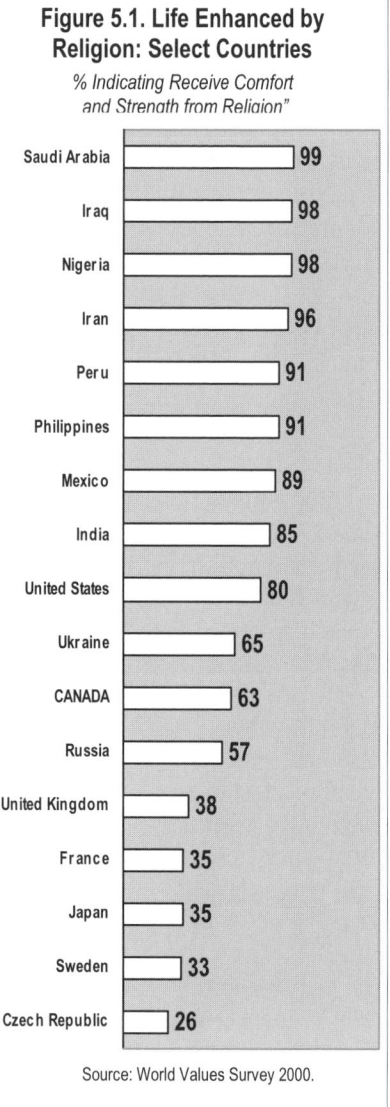

Figure 5.1. Life Enhanced by Religion: Select Countries

% Indicating Receive Comfort and Strength from Religion"

Saudi Arabia	99
Iraq	98
Nigeria	98
Iran	96
Peru	91
Philippines	91
Mexico	89
India	85
United States	80
Ukraine	65
CANADA	63
Russia	57
United Kingdom	38
France	35
Japan	35
Sweden	33
Czech Republic	26

Source: World Values Survey 2000.

However, while the relationships were consistent, the strength of the associations was very small. Similar to the situation in Canada, Americans who are not religious are clearly just about as likely to exhibit high levels of well-being as those who are religious.

When we look at the religion and well-being relationship worldwide, a different pattern is readily evident. To the extent that countries tend to know a relatively high level of affluence, their citizens express high levels of personal satisfaction.

The satisfaction level of Canadians is among the highest in the world.

Such a pattern for *subjective* measures of well-being is also apparent when we look at *objective* measures of standard of living via the United Nations Human Development Index.

Table 5.5. Salience & Satisfaction with One's Life: Select Countries		
[r = -.613]	Salience	Satisfaction*
Senegal	98%	26
Pakistan	98	28
Ethiopia	91	37
Malaysia	95	36
South Africa	82	36
India**	79	41
Italy	72	48
United States	67	65
Argentina	66	59
Poland	62	39
Israel	50	68
Spain	49	66
CANADA	45	71
Germany	44	48
Russia	34	23
France	30	57
United Kingdom	27	59
Sweden	17	72

*Percent rating personal life 7-plus on scale of 0 to 10
**BOLD: a G-20 country.
Sources: Salience - Gallup WorldView 2010;
Satisfaction – Pew Global Attitudes Project, July 24,

- The dominant pattern is *an inverse relationship* between the national levels of personal religious importance and place on the HD index.
- At the extremes, 96% of Nigerians say religion is personally important to them; yet the country ranks 158th in its standard of living.
- Conversely, Norway ranks 1st according to the HD index, yet only 20% of its people say religion is important to them.

In a stimulating synthesis of findings on happiness worldwide, Geoffrey Miller, an evolutionary psychologist at the University of New Mexico, has offered a number of summary points that help to clarify the context in which religion may be at work:

1. Almost all humans are happy almost all the time. That's been the case throughout history.
2. Major life events – such as winning the lottery or the death of a spouse – only affect happiness for six months to a year.
3. Many alleged factors such as age, sex, race, income, education, and national residence have little effect on happiness. Some key exceptions are hunger, health, and oppression. Yet, once minimum standards are met in each case, further increases – greater affluence, for example – do not appreciably increase happiness.
4. For people who experience very low levels of subjective well-being (e.g., major depression), the most potent anti-depressants

Table 5.6. Salience & Quality of Life: Select Countries

UN Human Development Index 2009 Rankings

[r = .765]	Salience	Rank
Thailand	97%	87
Nigeria	96	158
Philippines	94	105
Saudi Arabia	94	59
United Arab Emirates	92	35
Pakistan	92	141
India	90	134
Brazil	87	75
South Africa	85	129
Iran	83	88
Mexico	73	53
Italy	72	18
Poland	69	41
United States	65	13
Ireland	54	5
Israel	51	27
Spain	49	15
Korea, Republic of	43	26
CANADA	**42**	**4**
Switzerland	41	9
Germany	40	22
Iceland	38	3
Cuba	34	51
Russia	34	71
Netherlands	33	6
Australia	32	2
New Zealand	32	20
France	30	8
Finland	29	12
United Kingdom	27	21
Japan	24	10
Hong Kong	24	24
Norway	20	1
Sweden	17	7
China	***	77

Sources: Salience - Gallup WorldView 2010; HDI: UN Human Development Report, 2009.

are not social or economic but pharmaceutical. The effects of such drugs are stronger than increases in wealth or any other changes in conditions.[21]

Given that happiness knows something of "a set-point," Miller concludes by pointing out that the consumption of products and services marketed as happiness boosters is usually futile. Increasing GNP per capita also will not have positive effects on well-being once a minimum standing of living is in place. And runaway consumerism not only fails to make us happier but can impose high environmental costs on everyone else.

One practical implication: "Every hundred dollars that we spend on ourselves will have no detectable effect on our happiness; but the same money, if given to hungry, ill, oppressed developing-world people, would dramatically increase their happiness." Miller adds, "The utilitarian argument for the rich giving more of their money to the poor is now scientifically irrefutable." [22]

So it is that recent research carried out by the Pew Global Attitudes Project, for example, has confirmed the findings of a variety of academic studies showing that, in more affluent countries, happiness seems to rise up to a point, but not beyond it. Researchers refer to the pattern as the "Easterlin paradox," named after Richard Easterlin, a University of Southern California economist. He concluded that gains in material well-being have little impact on satisfaction with life once a certain level has been achieved. [23]

Those things said, it also is clear that in many parts of the developing world – notably many countries in Africa - that happiness threshold has not been reached. In such places, people predictably indicate that they are not satisfied with their lives, even though their religiosity levels may be high.

One area, however, where religion is associated with a difference worldwide is suicide.

- Both females and males who live in countries characterized by high levels of service attendance are less likely than other individuals to commit suicide.

- The differences are particularly pronounced in the case of countries such as the Philippines, Mexico, Brazil, and Iran, versus China, Korea, and Japan.

Gallup, in a recent release, has noted the same pattern in looking at 67 countries. The pollster also reported that the relationship tends to hold *within* countries.

Gallup's conclusion? Religion may be a factor in reducing suicides that is at least as important as economics.[24]

Table 5.7. Religiosity and Suicide Rates: Select Countries

[A-SF r = -.461] [A-SM r = -.433]	Attend- ance	Suicide Rates Females	Males
Thailand	80%	3.8	12.0
India	73	9.1	12.2
El Salvador	68	3.7	10.2
Philippines	64	1.7	2.5
Poland	62	4.4	26.8
Mexico	60	1.3	6.8
Ireland	56	3.8	17.4
Dominican Republic	53	0.6	2.6
Italy	49	2.8	9.9
Brazil	49	1.9	7.3
Iran	45	0.1	0.3
United States	43	4.5	17.7
Israel	39	3.3	8.7
Spain	39	3.8	12.0
Japan	38	13.7	35.8
Korea, Republic of	35	14.1	29.6
Germany	30	6.0	17.9
Greece	29	1.2	5.9
New Zealand	27	6.3	18.9
CANADA	**26**	**5.4**	**17.3**
Netherlands	26	5.0	11.6
Ukraine	23	7.0	40.9
Australia	23	4.4	16.7
France	20	9.0	25.5
Cuba	20	4.9	19.6
United Kingdom	20	2.8	10.1
Hong Kong	19	11.5	19.3
Sweden	17	8.3	18.1
Finland	12	9.0	28.9
Czech Republic	15	4.3	22.7
Russia	15	9.5	53.9
China	9	14.8	13.0

Sources: Attendance – Gallup WorldView 2010; Suicide rates: per 100,000 population, World Health Organization, 2009.

Assessment

These findings indicate that, according to these measures of personal well-being – outlook, self-esteem, and concerns – there are few differences overall between Canadians who are religious and those who are not. The patterns in Canada are consistent with patterns worldwide.

This does not mean that religion is not an important source of personal well-being for some people. Of course it is. Even in poorer countries it may function to help people deal with economic deprivation.[25]

However, it does mean that, particularly in more advantaged situations – such as Canada – people who are not religious are just about as likely to find personal well-being through other sources.

This initial reading points to the fact that life could be significantly diminished for individuals who find personal well-being with the assistance of religion.

But to the extent that alternatives to religion exist, especially in highly developed countries including Canada, it is possible that personal well-being will not necessarily be negatively affected by increasing religious polarization.

There might be some good reasons why people seem to be able to find happiness both with and without religion. John Helliwell, a renowned economics professor emeritus at UBC, has been studying personal happiness for some time and continues to do so. He is a member of Canada's National Statistics Council and has provided counsel on Britain's new initiative to survey well-being.[26] In October of 2010, he visited Harvard and summarized happiness research, giving attention to its social contexts.[27]

Helliwell maintains that while happiness research is in its infancy, three major findings will ultimately emerge.

1. *The positive trumps the negative*: positive outlooks and positive activities lead to good health and longer lives. Two strangers who wave to each other in traffic go home happier than two people who give each other the finger.

2. *Community trumps materialism*: relationships enhance life more than the pursuit of things. Research shows a 1% improvement in a worker-boss relationship improves happiness as much as a 30% increase in salary.

3. *Generosity trumps selfishness*: people who give away more are happier than those who give away less – regardless of income. Those who did favours for others in the last year felt happier than those who received favours.

If Helliwell is right regarding the three leading determinants of happiness, one can see where religion might sometimes contribute to each of the three sources. But it also is clear that other factors contribute as well.

Religion can be one source of happiness. But it is not the only one.

Some people might be surprised by these findings. What may surprise many more are the findings concerning polarization's impact on the widespread pursuit of spiritual fulfillment.

6 Polarization & Spirituality

*"Spirituality is about what we do with the fire inside of us.
The opposite is not a person who rejects the idea of God.
It is to have no energy, to have lost all zest for living."*
–Ron Rolheiser

NE of the anomalous features of life in an era of post-religious dominance in Canada has been the privileged status of spirituality.

While religion has been scorned and stigmatized and rejected by many, spirituality has known something of celebrity status. Until fairly recently, it seems, spirituality was strongly associated with religion – something like a family member. But in recent decades in particular, it seems to have moved out of the house. It's as if it had been something like Cinderella, and finally has been freed from the grasp of the evil stepmother. These days, the past has been largely forgotten, and Cinderella is able to flourish on her own.

Spirituality has received fairly remarkable treatment.

- It is assumed to be something that exists apart from religion, as in the comment, "I am spiritual but not religious." In fact, the phrase has spawned the acronym, SBNR, complete with a large number of websites (e.g., SBNR.org) and Facebook and Twitter entries.
- It typically is viewed as superior to religion. "I'm spiritual but not religious" is often said and heard as a triumphant declaration – greeted on the talk-show circuit with a positive nod from the host and even a polite ovation.
- It doesn't carry any of the negative baggage of religion. When one says, "I'm spiritual," the slate is clean. People who say, "I'm Catholic," or "I'm Muslim," or "I'm born again," hardly receive the same response.

Some pro-religious individuals who link spirituality to religion decry the growing lack of religion in people's lives, and fear for a future of unmet spiritual needs.

Others who place importance on spirituality have no concerns about Cinderella out there on her own.

Without totally ruining the end of the story, let's just say at this point that the research likes the chances of the emancipated Princess doing quite well. Here's why.

The Autonomy of Spirituality

What do Mother Teresa, Janis Joplin, and Princess Diana have in common? In his best-selling book, *The Holy Longing*,[1] Ron Rolheiser says they all were spiritual; more precisely, all three had spiritualities.

He argues that the term "spirituality" is badly understood today. It's not about certain activities like going to church, praying, or engaging in a spiritual quest. Rather, all of us are born with a restlessness that is like a fire. "We have to do something about the fire that burns within us," he writes. "What we do with that fire, how we channel it, is our spirituality.[2]

The dominant choices the three women made were obviously very different, with life-giving versus destructive consequences. But, he explains, how they willed to direct their energies were their spiritualities.[3]

While Rolheiser attempts to clarify what spirituality "really" is, the use of the term in everyday life is pretty much up for grabs. One seemingly can be spiritual in ways limited only by one's imagination.

Few other concepts get such a definitional exemption. A tree is a tree; a puck is a puck; but spirituality – well, in our culture, it's whatever a person says it is.

The result is that we have spiritualities of every shape and form. The SBNR.org's "About Us" statement declares that it "is dedicated to serving the millions of people worldwide who walk a spiritual path outside traditional religion." Not linked to "any one spiritual tradition or religion," it offers to "honor your personal journey and offer inspiration, education and entertainment to aid your experience of being human. Site visitors are invited to "Enjoy what you like and what intrigues you."[4]

Spirituality seemingly is in the eye of the beholder.

When we have asked Canadians, "What do you mean by spirituality?" about the best our coders have been able to do is classify the responses into "conventional" and "less conventional" categories, and then add subcategories. The first refers to expressions of spirituality that have fairly traditional religious connotations. The second refers to – well, essentially everything else. What stands out about the "less conventional" responses is how subjective and individualistic they tend to be. One searches largely in vain for threads of commonality.

Table 6.1. What Canadians Mean by "Spirituality"

Conventional (52%)

"...living in fellowship with Christ...believing in God and the Bible...that God is there for us, hears our prayers and answers them... need God's spirit to guide, protect and support me in good times and bad...building a personal relation with Jesus Christ...nourishing our souls so we can be closer to God..."

Less Conventional (48%)

"...a matter relating to our inner-self or soul...peace of mind...a feeling of oneness with the earth and with all that is within me...the existence of an immortal soul that has to be cared for...positive thinking and excitement...appreciation of the beauty of nature...the love of family and friends...inner awareness..."

Source: Adapted from Bibby, *The Boomer Factor*, 2006: 186.

If we were to group 100 people at a conference into tables of five and ask them to discuss their views of spirituality, I think we would quickly discover that about all they have in common is the word. Incidentally, my research does not indicate that things are changing very much on the clarity front. The responses to the "what do you mean by spirituality" question are about as diverse today as they were a decade ago.

Charles Taylor cautions that while the expressions are highly varied, many young people today are "following their own spiritual instincts" in looking for a direct experience of the sacred. He writes that the search "often springs from a profound dissatisfaction with a life encased entirely in the immanent order," where people sense "that this life is empty, flat, devoid of higher purpose."[5]

Perhaps. But the diversity of what is available in what Wade Clark Roof calls "a spiritual marketplace"[6] makes one wonder where the cutting points are between meaning and marketing, searching and selling.

The choices seem unlimited – and are growing. A cursory look at book offerings, websites, and conferences provides a sense of the varied "takes" on spirituality.

- The conventionally religious can find titles such as Henri Nouwen's *Reaching Out*, Phyllis Tickle's *Spiritual Practices*, William Young's novel *The Shack*, or Brian McLaren's *Naked Spirituality*, as well as titles offering Islamic, Buddhist, Jewish, Hindu, and Sikh takes on spirituality.[7]
- For those who want something a bit different, there are books including *The Secret*, *Aboriginal Spirituality and Biblical Theology*, *Celtic Spirituality*, *Mormon Spirituality*, and *Wiccan Spirituality*.[8]
- But we are just getting started. There also are books available that bear such titles as *God Without God, The Little Book of Atheist Spirituality, Spirituality Without God, The Christian Atheist,* and *The Homemade Atheist* with the subtitle, *A Former Evangelical Woman's Freethought Journey to Happiness*.[9]
- Websites offer articles such as, "How to be a spiritual atheist," informing readers that "atheists don't have to be separated from spirituality." Tangible instructions follow.[10]
- The web postings on the home page of the Centre of Naturalism in the fall of 2010 included a summary of a talk given to the Humanist Association of Massachusetts earlier in the decade entitled, "Spirituality Without Faith."[11] The presenter raised the question, "To what extent can secular humanists be spiritual?" and proceeds to say that "just as we can be good without God, we can have spirituality without spirits."
- The Christian Cultural Center of Montreal sponsored a recent one-day conference that carried the title, "The spiritual quest: with or without God." It highlighted different roads to spirituality, and explored the possibility that "the spiritual dimension in human beings" can be deployed "without reference to a divine being."[12]

- A Jewish website, www.aish.com, recently featured a thought-provoking article entitled, "Spirituality Without God," by Sara Yoheved Rigler. "The advantages of spirituality without God are obvious," she wrote. "One can choose one's own direction, methods, and goals without the intrusions of the Divine. The 'inner voice,' which functions as the CEO of most New Age enterprises, rarely tells one what one doesn't want to hear." She reminds readers that a faith like Judaism speaks of a God who not only creates and sustains the universe but also issues orders about things like stealing and adultery. "Little wonder," she says, "that most people resist such encroachments on their personal lives."[13]
- Sam Harris, the well-known, best-selling atheist author with a background in neuroscience and philosophy, displays what John Allemang has called "a mystic streak that allows a little too much room for spiritual fuzziness."[14] By his own admission, Harris finds inspiration in Eastern religions and acknowledged in a 2010 *Newsweek* interview that his next project is a spiritual guide, explaining "how we can live moral and spiritual lives without religion."[15]

These days, the relationship between religion and spirituality is anything but clear-cut. That reality has been underlined by the results of our research in Canada.

A Canadian Reading

Across the country, some 7 in 10 adults and more than 5 in 10 teens explicitly indicate that they have spiritual needs.

- While the inclination is higher among Canadians who are religious according to our attendance, identification, and belief measures, sizable numbers of other people also say they have spiritual needs.
- Among adults, the latter include 1 in 2 individuals who never attend services and/or do not identify with a religious group, as well as 1 in 4 atheists.
- In the case of teenagers, the figures are lower, but still appreciable: some 1 in 3 who never attend services and/or say they have no religion, as well as about 1 in 7 atheist youth indicate that they have spiritual needs.
- Adult and young females are consistently more likely than males to express spiritual needs – but just slightly.

Table 6.2. Spiritual Needs and Religiosity by Gender							
"I myself have spiritual needs"							
		ATTENDANCE		ID		BELIEF	
		Weekly	Never	Yes	No	Theist	Atheist
ADULTS	**72%**	**94**	**51**	**76**	**47**	**91**	**27**
Females	78	96	61	81	60	92	23
Males	66	92	42	71	36	90	28
TEENAGERS	**54**	**84**	**36**	**66**	**30**	**82**	**14**
Females	57	88	40	69	31	84	15
Males	51	80	32	63	29	80	13

A common response of those who value faith is to see such findings as signalling both need and opportunity. Canadians, in numbers that readily exceed those who are actively involved in religious groups have spiritual needs. As a result, they, as religious groups, are positioned to respond.

However, here the caution flag needs to go up.

What large numbers of Canadians have in mind when they think of spirituality is not necessarily what the groups have in mind – and have to offer. It might be a situation that is analogous to people acknowledging that they have an appetite for food. But the kinds of food they have in mind are not necessarily what the specialty restaurants are offering.

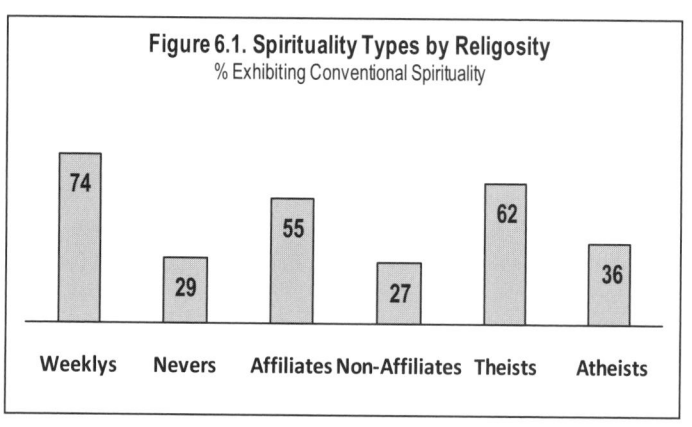

Figure 6.1. Spirituality Types by Religosity
% Exhibiting Conventional Spirituality

Weeklys 74 Nevers 29 Affiliates 55 Non-Affiliates 27 Theists 62 Atheists 36

The Alberta Case Example. In an effort to gain improved clarity on spiritual conceptions and spiritual needs, I carried out a brief Internet survey of 550 people in Alberta in the spring of 2010. The sample is highly representative, socially and demographically, and of sufficient size to permit generalizations to the provincial population with a high level of accuracy.[16]

For those readers not familiar with Alberta, it is worth noting that the province includes two cities (Calgary and Edmonton) with populations of more than 1 million people each. In addition, the province is characterized by considerable migration and immigration.

Consequently, the population is highly diverse with respect to community size, racial diversity, and provinces and countries of origin.

The spirituality survey provides some important findings that offer insights well beyond the province.

- More than 8 in 10 people say they have spiritual needs.
- However, rather than being in the market for religious groups or other groups that can respond, 86% of those with such needs say they are being met, at least for the most part.
- Some 95% of those who attend services weekly report that their spiritual needs are being met; but so do no less than 74% of those who never attend.

With respect to how they see the religion-spirituality balance in their own lives, equal proportions of 43% each say that they are either "religious and spiritual" or "spiritual but not religious." Relatively few describe themselves as "religious but not spiritual." The remaining 10% or so say they are neither religious nor spiritual.

- Those who view themselves as R & S are slightly more likely than the SBNR to say their needs are being met.
- Both levels of spiritual fulfillment are higher than those people who either see themselves as religious but not spiritual and – as would be expected – those who are neither spiritual nor religious. Still, 6 in 10 in this latter category say the spiritual needs they have are being met.

Table 6.3. Spirituality in Alberta

Do you feel you have spiritual needs? Yes		81%
Are your spiritual needs currently being met?	Yes	33
	Yes, for the most part	53
	Not really	11
	Not really at all	3
Spiritual needs being met by attendance	Weekly	95
	Never	74

			Met
Which of the following describes you best?/	Religious and spiritual	43	93
	Spiritual but not religious	43	85
	Not religious and not spiritual	12	61
	Religious but not spiritual	2	75

Source: The Alberta Spirituality Survey, 2010.
Carried out with the assistance of Courtney Kitachuchi and Carly Seibel.

The Alberta survey further reveals that a disproportionate number of "SBNR" individuals are females in their 40s and 50s with no religious affiliation, who never or seldom attend services.

That said, the female-male difference is small and note-worthy numbers of people of all ages identify themselves as SBNR. They also include close to 1 in 5 weekly attenders and 1 in 3 Catholics, Mainline Protestants, and Conservative Protestants, as well as a slightly higher pro-portion of people who identity with other major world faiths.

Overall, these findings underline the fact that very large numbers of people are pursuing spiritual needs. But many are looking in places other than conventional religion – and claiming they are coming away satisfied.

Table 6.4. SBNR Demographics

Gender	Female	45%
	Male	40
Age	<30	38
	30-39	41
	40-49	44
	50-59	55
	60+	37
Attend-ance	Never	65
	Yearly	57
	Monthly	32
	Weekly	16
Relig Family	None	68
	Other Faith	42
	ML Prot	36
	Cons Prot	34
	RC	32

Source: The Alberta Spirituality Survey, 2010.

- More than 1 in 2 Canadian teenagers indicate that they personally have spiritual needs.
- Such an acknowledgement is somewhat higher among Conservative Protestants, unspecified "Christians," and teens who identify with Aboriginal spirituality. It is somewhat lower among Quebec Catholics and Jewish young people.
- The figure drops to 30% among teens with no religion.

Polarization in the Mosaic
Personally Have Spiritual Needs

NATIONALLY	**54%**
Roman Catholicism	**62**
Outside Quebec	67
Quebec	50
Protestantism	**77**
Conservative	89
Mainline	66
Orthodox	**69**
Christian *unspecified*	**83**
Other World Faiths	**65**
Aboriginal Spirituality	78
Hinduism	70
Buddhism	67
Islam	67
Sikhism	61
Judaism	48
No Religion	**30**

The Global Situation

When we turn to the topic of spirituality, it is difficult to find global data akin to the religion data that we have been accessing. Gallup has been inclined to conceptualize spirituality in terms of religion. In fairness to Gallup, much of the world has likewise not made a sharp dichotomy. In fact, it is only in recent years that academics and others who observe religion have noted that average Americans, Canadians, and Europeans, for example, have been making such a clear distinction.

Significantly, the distinction has been closely tied to the recognition that secularization has not eliminated a sense on the part of large numbers of people that they have needs that continue to outlive their involvement and interest in organized expressions of religion.

So it is that in some settings where secularization is seen as fairly rampant, increasing attention has been given to exploring how people continue to pursue ways of addressing their spiritual needs, versus focusing only on involvement in religious groups.

One might argue that if spiritual needs are fairly pervasive, then to the extent that interest in organized religion in any society declines, individuals would be expected to seek more specific, personal, and customized ways of having such needs addressed.

Highly-respected sociologist Wade Clark Roof, for example, has written extensively on how the American Baby Boomer era has seen a major shift from involvement in organized religion to highly individualistic spiritual quests. Moreover, he has described how a burgeoning spirituality industry has emerged in response to such interests, resulting in lively "spiritual marketplaces."[17]

For Roof, three features in the U.S. have stood out.

The first is the sheer numbers of people involved in pursuing spiritual needs. Many who have lost traditional religious groundings are looking for new and fresh moorings. Others who are still religiously grounded are looking for further enrichment.

Second, a dominant theme is self-understanding. Consequently Roof speaks of quest, seeking, and searching.

Third, somewhat paradoxically, the spiritual yearnings are leading many beyond the self-focused, self-fulfillment themes of the 1960s and 70s. Now, he says, that quest has moved beyond consumption and materialism. "Popular spirituality may appear shallow, indeed flaky," Roof writes. But it also "reflects a deep hunger for a self-transformation that is both genuine and personally satisfying." His reading is that the current religious situation among American Boomers "is characterized not so much by a loss of faith as a qualitative shift from unquestioned belief to a more open, questing mood." [18]

Prominent Princeton sociologist Robert Wuthnow has been giving research attention to post-Boomers, focusing on people between the ages of 21 and 45. In his book, *After the Baby Boomers*, released in 2007, he reminds readers that the availability of choices and the inclination to engage in seeking have never been greater.

In exploring the extent to which young adults are spiritual but not religious, Wuthnow noted that 55% of his sample were attending religious services less than once a month. Of these, 6 in 10 indicated that spiritual growth is important to them, and 3 in 10 said they had devoted at least a fair amount of attention to their spiritual life in the previous year. Many were what Wuthnow calls "spiritual tinkerers" who, like their Boomer parents, piece together ideas about spirituality from many sources."[19]

Consistent with the findings of Roof and Wuthnow, the National Opinion Research Center's Tom Smith reports that poll data spanning just the last decade or so document a shift towards a "spiritual but not religious" outlook. A majority of people of all ages, he says, now describe themselves as "equally spiritual and religious."

But a growing number are reporting that they are "more spiritual than religious." The latter include 31% of Americans under 30 – double the 16% figure for those over 70.[20]

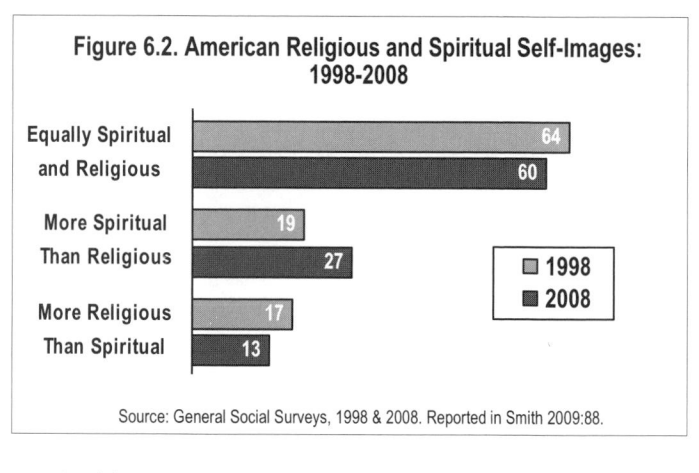

Figure 6.2. American Religious and Spiritual Self-Images: 1998-2008

Source: General Social Surveys, 1998 & 2008. Reported in Smith 2009:88.

Smith notes that in Europe, the argument for the movement toward personal spiritual expressions has been summed up in the phrase, "believing without belonging."[21]

Other European observers going back almost fifty years ago to Thomas Luckmann have spoken of "invisible religion,"[22] while the concept of "implicit religion" has become increasingly popular in recent decades, in large part through the efforts of Edward Bailey.[23]

A recent survey of European Common Market countries shows that interest in spirituality extends well beyond the parameters of conventional religion. As would be expected, there is a fairly strong relationship between attendance and spirituality, but there are also lots of exceptions to that pattern.[24] In all but one instance (Poland), levels of interest in spirituality fairly readily exceed attendance levels.

Consequently, there is every reason to expect that any movement away from organized religion will typically not result in the demise of spiritual interest.

On the contrary, "religious defection" will see many individuals move toward highly personalized forms of spirituality, and cultures will respond with increasingly lively "spiritual marketplaces."

Table 6.5. Attendance and Interest in Spirituality: 20 Select European Countries

"Whether or not you think of yourself as a religious person, how spiritual would you say you are, that is how strongly are you interested in the sacred or the supernatural?"

% Indicating They Are "Very" or "Somewhat" Interested"

$r = .418$	Attendance	Spirituality
Poland	62	52
Ireland	56	63
Slovak Republic	44	54
Spain	39	50
Portugal	38	59
Germany	30	36
Greece	29	57
Hungary	26	45
Switzerland	26	56
Netherlands	26	61
Luxembourg	26	53
Switzerland	26	56
Belgium	24	47
Ukraine	23	68
France	20	42
Bulgaria	16	53
Denmark	16	40
Czech Republic	15	32
Russia	15	40
Finland	12	47

Sources: Attendance - Gallup WorldView 2010;
Spirituality – European Values Survey 2008.

In looking for a current informed overview of spirituality developments worldwide, we have the benefit of the thinking of an acclaimed Canadian journalist and author, Douglas Todd of the *Vancouver Sun*, who specializes in spirituality. Over the years he has become a valued associate. Todd has been keeping a careful eye on developments relating to spirituality in Canada and abroad. His books on the topic include *Brave Souls* (1996) and *The Soul-Searcher's Guide to the Galaxy* (1994). His many awards include receiving the Templeton Reporter of the Year Award twice as the top religion reporter in North America.

In January of 2009, he penned a stimulating piece entitled, "Five spiritual trends to watch for in 2009." A year later, he reaffirmed the trends, writing: "I'm coming to the conclusion the five trends have real staying power, which could see them sticking with us to 2020 and beyond."[25]

The five "religious and spiritual shifts" that Todd sees?

1. Eastern spirituality will flower.
2. Religious terrorism will be the new normal.
3. Religious liberals will build on advances.
4. The religious right will regroup.
5. Secular spirituality will strengthen.

Eastern spirituality, he says, has gone mainstream in the West. Once an East-West dialogue piece for a small number of intellectuals, Asian spirituality is being embraced by growing numbers of people around the world. "Small spiritual armies of young Buddhists, calling themselves Dharma Punx, are spreading around North America." But Todd says that "it's not only whites jumping on the Eastern spirituality train." Growing numbers of Asians, inspired by the Dalai Lama, Thich Nhat Hanh and Thailand's Sulak Sivaraksa, are transforming Eastern spiritual traditions with a commitment to an "engaged Buddhism" that emphasizes justice. He notes that the Taiwan-based Chi Tzi movement has millions of followers in 40 countries, including Canada. It downplays religious rites and zealously pursues international charity projects.

Religious terrorism. Todd draws on Pew Forum findings in noting that 9% of countries are experiencing some form of terrorism – "not only from Muslims, but from Christians, Hindus, atheistic leaders and others." Surveys show that Islamic anger is based largely on a sense that Muslims are being oppressed by Western financial, political and military powers. But anger is also being felt much more widely.

Religious liberals. Spiritual searchers are yearning for alternatives to conservative versions of Western religion. Todd notes that they are finding it in progressive Christian and other writers who include Marcus Borg, Jim Wallis Tariq Ramadan, and Ron Rolheiser. He suggests that, as civil rights, South African apartheid, and the Vietnam War brought religious progressives together in the 1960s and 70s, "possible environmental disaster now galvanizes them."

The Religious right. The religious right, in Todd's words, "has been hit some body blows," including the rise of Obama, the failure of the Iraq war they backed, the defeat of Sarah Palin, and – in both the U.S. and Canada – same-sex union legislation. Nonetheless, its passion, anger, money, followers, and political and media connections will see it continue to be a societal force.

Secular spirituality. The inclination for people to dichotomize between religion and spirituality will persist. It is becoming increasingly common to reject organized religion, yet embrace a host of spiritual practices and beliefs. Todd sees "secular spirituality" manifesting itself in mainstream publishing, academia, widespread nature reverence, and pop culture figures, including Oprah, Eckhart Tolle, and Deepak Chopra.

He adds that polls – as we saw with Wuthnow's work – show more and more people are becoming "spiritual tinkerers" who "mix and match an often dizzying variety of beliefs and practices." Secular spirituality also is appearing in movies. Todd cites the example of *Avatar*, with its eco-spiritual theme, where the Na'vi humanoid heroes "practice a powerful indigenous form of nature spirituality that holds the potential to heal the universe." He notes that Canadian director James Cameron took the title of his movie from Indian religion – that "an 'avatar' is an incarnation of a Hindu god."

Assessment

These findings document the fact that spiritual interest and needs are widespread. That said, how spirituality is conceptualized varies considerably across the population.

Large numbers of Canadians of all ages who are not religious in conventional ways nonetheless express spiritual needs. At the same time, this does not mean that they necessarily are looking in the direction of conventional religion to have them met. In fact, many are finding alternatives to religion when it comes both to the conceptualization and nurturing of spirituality.

It seems clear that as polarization intensifies in Canada, spiritual needs and responses will persist – with and without the presence of religion in people's lives.

Because of the subjectivity associated with spirituality, its nature will probably best be understood with the help of a good number of adjectives.

We will find ourselves thinking, for example, of Catholic spirituality, Baptist spirituality, Buddhist spirituality, Islamic spirituality, and so on.

But we also will find that a variety of atheistic and agnostic spiritualities exist, as do more generic forms of theistic and non-institutional spirituality.

To the extent that spirituality finds expression both within existing religions and apart from religion, there is no doubt that it will persist on a global basis. One would expect that its expressions will only become more and more diverse as it moves outside the parameters of formal religion in an increasing number of cultural settings around the world.

And like products of every kind, we can expect those expanding expressions to be exported, further expanding spirituality marketplaces pretty much everywhere.

Growing religious polarization in Canada will do little to reduce the apparent fascination most people have with spirituality.

That's not to say that all expressions of spirituality "are born equal" when it comes to functionality. Many expressions of spirituality, for example, along with "civil religions" and "implicit religions," have little or nothing to say about the death question.

On a number of occasions, Todd has reflected on the extent to which something like hockey, for example, has been said to be a Canadian "religion" – an idea that actually has been posited by some academics.[26] Obviously hockey – like sports such as soccer in many parts of the world – can call forth personal and collective emotions and bind people together. Sports also are replete with symbols and rituals.

But let's not get carried away. Whatever the functions of sports and other potential "invisible religions" to which we direct our energies – such as careers, materialism, or family life, they fall far short of being substitutes for religions that can address the "big questions of our existence." Such a reality was underlined in the aftermath of the tragic death of NHL executive Brian Burke's son, Brendan, in early 2010, when *Hockey News* writer Sam McCaig commented, it "makes things like trade deadlines, NHL playoff berths and Olympic tournaments seem like little more than surreal, meaningless pastimes."[27]

Bell – and McCaig – are right. In the face of things like tragedy and death, most of us need much more.

Dating back to *Fragmented Gods* almost three decades ago, I have been among those who have argued that religion is only one source of meaning. People can obviously find ways of making life meaningful and do – without exclusively or even necessarily turning to religion. In the words of Bertrand Russell that I cited back then, "I do not think that life in general has a purpose. It just happened. But individual human beings have purposes."[28]

In a recent polling of 84 countries, the Gallup organization confirmed the fact that meaning does not require religion. Only 2% of all respondents worldwide said they were secular or nonreligious. Nevertheless, 83% of these same people indicated that their lives have an important meaning or purpose – about 5-10% below Christians, Hindus, Muslims, Buddhists, and Jews, but still extremely high.[29]

The gods are not indispensable to finding purpose. But they do not appear to have many equals when it comes to addressing with certainty what happens when we die.

Spiritual needs and spiritual expressions will outlive religion. What they will add to people lives, and the extent to which they will come up short, remains to be seen.

~

A closing thought. I have found that the research news about various conceptions of spiritual needs that in turn are widely being met brings a fairly predictable response from religious leaders in particular. "People might be into spirituality," they protest. "But what they are embracing is not "real" or "genuine" spirituality.

Maybe so. But the job of the sociologist is not to tell people of faith what "true" spirituality looks like. If the wide range of spiritualities is not viewed as bona fide, the onus is on those who feel that way to find ways of getting the word out to the growing number of people in Canada and elsewhere who feel otherwise.

The research suggests that large numbers are not only finding alternatives to conventional expressions of spirituality, but are also finding those alternatives to be highly functional.

Consequently, if they are travelling up the wrong mountains, they need to hear from some extremely persuasive and credible guides.

Many of them are quite happy with both their paths and their destinations.

7 Polarization & Social Well-Being

"It is doubtful whether men were in general happier when religious doctrines held unlimited sway than they are now; more moral they certainly were not." – Sigmund Freud

EVERYONE has heard the argument in one form or another. Are people who are religious *more* compassionate than people who are not religious? Or are they actually *less* compassionate? Does the valuing of God result in people being better people when it comes to how they relate to others? Even if that's the case, can't people be good without God?

Old questions, tough questions. Here again, if we opened up the mic to people in any audience, we know the input would be extremely varied and probably emotional. The data sources would be extensive.

- We can readily draw on *personal experience* – and why not? We all have known people who are religious and not religious. Some of them have been terrific people, others less than terrific.
- We can reflect on *history*. Some could offer stories of how religious groups helped their parents and grandparents when they arrived in Canada from other countries. A number of Aboriginals in the audience might remind us of what they know about residential schools, and decry what religious groups did to children in days gone by. Still others would raise the issue of religion having contributed to wars and conflict in many parts of the world, and go so far as to say that the world would have been a far better place without religion.
- A speaker or two might say that *they themselves* have been motivated to be better and kinder people because of their faith.

- An academic might try to inform us that *research* offers mixed reviews regarding the relationship between religion and compassion.

The discussion would get even more complex if we tried to carry out the Herculean task of not only comparing things personally and historically but also cross-culturally.

What about societies, past and present, where religion has been pervasive, versus those where religion has seemingly been absent – the United States, for example, versus the Soviet Union prior to the demise of the communist bloc in the late 1980s?

Would a person who lived in Chicago in the 1970s have found America to be a more compassionate place to be than his or her counterpart in Moscow? Today, ideology aside, is interpersonal life in a theocratic Iran more civil than in a highly secularized Sweden? How about life in predominantly Catholic countries like the Philippines or Ireland versus the Czech Republic or China?

Very big questions that conjure up very long answers, and, I suspect, very little consensus.

New Arguments from Science

Since the 1970s, science has accelerated its participation in the fray. The burgeoning disciplines of social and evolutionary biology, along with moral psychology, have led the way in giving increasing attention to the scientific study of human nature. The focus has been morality. In my mind, it is a short path from talking about what is right and wrong to talking about social well-being.

Much of this emphasis on "the new science of morality" has originated at Harvard University with faculty and graduates including Robert Trivers, Steven Pinker, Edward O. Wilson, Daniel C. Dennett, and Marc Hauser. In 1975, Wilson predicted that ethics would someday be taken out of the hands of philosophers and incorporated into the new synthesis of evolutionary and biological thinking.[1] Theologians seemingly had little say in the matter.

A 2010 gathering in Connecticut sponsored by the Edge Foundation brought together nine leading thinkers in exploring "the New Science of Morality." John Brockman, the editor and publisher of *www.Edge.org,* noted that "it seems like everyone is studying morality these days, reaching findings that complement each other more often than they clash." In introducing what people had to say he asked, "What do we have to offer a world in which so many global national crises are caused or exacerbated by moral failures and moral conflicts?"[2] Some of the participants included:

- Yale psychologist *Paul Bloom*, who maintains humans are born with hard-wired morality and have a deep sense of good and evil bred in the bone;
- University of Virginia psychologist *Jonathan Haidt*, who asserts that morality has evolved out of five or more innate foundations: harm, fairness, ingroup, authority, and purity – the highly educated tend to rely on the first two, more religious and lower class people rely on all five;
- Florida State social psychologist *Roy Baumister* cautioned against reductionism, offering the reminder that a focus on the individual and nature needs to be complemented by an emphasis on the interpersonal – nature and culture – where morality is an attempt to get people to overcome their natural selfish impulses.

Two others among the nine were Marc Hauser and Sam Harris. Here is a sampling of their thinking.

Marc Hauser. In his 2006 book, *Moral Minds: How Nature Designed Our Universal Sense of Right and Wrong,*[3] this Harvard evolutionary biologist and neuroscientist challenged the widespread assumption that morality is the product of learning, primarily through families, education, and religion.[4]

Hauser argued that, with evolution, humans have developed a universal, unconscious moral instinct. In an interview in 2006, he explained that we are born with "a universal moral grammar" or set of principles for making judgments about right and wrong. Those principles are "built into the brains of all humans."

This sense of right and wrong consequently precedes everything, including our experiences and our judgments. Variables such as education and reflection colour our moral verdicts, but do not determine them. In fact, such moral principles are immune to commandments handed down by religions and governments and presumably everything else.

Similar to language, cultural variations can be expected. But, says Hauser, "the moral faculty will place constraints on the range of cross-cultural variation and thus limit the extent to which religion, law or teachers can modify our intuitive moral judgments."[5]

For example, he points out that his research demonstrates considerable consensus on moral judgments concerning the permissibility of harming other individuals, with little variation by education or religion including – specifically – people who are religious and those who are atheists.

Hauser brings the resources of a wide range of disciplines to his research task, including evolutionary biology, neuroscience, moral and political philosophy, primatology, linguistics, anthropology. One of his primary research methods is to pose "artificial moral dilemmas," where people are presented with situations calling for moral responses. His assumption is that intuition plays a major role in shaping their responses. An Internet version of his "Moral Sense Test" (MST) is available to potential participants.[6]

In short, for Hauser, our principles for determining morality are present at birth. They are not the product of either learning or reflection.

Following a three-year investigation, Harvard put Hauser on a year's leave in August of 2010 for eight instances of scientific misconduct. For many observers, such developments called much if not almost all of Hauser's work into question.[7] For his part, Hauser maintained that he had "made some significant mistakes." He indicated that "after taking some time off, I look forward to getting back to my work."[8]

Sam Harris. The ideas of Harris are offered in a number of books, the latest of which is *The Moral Landscape: How Science Can Determine Human Values* (2010)[9]. He further offered a succinct overview of his views on moral values in the 2010 Edge event just discussed.[10] Science's failure to address questions of meaning, morality, and values, says Harris, has provided the primary justification for religious faith. Such an abdication has resulted in religious dogmatism, superstition, and sectarian conflict. "We have convinced ourselves that somehow science is by definition a value-free space," he continues, "and that we can't make value judgments about beliefs and practices that needlessly derail our attempts to build happy and sane societies."

Science consequently should not limit itself to merely describing existing moral systems but needs to be engaged in persuasion – persuading people who are committed to harmful things in the name of "morality" to change their commitments and lead better lives. He sees this as no less than "the most important project facing humanity at this point in time." I'm not exaggerating. Harris argues that "it subsumes everything else we could care about – from arresting climate change, to stopping nuclear proliferation, to curing cancer, to saving the whales."

"Project Two" for Harris is understanding right and wrong in universal terms. He notes that this is a particularly difficult task, since the pervasive idea exists that there is no intellectual basis for claiming there is "moral truth."

Harris uses a poignant illustration to make his point. "In 1947, when the United Nations was attempting to formulate a universal declaration of human rights, the American Anthropological Association stepped forward and said, it can't be done. Any notion of human rights is the product of culture. This was the best our social sciences could do with the crematory of Auschwitz still smoking."

Harris challenges such a relativistic assumption. He maintains that we need to converge globally on the question of how we should treat each other. The point of consensus for Harris is well-being: "The concept of 'well-being' captures everything we can care about in the moral sphere."

Harris is convinced that there are right and wrong answers to questions of human flourishing, and morality relates to that domain of facts. In his mind, science needs to give top priority to exploring and developing a universal conception of human values.[11]

Rather than questions of meaning, morality, and purpose being outside the limits of science, Harris believes that science alone can uncover the facts that are needed to enable humans to flourish. Religion not only does not have the answers; it is a major source of world problems.

My re-reading of this brief exposition leads me to think I have made Harris sound more charitable toward religion than he is. In a back cover endorsement of The *Moral Landscape*, Richard Dawkins writes, "As for religion and the preposterous idea that we need God to be good, nobody wields a sharper bayonet than Sam Harris." *Newsweek*'s Jerry Adler sums things up this way: "Dawkins and Harris are not issuing pleas for tolerance or moderation, but bone-rattling attacks on what they regard as a pernicious and outdated superstition."[12]

Clarifying the Question

Undoubtedly, social compassion – concern for others – has a large number of possible sources. A starting point is to agree on that.

Let's also be clear on some additional matters, and save ourselves considerable time and energy by not treating them as issues in question.

✓ Neurological or biological determinism can be treated and greeted as a scientific breakthrough. However, it really re-opens a very old claim – that nature can explain everything, with no recourse to nurture. Sociologists are equally adamant that social environment plays an important role in shaping individuals. A much more productive approach is to combine the insights of both perspectives, as the new area of "social neuroscience" is attempting to do."[13]

✓ Religion is one source of compassion for some people in some situations. Religions often and perhaps even typically call on their followers to care about other people. Besides expecting them to adopt such ideals, they expect them to put them into practice. It therefore is hardly a shocker that people who are taught "to be good" and taught "to be kind" sometimes come through. American President Barack Obama recently acknowledged that he "came to Christian faith later in life and it was because the precepts of Jesus Christ spoke to me in terms of the kind of life that I would want to lead – being my brothers' and sisters' keeper, treating others as they would treat me."[14]

✓ Do interpersonal values always translate into behaviour? Of course not. In causation parlance, values *are not* sufficient causes of behaviour. But they *are* necessary causes: a person who acts compassionately values compassion, even if someone who values compassion is not always compassionate. If the value is in place, compassionate behaviour is at least a mathematical possibility. Conversely, "no value = no compassion."

✓ Does religion sometimes contribute to the lack of compassion – to pain, suffering, and even the death of other people? Unfortunately, the answer is yes.

✓ Do individuals who are not religious also sometimes treat other people in negative ways, spanning rudeness and exploitation to death? Here again, the answer is, unfortunately, yes.

So the question I want to bring to the Canadian scene assumes all of the above realities. What I want to know is this: *at this point in history in Canada, to what extent is religiousness associated with compassionate values and behaviour?*

An important related question, given the increasing religious polarization is: *how does the level of compassion of those who are religious compare with the level of compassion of those who are not?*

The answers will help us to assess the immediate implications of religious polarization for interpersonal life in Canada.

Civil societies require the adoption of values and norms that make for good interpersonal life. Consequently, the question of civility sources is an extremely important one.

In the fall of 2010, Hockey Calgary, the organization that oversees minor hockey in Calgary, became the first in the country to require parents to complete a one-hour on-line course before their children could play.

The president of Hockey Calgary, Perry Cavanaugh explained that cases of unruly parents and violence on the ice required exposure to standards to guide everyone toward mutual respect at the rink. He cited such things as hockey parents yelling at referees, climbing the glass, and throwing coffee cups on the ice, and a significant number of players being suspended because of illegal hits, fighting, and roughing penalties.

Thinking like a sociologist, Cavanaugh noted that "Calgary has gone through a period of negative activity in terms of violence in the community," with those changes "propagating more and more into local arenas. We're seeing less respect to individuals, players, coaches, parents, and we need to send a message that this kind of behaviour is not tolerated."[15]

By the time the season started, 99% of Calgary's 13,000-plus young hockey players had "Respect in Sport" – certified parents (at least one had to take the course). Cavanaugh commented that, even if some parents didn't like the program, they were "putting their egos aside and getting the kids on the ice."[16]

It seems that when it comes to social well-being, we need all the help we can get.

A Canadian Reading

Values. Going back to the 1980s, we have been asking adults and teenagers about the importance they give to a number of values. Some pertain to goals or objectives, such as a comfortable life, friendship, and success. Others focus on means or norms for living and relating to other people, such as honesty, politeness, and generosity. Findings regarding the latter offer information on the extent to which Canadians of all ages place importance on traits that make for positive interpersonal life.

The most recent Project Canada surveys show that the majority of Canadians place a very high level of importance on almost all of these interpersonal values – although the size of those majorities vary considerably.

When one looks at the findings by age, some slight variations are apparent between older and younger adults – but perhaps not as much as some would expect.[17] The major difference is the extent to which these traits are highly valued by adults versus teenagers.

Table 7.1. Interpersonal Values by Age Cohort % Indicating "Very Important"				
	Pre-Boomers	Boomers	Post-Boomers	Teenagers
Honesty	95	92	89	81
Concern for others	75	73	77	65
Politeness	79	76	70	64
Forgiveness	75	75	75	60
Generosity	53	54	57	---

Sources: Project Canada 2005 and Project Teen Canada 2008.

Another variable that has some predictability is gender. Adult and teenage females are consistently more likely than their male counterparts to highly value all of these interpersonal characteristics.

Table 7.2. Interpersonal Values by Gender: Adults & Teens % Indicating "Very Important"				
	ADULTS		TEENAGERS	
	Females	Males	Females	Males
Honesty	95	89	87	74
Concern for others	83	67	72	56
Politeness	80	69	70	57
Forgiveness	81	69	66	53
Generosity	64	46	---	---

*Shaded: a difference of 10 or more percentage points or more; viewed as substantively significant. The r's for adults, respectively: .113, .185, .128, .145, .184. Teens: .176, .180, .153, .146.

Source: Project Canada 2005 and Project Teen Canada 2008.

Beyond these age and gender variations, what we want to know is whether or not religion is also associated with differences in the importance given to these values.

An examination of values by attendance, identification, and belief reveals a consistent pattern: Canadians who are religious according to these three indicators are consistently more likely than other people to place a high level of importance on these interpersonal traits.

A number of quick observations.

1. The relationships between religiosity and these interpersonal values are not always overly strong, but they are consistent. Overall, it is fair to say that people who are religious tend to be more likely to value these traits that make for civility than people who are not religious.

2. Not everyone who is religious places a high level of importance on these values. Conversely, large numbers of people who are not religious see these traits as "very important." Such basic findings help us to understand why generalizations about people in both categories typically need to allow for considerable exceptions.

3. In general, these findings support the idea that, all sources considered, religion – measured here in three different ways – has *a unique impact* on the importance that Canadians place on these interpersonal values.[18] (This note offers clarification on the statistics used for this analysis.)

Table 7.3. Interpersonal Values by Religiosity: Adults & Teens
% Indicating "Very Important"

	■✚■	ATTENDANCE		IDENTIFN		BELIEF	
		Weekly	Never	Yes	No	Theist	Atheist
ADULTS							
Honesty	92%	96	92	92	89	94	89
Concern for others	75	83	72	75	75	85	74
Politeness	75	80	71	75	71	81	63
Forgiveness	75	88	69	76	63	77	65
Generosity	55	76	44	56	45	67	37
TEENAGERS							
Honesty	81%	86	79	83	77	86	75
Concern for others	65	74	60	67	60	72	54
Politeness	64	69	61	68	58	71	57
Forgiveness	60	77	52	64	51	72	44
Patience	44	57	39	48	37	55	35

*Shaded: indicates a difference of 10 percentage points or more; viewed as substantively significant.

Source: Project Canada 2005 and Project Teen Canada 2008 national surveys.

A particularly interesting test of these findings is to see whether or not they hold up by gender, and also if they apply in Quebec, where secularization has been extensive. The teen data obviously also have a built-in control for age.

When we use belief in God as a non-organizational measure of religiosity, we see that positive relationships exist between theism and values in both the gender and regional instances. Teens who are theists are consistently more likely than others to place a high level of importance on interpersonal values. Something is happening "out there" with religion and interpersonal values that transcends region, gender, and age.

Table 7.4. Values of Theist & Atheist Teens by Gender
% Indicating "Very Important"

| | Female | | Male | |
	Theist	Atheist	Theist	Atheist
Trust	94	86	82	71
Honesty	91	79	80	71
Concern	80	61	63	49
Politeness	76	60	65	54
Forgiveness	77	49	66	41
Hard work	64	48	58	50
Patience	59	30	49	39

Source: Bibby, *The Emerging Millennials* 2009:172.

Table 7.5. Values of Theist & Atheist Teens: QC & Elsewhere
% Indicating "Very Important"

| | Quebec | | Elsewhere | |
	Theist	Atheist	Theist	Atheist
Trust	83	80	89	77
Honesty	86	73	86	76
Concern	58	47	75	58
Politeness	74	62	71	54
Forgiveness	62	37	73	48
Hard work	60	53	62	48
Patience	48	33	56	36

Source: Bibby, *The Emerging Millennials* 2009:172.

Behaviour. We all know that one of the shortcomings of surveys is their inability to capture actual behaviour. There is nothing surprising about that limitation. As I so often remind people, surveys at their best are simply good structured conversations. As such, they have no equal when it comes to understanding what's going on in people's heads – their thoughts including their beliefs, attitudes, values, expectations, and so on. In probing ideas, surveys have no equal.

When we want to get a good reading on behaviour, however, we all know that it can be precarious to simply rely on what people tell us they do or have done. We can ask them questions about how much money they give to charities, whether or not they ever have used marijuana, how often they work out, the last time they received a speeding ticket, whether or not they ever gamble, how often they have sex, if they ever lie, and on and on.

But – and this is going to sound excessively cynical – we can only put a percentage of certainty on whether or not they have told us the truth. That percentage obviously depends on factors such as how well we know the person, whether or not we think they feel comfortable with us, and the risk involved in their providing the information.

That's my long way of saying that it is difficult to gather reliable data through surveys on how people actually behave. Nonetheless, we try.

For example, in our latest youth survey, we again asked participants to imagine that they have bought something and have received $10 more in change than they were supposed to receive. We asked them if they would be inclined to (a) keep the $10 and keep walking, (b) go back and return the extra $10, or (c) feel that what they would do would depend on factors such as the size of the store, whether they expected to shop there again, and whether or not they knew the sales person involved. [19]

It's not behaviour – but maybe at least something in the way of anticipated behaviour.

- What the survey found is that some 4 in 10 teens claim they would return the $10, while the remainder were almost evenly divided between those who said "it would depend" and those who admitted that they would probably simply keep the ten bucks.
- However, an examination by our three religiosity variables shows a consistent, positive relationship between attendance, identification and belief and the inclination to return the $10.

Perhaps the findings reflect what young people *would do*; at minimum they reflect what they *think they should do*.

This takes us back to the argument about values functioning something like "good intentions." Behaviour doesn't necessarily follow; but the values have to be present in order for the behaviour to occur.

Our findings so far point to religion helping to at least instill positive interpersonal values. With our "$10 data," we are going a bit further in maintaining that the findings support the argument that religion is also related to Canadians holding some positive interpersonal intentions.

Table 7.6. Honesty in Action by Religiosity: Teenagers *"Do you think you would be inclined to..."*								
	I✦I	**ATTENDANCE**		**IDENTIFN**		**BELIEF**	
		Weekly	Never	Yes	No	Theist	Atheist
Return the $10	38%	56	36	42	33	47	26
It would depend	31	22	34	30	37	27	36
Keep the $10	31	22	30	28	30	26	38

Source: Project Teen Canada 2008.

Civility. Most people, I think, would fairly readily concede that some kinds of behaviour reflect a measure of civility while others do not.

For example, there would seem to be some basic courtesy ideals associated with such things as people not walking on a red light and making traffic wait (apart from getting a ticket), saying sorry when we accidentally bump into someone, not parking in a stall reserved for those who are handicapped when one is not handicapped, and resisting the urge to "give someone the finger."

The Project Teen Canada survey in 2008 asked young people across the country how they felt about such kinds of behaviour.[20] Participants were asked to indicate whether they approved, disapproved, or didn't care either way.

Adults who are cynical about the civility levels of teenagers would be wise to take a close look at the results.

- Large majorities of around 80% disapprove of people misusing parking stalls for the handicapped, or not apologizing for bumping into someone.
- A two-thirds majority doesn't approve of people walking on a red light at the expense of oncoming traffic.
- However, only 45% act troubled about people occasionally giving someone "the finger."

Interestingly, differences by attendance, identification, and belief are consistently positive but extremely small – with the sole exception of extending the famous "finger."

Clearly there are a variety of sources of such basic civil attitudes, besides religion.

Table 7.7. Select Behaviour Attitudes: Teenagers % Indicating Disapproval							
	🍁	ATTENDANCE		IDENTIFN		BELIEF	
		Weekly	Never	Yes	No	Theist	Atheist
Parking handicapped	82	85	79	84	80	85	77
No 'sorry' for bumping	77	77	77	79	76	78	74
Walking on a red light	63	66	61	63	63	64	58
Giving the finger	45	62	38	49	36	53	34

Source: Project Teen Canada 2008.

Being Good. A basic hope for almost every parent is that their children – in the phrase of one of my former students – "will turn out OK." Related to that essential hope, parents and other adults, along with our schools, churches, and other institutions want to see young people "stay out of trouble."

How is everyone faring?

The 2008 national youth survey included a number of items that probe both self-image and behaviour with respect to the stereotypical notion of "trying to be good" or "trying to stay out of trouble."

Teens are almost unanimous in claiming that they "are kind to other people." The numbers drop a bit, as would be expected, when they are asked how well the two statements, *"I have never got into trouble with the police"* and *"I try to stay out of trouble"* describe them personally. Gender differences, by the way, are fairly small in both of these cases – 86% for females vs. 78% for males re: having not had police problems and 83% vs. 77% for staying out of trouble.

When we look at these variables through the eyes of religiosity, what we find is that almost all young people, whether they are religious or not, see themselves as kind to other people.

Where religion makes an appearance is when we look at experiences teens have had with the police.

- The differences are not overly large, but nonetheless smaller percentages of teens who attend weekly, identify with a religious group, or believe in God say they have got into trouble with the police.
- Those who are cynical about those self-reports need to take note of the fact that young people who are religious are also more inclined to say that they consciously try to stay out of trouble – a motivational difference that they would not seem to have any particular point in exaggerating.

Religion here again appears to be having a unique impact on teens, beyond other social and cultural factors.

Again I rush to emphasize that these data documenting the inclination of most teens to value "goodness" support the reality that there are many sources at work. Religion is certainly not the only source – but it *is* one source.

Teenagers clearly can be good without God. But God seems to increase the number of good teenagers.

Table 7.8. Teenage Goodness by Religiosity
% Agreeing

	■✦■	ATTENDANCE		ID		BELIEF	
		Weekly	Never	Yes	No	Theist	Atheist
I am kind to other people	94	96	93	95	93	95	89
I have never got into trouble with the police	83	90	78	86	79	86	75
I try to stay out of trouble	80	87	75	84	74	86	65

Source: Project Teen Canada 2008.

Social Concerns. Over the years, teens and adults have been asked about the extent to which they regard various issues to be serious problems. Lists of 15 or more areas have been given, with respondents indicating their severity.

A look at a sampling of such issues by religiosity among teens, for example, reveals a consistent pattern. Those who are religious tend to be more likely than those who are not to see issues with very direct personal and interpersonal consequences – such as drugs, school violence, and bullying – as serious problems. Differences tend to be slight, however, in the case of more general issues, such as the environment or American influence.

Table 7.9. Canadian Concerns by Religiosity: Teenagers
% Indicating Are "Very Serious" Problems in Canada

	🍁	ATTENDANCE		ID		BELIEF	
		Weekly	Never	Yes	No	Theist	Atheist
Environment	54	48	56	55	55	53	55
Drugs	42	48	39	45	36	51	36
Violence at school	42	47	40	45	38	48	39
Bullying	34	38	31	36	31	39	29
American influence	24	25	25	25	22	27	24

Source: Project Teen Canada 2008.

Indicative of the pervasiveness of current attention being given to environmental and sustainability issues, there are no significant differences in levels of interest and concern being expressed about related topics on the part of teens who are religiously involved and those who are not.

"Thinking green" and being conscious of sustainability are widespread emphases in our culture. Here, even for the devout, religion is typically only one of many potential sources, and seldom a prime source at that.

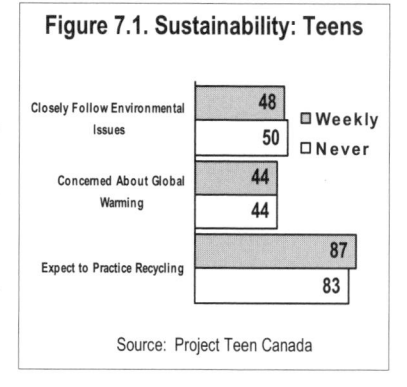

Figure 7.1. Sustainability: Teens

	Weekly	Never
Closely Follow Environmental Issues	48	50
Concerned About Global Warming	44	44
Expect to Practice Recycling	87	83

Source: Project Teen Canada

Social Compassion. The Project Canada surveys have also included numerous items that have probed the prevalence of social compassion.

For example, given that Canada has had a publicly funded health care system for some time, it is not surprising that nearly all adults and teens agree that *"people who cannot afford it have a right to medical care."* This is a good example of a compassionate outlook that has been engrained in Canadians. Religion would not be expected to be a unique source – and it is not.

Being concerned about people outside of Canada, however, is not an outlook endorsed by everyone. Some 25% of adults and approximately 30% of teenagers agree with the statement, *"We need to worry about our own country and let the rest of the world take care of itself."*

- Among *adults*, disagreement with such a focus on taking care of ourselves varies little by the religiosity measures.

- However, *teenagers* who are religious are more likely than those who are not religious to be *opposed* to such an isolationist position. The differences are small, yet consistent across all three measures.

- For many teens, non-religious and religious, the Internet's role in further reducing the size of the global village, making needs across the planet more visible, has *not* resulted in a particularly compassionate outlook toward "the rest of the world."

Table 7.10. Social Compassion by Religiosity: Teens & Adults							
		ATTENDANCE		ID		BELIEF	
		Weekly	Never	Yes	No	Theist	Atheist
People who cannot	**Agree**						
afford it have a right	**ADULTS** 98%	97	98	98	98	98	99
to medical care	**TEENS** 94	93	94	94	93	94	92
We need to worry about our own	**Disagree**						
country and let the	**ADULTS** 73	78	70	72	79	76	79
rest of the world	**TEENS** 67	74	62	70	64	71	59
take care of itself							

Sources: Project Canada 2005 & Project Teen Canada 2008.

Global Concerns. Such an observation is further borne out by data from the 2008 national youth survey regarding the extent to which young people are concerned about a number of issues on a global basis.

Only about 40% indicated they are "very concerned" about issues like human rights violations, poverty, and AIDS "in the world generally," while just under 30% expressed a similar level of concern about terrorism.

In each instance, religious teens are more inclined than others to express concern about these issues – especially in the case of poverty, AIDS and terrorism.

Table 7.11. Global Concerns by Religiosity: Teenagers							
% Indicating "Very Concerned" About...							
	■✹■	ATTENDANCE		ID		BELIEF	
		Weekly	Never	Yes	No	Theist	Atheist
Human rights violations	42	43	40	42	41	45	41
Poverty	40	48	35	43	34	49	33
AIDS	37	40	35	39	32	41	33
Terrorism	27	31	23	30	21	33	21
Source: Project Teen Canada 2008.							

These findings point to a significant preliminary conclusion: religion is one importance source of positive interpersonal life. Those who are not religious do not lack for civility and compassion. But, collectively, they tend to lag slightly behind Canadians who are religious.

To the extent that religion is making a contribution to social compassion in Canada, a decline in the proportion of people who embrace religion will be associated with a decline in the values and behaviour that make for social well-being.

It's not that religion's contribution cannot be made up by other sources. But until such sources are located and are operative, social well-being in Canada is going to take a significant hit.

Religious groups can easily be attacked and belittled. It is a far more difficult task to identify the functional alternatives that will fill the social well-being void.

Civility and Compassion Among Canadian Youth

- Conservative Protestant teens, along with their "Christian unspecified," Islam, and Hindu counterparts, are more likely than others to say they would return the 10 bucks and to disapprove of people using "the finger." Some 1 in 2 Catholic, Orthodox, Mainline Protestant, and Buddhist teens also give the finger a thumbs down.
- World poverty is a particular concern for young Muslims, Hindus, Jews, Protestants, and Catholics outside Quebec.

Teenage Polarization in the Mosaic
Social Civility and Compassion

	Return the $10	Disapprove of the Finger	Concerned About World Poverty
NATIONALLY	**38%**	**45**	**40**
Roman Catholicism	**38**	**46**	**42**
Outside Quebec	40	44	47
Quebec	32	51	32
Protestantism	**51**	**56**	**43**
Conservative	60	64	45
Mainline	46	48	43
Orthodox	**29**	**47**	**41**
Christian *unspecified*	**53**	**58**	**49**
Other World Faiths	**43**	**49**	**47**
Islam	54	60	57
Hinduism	53	63	55
Judaism	38	32	46
Sikhism	34	38	32
Buddhism	33	54	39
Aboriginal Spirituality	32	32	39
No Religion	**30**	**36**	**34**

The Global Situation

Helping Behaviour. In 2007, Gallup released survey findings on acts of compassion for three settings – Canada, the United States, and Britain. The pollster asked people if they had donated money, volunteered time, or helped a stranger "in the past month." They then looked at the results by the importance that respondents said religion has in their daily lives.

Gallup found people in Britain were most likely to donate money, while Americans and Canadians were more likely to volunteer their time. Differences in helping a stranger were fairly small.

In all three settings, without exception, people who placed importance on religion were slightly more inclined than others to donate money, volunteer time, and help a stranger. Religion was making a small but consistent difference.

Table 7.12. Helping Behaviour by Religiosity: Canada, the U.S. & Britain

% Who in the Past Month Have...

	ALL			Religion NB			Religion Not NB		
	Canada	US	UK	Canada	US	UK	Canada	US	UK
Donated money	60	64	73	66	71	82	56	50	67
Volunteered time	39	44	23	45	50	32	34	34	18
Helped a stranger	64	59	66	65	67	70	62	63	53

Sources: Gallup Poll analysis by English 2007.

Buster Smith and Rodney Stark have recently noted that "studies on the relationship between generosity and religiosity have been largely confined to examinations of developed countries." They point out that Gallup's worldwide data "make it possible to expand these analyses to countries in all regions of the world."[21]

Brett Pelham and Steve Crabtree have used the Gallup data to examine the relationship between religion and "helping behaviour" worldwide. They report that people who are highly religious are more likely than others to have engaged in each of the three kinds of behaviour. What's more, they say that the relationships are consistent not only across global regions but also are "consistent across the world's largest faith traditions, including Christianity, Islam, Hinduism, and Judaism." For example, they report that "differences for helping a stranger" range "from 7 percentage points among Buddhists to 15 points among Jews."[22]

Table 7.13. Helping Behaviour by Religiosity: Globally						
% Who in the Past Month Have…						
	DONATED		VOLUNTEERED		HELPED A STRANGER	
	Highly Religious	Less	Highly Religious	Less	Highly Religious	Less
Europe	43%	28	24	17	42	36
Asia	41	26	24	19	46	37
Americas	39	28	29	18	56	49
Africa	23	15	27	17	52	43

Note: Gallup defines "highly religious" people as those who report that religion is important to their daily lives and also report having attended a religious service in the week prior to being surveyed. All others are categorized as "less religious."

Sources: Gallup World Poll analyses by Pelham and Crabtree 2008.

Incidentally, Smith and Stark have carried the analysis a bit further, looking at generosity by attendance and salience separately. They have found the relationships to hold for both measures, controlling for variables such as gender, age, and marital status. They note that in each of the three instances, the associations with attendance are higher than they are for salience.[23] Such a finding, they suggest, points to the importance of community – and not just the subjective importance of religion – to individuals.

Development Assistance. On a national level, to what extent are countries that are relatively affluent showing generosity to countries that are in need of assistance?

The results are mixed. According to current figures provided by the key monitoring body, the Organisation for Economic Co-operation and Development, *in absolute terms*, the top 10 donors are the U.S., Britain, Japan, France, Germany, the Netherlands, Sweden, Spain, Canada, and Italy. The overall correlation between service attendance and giving in real dollars is both positive and appreciable (r= .412).

However, if giving is computed *as a percentage of Gross National Income*, the correlation between attendance and giving is actually negative (r = - .441).

One's conclusion here is based on one's judgment as to whether appropriate and significant giving is "how much" versus "what proportion" based on capabilities.

Attendance gets a a "B" on the former, a "D" on the latter.

Table 7.14. Development Assistance: 22 Member Countries National Contributions - 2008			
	Attendance	Real USD millions	% of GNI
Average	*29%*	*5.5*	*.48*
Ireland	56	1.3	.59
Italy	**49**	**4.9**	**.22**
United States	**43**	**26.8**	**.19**
Spain	39	6.9	.45
Portugal	38	0.6	.27
Japan	**38**	**9.6**	**.19**
Austria	34	1.7	.43
Germany	**30**	**14.0**	**.38**
Greece	29	.70	.21
New Zealand	27	.35	.30
Luxembourg	26	0.4	.98
Switzerland	26	2.0	.42
CANADA	**26**	**4.8**	**.32**
Netherlands	26	7.0	.80
Belgium	24	2.4	.48
Australia	**23**	**3.0**	**.32**
France	**20**	**10.9**	**.39**
United Kingdom	**20**	**11.5**	**.43**
Sweden	17	4.7	.98
Denmark	16	2.8	.82
Norway	13	4.0	.88
Finland	12	1.2	.44

Real USD r = .412; % GNI r = -.441
BOLD: G-20 Countries.
Sources: Attendance - Gallup WorldView 2010; Contributions - Organisation for Economic Co-operation and Development 2010.

Trust and safety. Still other measures of positive interpersonal life might take the form of trust and lack of crime.

An examination of attendance, trust, and crime in a sample of 29 countries reveals that a modest positive relationship exists between trust and a lower crime rate (r = .275). But attendance all by itself is *not* positively associated with either trust (r = -.468) or a low crime rate (r = -.195).

In countries like Ethiopia, the Philippines, South Africa, and Brazil, for example, service attendance is fairly high – well above the levels in places such as Canada, Britain, and Sweden. Yet crime rates in all four of those settings are significantly above those of Canada and the other two countries, and – predictably – trust levels are much lower.

Table 7.15. Attendance, Trust, and Crime Rates: Select Countries

"Most people in society are trustworthy"/ Crime rates per 100,000 population

	Attendance	Trust	Crime Rates
Nigeria	89%	32%	1.3
Ethiopia	78	47	6.4
India	73	54	2.8
Malaysia	73	56	2.3
Poland	62	48	1.2
Philippines	64	--	6.4
Mexico	60	46	11.6
South Africa	57	42	36.5
Pakistan	56	54	6.8
Palestinian Territories	55	34	3.9
Italy	49	41	1.2
Brazil	49	35	22.0
Iran	45	----	2.9
United States	43	58	5.2
Israel	39	42	2.4
Spain	39	43	.9
Japan	38	43	.5
Korea, Republic of	35	46	2.3
Germany	30	56	.8
CANADA	**26**	**71**	**1.7**
Ukraine	23	47	6.3
Australia	23	--	1.2
France	20	45	1.4
United Kingdom	20	65	1.4
Sweden	17	78	.9
Czech Republic	15	42	2.0
Russia	15	50	14.2
Norway	13	--	.6
China	9	79	1.2

Sources: Attendance - Gallup WorldView 2010; Trust – Pew Global Attitudes Project, 2008; Crime rates – United Nations Office on Drugs and Crime 2010.

These global findings underline the complexity of religion having an impact on both trust and crime in every social or geographical setting around the world.

In some countries where cultures of crime, violence, and corruption have been rampant historically – such as the Philippines, Mexico, South Africa, and Brazil – people have been attending churches in large numbers. However, religion all by itself has hardly turned those societies around.

Conversely, countries such as Canada and the United States, along with European countries including Britain, France, Poland, Germany, and Sweden, seemingly have come to know high levels of safety and civility, with religion being one of the contributors.

In short, the global portrait shows religion sometimes being an important source of enhanced interpersonal life, in other instances, having little effect.

The findings remind us that religion typically has an impact on individuals and societies to the

Table 7.16. View Theism Makes for Better People by Belief in God: 10 Select Countries

"Belief in God or a higher power makes for a better human being"

[r = .498]	Agree	Believe in God
Nigeria	96%	99
Indonesia	96	96
Lebanon	92	92
India	91	99
United States	82	88
Russia	81	91
Mexico	80	97
Israel	71	95
South Korea	70	98
United Kingdom	56	86

Source: ICM poll conducted for the BBC Two program, "What the World Thinks of God." 2004. Belief in God: computed from the World Religion Database in Smith 2009:284-287.

extent that it is able to work with and through other institutions, such as families, schools, governments, private industry, and media that are positioned to influence personal and collective life.

Without that kind of social reinforcement, religion finds it difficult to have a significant impact in any setting.

Assessment

These findings point to a fairly consistent pattern in both Canada and around the world: people who are religious are more likely than those who are not to endorse positive interpersonal values and exhibit positive interpersonal behaviour.

Put far more succinctly and provocatively, on balance, religion appears to be making a noteworthy contribution to social well-being.

Yet, religion typically has a positive influence to the extent that it also is associated with other institutions that have a positive impact on interpersonal life. American political scientist Walter Russell Mead comments that, in various parts of the world, one can readily uncover "young Muslims who have only a narrow and sectarian education, and young Pentecostals who know very little outside of their Bibles. God may have a special love for the poor," he says, "but that does not mean that the poor get sophisticated religion. They get strong religion and hot religion more than they get subtle religion and sophisticated religion." The result can be a dangerous world.[24]

The findings also make it very clear that religion is not the only source of civility. Far from it. Without question, people can be good without God.

Nonetheless, on balance, religion, for all its downsides and darksides, is one important source of civility.

Such a finding should hardly come as a surprise. When we stop to think about, it is fairly readily apparent that there are few institutions and organizations that exist with one of their foremost goals being the enhancement of interpersonal life. Religions typically have such a goal. It is a central part of what they are about.

Consequently, if religion ceases to be practiced by significant numbers of Canadians, some equally effective sources of social well-being will have to be found.

At this point in our history, it is not at all clear that such functional alternatives are anywhere in sight.

Some might argue that Canada and much of Europe benefit from "the shadow effect" of Christian legacies – sort of like the after-effects that our parents and grandparents have on our lives, long after they are gone. Historian Mark Noll, for example, has suggested that Canada has not abandoned its "communal social order" - just "the Christian presence that did so much to build" it.[25]

Those claims undoubtedly carry some truth. But one can also argue that shadows disappear with time – that some semblance of their sources needs to exist if they themselves are to live on.

Such would seem to be the case with religion in Canada.

Highly-respected *Toronto Star* journalist, Carol Goar, pointed out a short time ago that "faith-based organizations are the bedrock of Canada's charitable sector." She noted that they run homeless shelters and transition homes for abused women, offer asylum to refugees and settlement assistance to immigrants, set up after-school programs for kids in troubled neighbourhoods, organize soup kitchens, open their doors to seniors, community groups and service clubs, raise millions of dollars "for good works" and mobilize thousands of volunteers. But, Goar wrote, "as their membership rolls shrink and their collection plates lighten, they are struggling to maintain this network of charitable activities."

She concluded with these strong words: "It is fine to say – as the majority of Canadians do – that you prefer to explore your own spirituality, practise your religion privately and ponder metaphysical questions in solitude. But, she says, "Look around. There's a world in need out there. Church members are on the front lines, putting their faith to work. They could use some help."[26]

The concerns raised by Goar have received considerable support in an important analysis released in 2009. Ray Pennings and Michael Van Pelt of Cardus – a think tank that examines cultural, social, and religious intersections in Canada – note that the vitally important civic sector, with its array of charitable and nonprofit organizations, accounts for just under 10% of Canada's gross domestic product. This "Third Sector," distinct from the public and private sectors, is driven disproportionately by a small core of citizens: some 20% of adults donate 80% of the money given to charities, while about 10% of adults provide 80% of the hours volunteered.[27]

The imminent problem raised by Pennings and Van Pelt is that the vast majority of people in this "civic core" are older and often religious. As they pass from the scene, many organizations and charities will feel the effects.

An ongoing Statistics Canada survey series on giving and volunteering corroborates such an assertion. The latest survey in the series, conducted in 2007, found that Canadians who attend weekly services were more likely than other people both to be among top donors (25% vs. 15%) and top volunteers (25% vs. 9%).[28]

Maclean's offered this provocative take on the findings: "If religion is simply a license for bad behaviour, how does one explain the mammoth gap between the charitable acts of those who believe and those who do not?" The magazine then posed the important question: "If organized religion continues to fade from mainstream practice, how will society ever replace the massive contributions of time and money that believers currently provide?" *Maclean's* concluded, "Spirituality and altruism share an obvious and welcome concern for humanity and its future. Do atheists?"[29]

In the midst of our debating whether or not religion contributes more or contributes less to optimum social life, perhaps we would be wise to recognize that religion has the potential to be one important source of social well-being, and give greater attention to identifying additional sources that also can be effective.

~

A quick footnote with respect to the response I expect I will receive to this chapter. Sam Harris has said that when he wrote his first book, *The End of Faith*, the most hostile communications came from Christians – ironic, he felt, given that "Christians generally imagine that no faith imparts the virtues of love and forgiveness more effectively than their own."[30]

In October of 2007, some of the preliminary findings presented in this chapter were released in a story by Charles Lewis in the *National Post*.[31] In this case, the most hostile and mean-spirited responses came from atheists.

I would suggest that one measure of compassion will be found in people who are religious suppressing the urge to gloat, and those who are not religious suppressing the urge to slay the messenger.

8 Polarization & Death

"If mortals die, will they live again?" – Job 14.14, RSV

BABY BOOMERS increasingly have been having to come to grips with mortality in recent years – while people following them have been pondering the strain they will be putting on health care and social services. The oldest in the cohort were born about 1946 and turned 65 in 2011. The youngest, who arrived around 1965, hit 45. As a "borderline Boomer," I know how many of them were feeling.

We all know the folk wisdom, but most of us ignored it when we were younger. "Life is short." "Take time to smell the flowers." "If you've got your health, you've got everything." "Enjoy people while you can." Those things all sounded so trite.

But in the last while, lots of Boomers have had to deal with aging and ailing grandparents, parents, and other relatives and friends. There also have been quite a few deaths. It's not just the older people. Friends and acquaintances who were supposed to be around are no longer here, reduced to memories far too early. What has been particularly difficult to deal with has been the loss of the very young, whose lives were just beginning.

There has been something so random, unpredictable, and surreal about it all. One year or one day people are with us. The next year or the next day they are so gone.

The fact that we know that aging and death are facts of life provides little comfort. Watching such things unfold as an inevitable part of life and life cycles does not make them any easier to accept.

Few things underline limits, helplessness, and finality with more vividness than death.

So it is, writes Tom Harpur, that "surely the most momentous personal question of our day – or indeed any other – is, having once died, is that the end or do we somehow live again?"[1]

The Problematic Death Question

The Boomers have been problem-solvers. They have been a generation that collectively has worked hard, pursued a good education, set challenging goals, and achieved many of them. In Canada and the United States, they have been part of social and technological revolutions that have elevated the quality of life for millions of people. Few things have been outside of what's doable.

Contrary to excessively enthusiastic commentators, the Boomers haven't done it all and they haven't achieved it all. They have accomplished much and provided a rich legacy upon which Post-Boomers can build.

But as they have to come to grips with death, they don't appear to have any particular advantages over generations before them. As one Boomer, Michael Coren, has put it, death as "the great egalitarian blade comes to us all. We can shout and moan and complain, but in the end we can do nothing. We slide and slip into the beyond."[2]

The Limits of Science

The information explosion has not resulted in our knowing much more than earlier generations about death.

When we think about it, it's rather strange. Science can enable us to explore the universe. It can provide us with miraculous technologies for carrying out our work, performing life-saving medical procedures, and transmitting music, images and messages.

Yet while science and technology can combine to equip us, inform us, entertain us, and prolong our lives, the mighty duo have few trustworthy product lines to offer when it comes to understanding the reality for which no one gets an exemption – death.

It remains as much a mystery as ever.

The difficulty, of course, is that we as humans have to rely on what we can know. And as long as the rules of science limit the knowable to what we can see, touch, hear, smell, and taste, we remain remarkably clueless in the face of death.

There could be something more. But science throws up its hands and declares, "There is no way of knowing."

It may not be an exaggeration to say that, rather than being less troubled by death, the Boomers find it all the more frustrating to accept.

They have been a generation accustomed to finding solutions to problems, including the need to respond to physical deterioration. Much has been written about their age-defying outlook and their co-opting of technology to enable them to deal with declining hearing, sight, mobility and sexual abilities. Their generation has been replete, as well, with people who can tell them what the weather will be like next month, with social forecasters who allegedly can tell them what will happen decades from now.

Why should death be any different?

Alas, with death Canada's Boomers meet their resource match. And the fact that many of them decided to take a pass on religion along the way doesn't exactly help. To borrow the poetry of songwriter Randy Newman, they won't have any God to greet them, having already taught their children "not to believe those lies."[3]

Efforts to go lightly with death do not help much. *Globe and Mail* columnist Margaret Wente recently put things this way: "I hate the modern loss of ritual and solemnity surrounding death. Something's lost when people get together and have a party and pretend the loved one has done nothing more dramatic than move to Cleveland. She adds, "These are serious matters, and we shouldn't pretend they're not."[4]

Death and Religion

If science can't help us with the question of death, what options do we have?

Option 1 would seem to be to take the advice of someone like Freud.[5] He reminded us that it would be great to be able to believe that there is something out there after we die – that there is life after death.

Unfortunately, he says, there isn't. Consequently, we have to take a deep, last breath and realize, "That's it." No more. It's over. It's not great. But things are what they are. Christopher Hitchens, at 61, found out in 2010 that he had cancer. Somewhat stoically, he told Noah Richler of *Maclean's* that he had been "looking forward to some good sixties. I really didn't want more than a decade" when "I'd cash out a bit. And now I'm not going to get that."[6]

Option 2 would be to plead ignorance – to take an agnostic position toward death and declare we just don't know. Maybe there's life after death; maybe there's not.

This second option likewise doesn't do much for morale. But perhaps "maybe" is better than "no" – akin to something being better than nothing. .

Option 3 would be to believe that death is not the end, that there actually is life after death. Obviously this has been an option that many religions have posed.

The difficulty here for those who are empirically minded is that we don't have much, if any, reliable scientific data on which to base such a possibility.

Lots of people have claimed that they have had near-death experiences that allowed them to observe first-hand what life after death is like. A religion such as Christianity, of course, makes the claim that Jesus died and was raised from the dead, providing a concrete example of what can be experienced.

What the choices come down to is this: is one going to rely exclusively on what is known scientifically, or is one open to the possibility that faith is also a way of knowing?

Since science cannot speak to the non-observable, it really is unable to address the question of life after death.

Religions, to varying degrees, claim to have insight into what happens after we die.[7] In lieu of being accompanied by observable evidence, those claims have to be taken on faith.

Option 1 goes with science, option 3 with religion. Option 2 is the choice of the undecided.

As we will see, these are more than just belief choices. The directions that people choose to go have very important emotional and outlook consequences.

A Canadian Reading

A few months ago, I sat in a food fair in the West Edmonton Mall, reflecting on the extent to which young people reflect. Over to my left? Live data. Two buoyant teenage females ostensibly were having lunch with each other. What intrigued me was that both were text-messaging the whole time. As they got up from their table, they were still texting, taking a few seconds out to simultaneously pop in earbuds as they returned to the mall.

I thought to myself, "Are my surveys really capturing what's going on in the world? When would two people like that possibly give time to thinking about life's 'big questions'? They barely give time to each other."

I can almost hear someone saying, "Those teens were multi-tasking." I'm not so sure. Ron Rolheiser's observation seems more apt – that multi-tasking is really the ability to be inattentive to more than one thing at the same time.

Deep Thoughts. Actually, my West Edmonton Mall data reflected a number of realities – beyond multi-tasking. The percentage of teens who admit that they seldom or never take time to "sit and think" has doubled from 13% in 1984 to 26% today. Further, the percentages who say they *never* think about issues like death, suffering, and purpose have risen slightly.

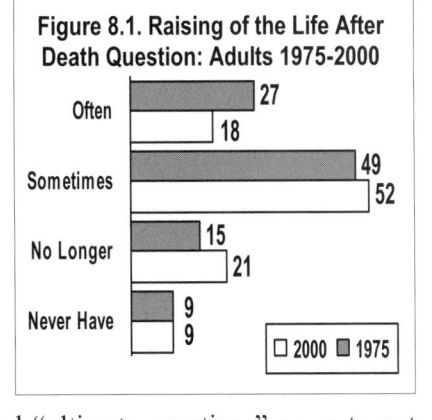

Figure 8.1. Raising of the Life After Death Question: Adults 1975-2000

Still, these so-called "ultimate questions" seem to get squeezed in – maybe because they sometimes simply force themselves in. Dating back to our first surveys in the 1970s and 80s, we have found that a consistent 9 in 10 Canadians of all ages say that they raise questions about meaning and purpose, suffering and death.

Table 8.1. Raising of Ultimate Questions: Teens, 1984 & 2008 (%)							
	Often/Sometimes		No Longer		Never Have		TOT
	1984	2008	1984	2008	1984	2008	
What happens after death?	84	78	11	15	5	7	100
Why suffering in the world?	82	75	12	16	6	9	100
What is the purpose of life?	79	75	13	15	8	10	100

Source: Bibby, *The Emerging Millennials*, 2009:173.

Undoubtedly, the reflections are typically periodic – often the result of teens and the rest of us having to come to grips with illness and death, other times the result of events that receive extensive media attention. But, either way, the questions are raised, regardless of how full lives might be.

What *has* changed slightly over the past few decades is the inclination for adults, in particular, to put these so-called "ultimate questions" aside a bit faster. It appears to be necessary not because they think they have found answers, because most indicate they have not. Rather, they either have not been able to find satisfactory answers, or don't believe it is possible to find them. As a result, they simply have moved on to more tangible and doable things – led by those pragmatically minded Boomers.[8]

In the case of life after death specifically, more than 9 in 10 adults and teens say they have raised the question. Needless to say, good answers have been hard to come by.

Close to 5 in 10 adults admit that "dying" concerns them "somewhat" or more. Such concern levels have remained the same in recent years. Perhaps surprisingly, concern about dying also differs very little by age group.

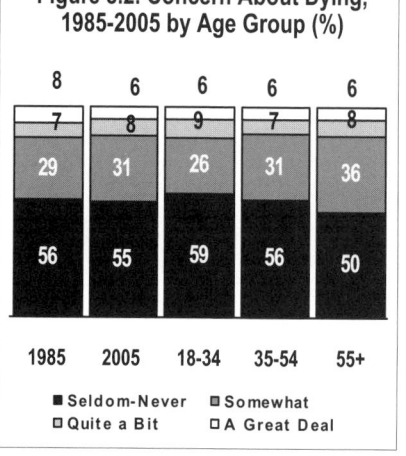

Figure 8.2. Concern About Dying, 1985-2005 by Age Group (%)

	1985	2005	18-34	35-54	55+
A Great Deal	8	6	6	6	6
Quite a Bit	7	8	9	7	8
Somewhat	29	31	26	31	36
Seldom-Never	56	55	59	56	50

■ Seldom-Never   ▨ Somewhat
▫ Quite a Bit   ▫ A Great Deal

Belief in Life After Death. Currently, some 67% of Canadian adults indicate that they believe in life after death, 12% that they definitely do not. The comparable figures for teenagers are 78% and 8% respectively. The adult numbers are virtually unchanged from the mid-1980s. In fact, the 12% figure for disbelief is identical to what Gallup found when it first put the question to Canadians way back in 1945.

What our polls since the mid-70s have documented is the ongoing reluctance of people to rule out the possibility of life after death, but their ongoing ambivalence as to whether it actually exists.

Such lack of clarity should hardly come as a surprise. After all, we don't know anything more for sure about the chances of a hereafter today than we did in the past.

Table 8.2. Belief in Life After Death: Adults, 1985-2005		
"Do you believe in life after death?		
	1985	2005
Yes, I definitely do	36%	36
Yes, I think so	29	31
No, I don't think so	20	21
No, I definitely do not	15	12
Source: Bibby. Project Canada Survey Series.		

Those things said, if religion offers some "market entries" on the topic, we would expect that differences in belief would certainly vary by religiosity.

And they do. Canadian adults and teens who are theists are considerably more likely than atheists to believe in life after death. Relationships between belief in the hereafter and both attendance and identification are also sizable.[9]

One might assume that the link between atheism and belief in life after death is obvious: one has to believe in the gods in order to believe we will live after we die. Actually, as we will see shortly, it's not quite that straightforward.[10] Many atheists, for example, are among those who believe contact with the spirit world is possible.

Table 8.3. Belief in Life After Death: Adults & Teenagers							
[🇨🇦]		ATTENDANCE		IDENTIFN		BELIEF	
		Weekly	Never	Yes	No	Theist	Atheist
ADULTS							
Yes, I definitely do	36%	72	17	41	9	67	3
Yes, I think so	29	17	29	32	26	20	10
No, I don't think so	20	7	29	19	33	9	10
No, I definitely do not	15	4	25	8	32	4	77
Teenagers							
Yes, I definitely do	34	64	21	43	16	69	11
Yes, I think so	41	24	44	41	41	22	25
No, I don't think so	17	8	23	12	27	5	29
No, I definitely do not	8	4	12	4	16	4	35

- **Shading:** differences are *not* at least 10 percentage points.

Source: Project Teen Canada 2008 national survey.

Views of What Happens After Death. About 6 in 10 Canadian adults believe in *heaven* and 5 in 10 believe in *hell*. Believing in one usually means one believes in the other. But not always.

- No less than 99% who "definitely" believe in hell also "definitely" believe in heaven.
- That said, among those who are certain there is a heaven, a lower figure of 76% are also certain there is a hell. Who said we have to take the bad with the good?

Illustrative of the belief complexities of Canadians, if a person believes in heaven or hell, that must mean they believe in life after death. Right? Well, usually, but....

- About 8% who are certain that there is a hell don't think there is life after death. If hell is associated with some kind of non-existence, I guess that makes sense.
- But some 8% who believe in heaven also don't believe in life after death. Presumably heaven is something else.[11]
- Among teenagers, belief in heaven (75%) is even more prevalent than among adults. So is belief in hell (60%) – although it is slightly less "popular."
- As would be expected, adults and young people who are religious according to our three measures are generally considerably more likely than others to embrace beliefs about heaven and hell, angels and spirit world contact.

Table 8.4. Belief in Elements of Life After Death: Adults & Teens

	▌✦▌	ATTENDANCE Weekly	ATTENDANCE Never	IDENTIFN Yes	IDENTIFN No	BELIEF Theist	BELIEF Atheist
ADULTS							
Heaven	62%	94	32	72	12	89	4
Angels	62	94	34	71	18	88	3
Hell	48	82	24	55	8	72	4
Spirit world contact	46	53	37	48	33	57	9
Teenagers							
Heaven*	75	93	57	84	47	96	18
Good people rewarded	61	76	47	72	37	84	19
Hell*	60	82	44	67	37	80	15
Spirit world contact	46	45	45	48	43	53	31

- **Shading:** differences are *not* at least 10 percentage points.

Sources: Project Canada 2005 and Project Teen Canada 2000* and 2008 surveys.

One interesting pattern that is even more pronounced among teens than adults is the inclination to believe in life after death, without necessarily believing in God.

- Among adults, 91% who say they "definitely" believe in life after death express the same certainty about the exist-ence of God.
- In the case of teenagers, just 75% who are certain there is an afterlife express the same certainty about God.

Such findings point to the fact that our culture – notably the music and video game industries – gives

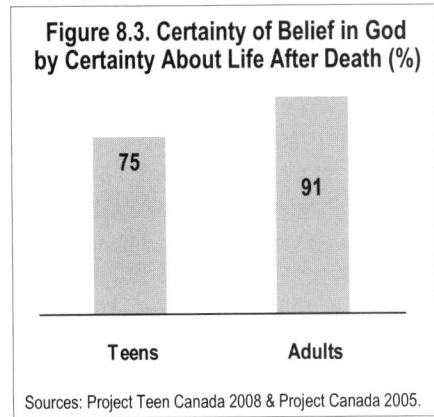

Figure 8.3. Certainty of Belief in God by Certainty About Life After Death (%)

75 — Teens

91 — Adults

Sources: Project Teen Canada 2008 & Project Canada 2005.

credence to super-natural phenomena generally, including spirits, angels, demons, and the like. God? Not so much.

Sara Yoheved Rigler sums up the situation this way: "The popularity of angels, psychic phenomena, faith healing, meditation, and near-death experiences testifies to a paradigm shift in our concept of reality," she writes. "But somehow God has gotten lost in the shuffle."[12]

Some 6 in 10 teens agree that *"good people will be rewarded after they die."* What's interesting to note here is that this idea is endorsed not only by young people who are religious but also by large numbers who are not.

- The latter include close to 50% who never attend services, 40% who say they have no religion, and 20% who are atheists.
- Those levels are fairly consistent with the proportion of non-religious teens who believe in heaven and hell.

The "afterlife" clearly is something that intrigues significant numbers of Canadians. For many, it seems to be almost "a justice issue necessity." If the universe is rational and fair – two pretty big assumptions – then the afterlife is necessary in order that "good people can be rewarded" and "wrongs can be made right."

However, for most atheists, it seems that the balancing out of things will have to take place this side of death. Atheists are particularly disinclined to think that how we live out life now will influence what we will experience after we die.

		ATTEND		ID		BELIEF	
		Weekly	Never	Yes	No	Theist	Atheist
Somehow, some day injustices will be made right	70%	86	53	73	51	86	30
How we live will influence what happens to us after we die	62	84	42	67	34	85	3

Table 8.5. Adult Views of What Happens When We Die
"Which of the following comes closest to your view of life after death?"

Source: Project Canada 2000.

Our findings on what people think will actually happen when we die leave one with the sense that religious groups either *don't have much to say* about life after death, or just *aren't saying much.*

Pushed on the specifics of their views:

- about 4 in 10 Canadians say that they "believe there must be something beyond death," but admit that they "have no idea what it may be like";
- another 3 in 10 think there probably is no such thing;
- 1 in 10 maintain we will experience reincarnation;
- the remaining 2 in 10 believe we will be looking at some combination of rewards and punishments.

The idea of rewards/punishments is most commonly held among weekly service attenders. That said, the "no idea" acknowledgment is the most common among everyone else who believes in life after death, including the 30% of weekly attenders – the same level as found among those who never attend services.

These findings document the fact that large numbers of people view life after death as a time when things will be made right – when good people, in particular, will be rewarded.

Beyond generalities, however, things are very vague.

Table 8.6. Adult Views of What Happens When We Die

"Which of the following comes closest to your view of life after death?"

	🍁	ATTEND Weekly	ATTEND Never	ID Yes	ID No	BELIEF Theist	BELIEF Atheist
Something, no idea what	36%	30	30	38	28	41	21
Rewards & punishment	18	45	4	21	5	22	1
Reincarnation	8	3	9	8	9	9	5
Rewards no punishment	4	8	1	4	<1	4	<1
No life after death	18	5	37	14	41	9	57
Unsure if life after death	16	9	19	15	17	15	16
Totals	100	100	100	100	100	100	100

- **Shading:** differences are *not* at least 10 percentage points.

Source: Project Canada 2000.

Responses to Death. We all are well aware that death brings with it an array of emotional responses. Foremost, initially at least, is sorrow. A life has been lost. A family member, a friend, an acquaintance, perhaps a stranger with whom we empathize, is gone. If a partner or a child is involved, maybe it's the thought of the pain that will be experienced by the ones we leave behind that pains us most. In his book, *The Last Lecture*, Randy Pausch wrote that as much as he was troubled about the fact he would not be able to see his three young children grow up, what was more disturbing to him was the fact they would grow up not having a father.[13] A survey respondent summed up another dimension of parental pain when he said he'd be troubled most by having any of his children die before him.

The prospect of our own death brings forth so many additional emotions…simply not being able to live, laugh, love…all the things we want to be able to do. Even someone so confident and enthusiastic about life after death as the Apostle Paul wrote that he nonetheless struggled with the fact that he needed to live life, and therefore on balance preferred to be able to live a little longer.[14]

In our Project Canada surveys, we have put the tough question to Canadians. In 1980 and again in 2000 we asked, *"What would you say your primary response is to the reality of death?"* We have offered five responses – fear, sorrow, mystery, hope, and no particular feeling; in the 2000 survey people were given the opportunity to cite any other primary responses.

- The surveys have found that *sorrow* (26%) and *mystery* (23%) are mentioned most often, followed by *hope* (19%) and *fear* (15%). About 1 in 5 have said they don't have any particular feeling, seemingly having many emotions.

Table 8.7. Primary Emotional Responses to Death

"What would you say your primary response is to the reality of death?"

| | 🍁 | | ATTEND | | ID | | BELIEF | |
	1980	2000	Weekly	Never	Yes	No	Theist	Atheist
Sorrow	20%	26	19	33	25	34	22	25
Mystery	24	23	17	21	22	30	22	29
Hope	**18**	**19**	**45**	**9**	**22**	**6**	**33**	**5**
Fear	18	15	10	13	14	11	13	14
No partic feeling	20	17	9	24	17	19	10	27
Totals	100	100	100	100	100	100	100	100

- **Shading:** differences are *not* at least 10 % points. The r's for hope & attendance 338, ID .141, belief .312.
Sources: Project Canada 1980 and 2000.

- What stands out when we look at the survey results by religiosity is the inclination of *weekly attenders* to cite *hope* (45%) more frequently than anything else.
- *Hope* also stands out as the dominant *theist* response, and the least common response for *atheists* and those with *no religion*.

An examination of the belief in life after death and the response of hope by religious groups and attendance reveals some important Canadian variations.

Generally speaking, attendance – which makes so much difference nationally – continues to have that same relationship across groups. The single exception is with belief in life after death among *Quebec Roman Catholics*. The percentage of Catholics who say they believe in an afterlife is the same (76%), regardless of how often they attend services. The belief obviously has been well-instilled.

In the case of *Protestants*, belief and hope levels are higher for Conservatives than Mainliners. Nonetheless, in both group cases, the levels go up with attendance.

Overall, Protestant hope levels are higher than that of Roman Catholics – especially in comparison to Quebec.

Table 8.8. Life After Death: Beliefs and Responses by Religious Families & Attendance

	Believe in Life After Death		Hope is Primary Response	
	Weekly	<Weekly	Weekly	<Weekly
🍁	88%	60	45	12
Roman Catholics	89	73	36	14
Outside Quebec	93	69	44	18
Quebec	76	76	24	10
Protestants	85	60	56	14
Conservative	88	76	65	30
Mainline	81	59	52	11
Other World Faiths	---	65	---	17
No Religion	---	35	---	5

Sources: Project Canada 2005 (life after death)
& Project Canada 2000 (hope).

A more detailed look at Catholic and Protestant responses to death reveals some important variations.

- The two most common responses of *Catholics outside Quebec* are hope and sorrow – *in Quebec*, mystery, sorrow, and fear, with hope relatively low.
- *Conservative Protestants* stand out in maintaining that their predominant response is hope, followed by mystery. Sorrow is fairly low.
- In the case of *Mainline Protestants*, the most common responses are sorrow, mystery, and no particular feeling. Hope is quite low.

These findings suggest that the country's historically dominant Catholic and Protestant groups vary considerably in providing their affiliates with a sense of life after death that creates feelings of hope and mystery, versus sorrow, fear – or no particular feeling at all.

Clearly funerals and funeral homes are reflecting the varied ways in which Canadians are understanding and responding to death. A perusal of death announcements provides a reminder of the range of choices involved – from people requesting nothing be done, through a gathering of celebration, to a traditional funeral. One local Alberta funeral home has run an ad recently showing an endearing father-son picture with the caption, "Dad wasn't really a churchgoer," and goes on to emphasize, "There are many options available...for whatever you think is best." [15]

Table 8.9. Life After Death: Catholics & Protestant Responses

	Sorrow	Mystery	Hope	Fear	No Partic Feelings	Totals
🇨🇦	26%	23	19	15	17	100
Roman Catholics	24	23	20	20	13	100
Outside Quebec	24	18	27	17	14	100
Quebec	25	28	13	23	11	100
Protestants	25	20	24	10	21	100
Conservative	12	23	50	9	6	100
Mainline	28	21	18	10	23	100

Source: Project Canada 2000..

Beliefs About Life after Death Among Canadian Youth

- Strong majorities of teens who identify with religious groups believe in life after death, as do 57% who have no religion.
- The idea that good people will be rewarded when they die is held by majorities in all religious categories, led by Muslims, Sikhs, Hindus, Buddhists, Orthodox, Catholics outside Quebec, and "Christians."
- Belief we can have contact with the spirit world is common among those who value Aboriginal Spirituality. It also is held by about 1 in 2 Catholic, Conservative, "Christian," Buddhist, Hindu, Sikh, and Muslim youth. Some 43% of those with no religion also endorse such an idea.

Teenage Polarization in the Mosaic
Life after Death

	Believe in Life After Death	Good People Are Rewarded After They Die	We Can Have Contact With the Spirit World
NATIONALLY	75%	61	46
Roman Catholicism	85	74	49
Outside Quebec	84	79	46
Quebec	85	62	55
Protestantism	88	65	39
Conservative	92	60	46
Mainline	85	69	39
Orthodox	85	81	38
Christian *unspecified*	89	76	52
Other World Faiths	80	78	48
Islam	85	94	44
Aboriginal Spirituality	85	51	72
Hinduism	81	78	54
Judaism	72	55	21
Sikhism	78	83	45
Buddhism	75	75	59
No Religion	57	37	43

The Global Situation

The reality of death and its social and emotional impact obviously is felt worldwide. Every culture since the beginning of time has had to find ways of responding to death. Every individual who has ever lived has had to find ways of coping with the loss of others, as well as the fact that one's own life eventually will end.

It therefore should surprise no one that reflecting on death is a universal phenomenon.

Just before the end of the 20th century, people in almost 50 countries were asked in the World Values Survey, *"Do you ever think about death?"* Some 80% indicated that they do – about 20% saying "often," 40% "sometimes," and the rest "rarely" or "never."

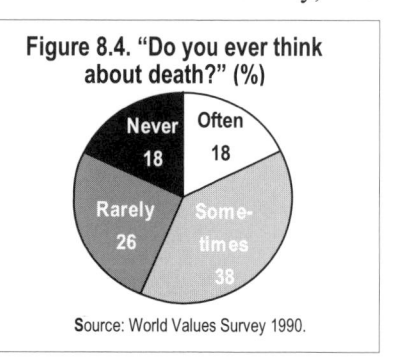

Figure 8.4. "Do you ever think about death?" (%)

Source: World Values Survey 1990.

The countries in the survey with the highest number of people indicating they "never" think about death? China (46%), Slovenia (36%), and Brazil (35%). Many countries with low attendance levels still had relatively few people who said they never raised the death question, including Sweden (11%), Great Britain (14%), and Norway (7%). The level in Canada was only 9%, in the U.S. 8%.

The same survey found that a solid majority of people (77%) took the position that because "death is inevitable, it is pointless to *worry* about it."

Reflection and anxiety levels aside, a majority of people around the world are inclined to give credibility to the idea of life after death. Another World Values Survey in 2000, involving people in some 75 countries, found that 61% said they believe in life after death while 28% indicated they did not; the remaining 11% were unsure.[16]

Here again, what's interesting to note is the tendency for people in countries where conventional religiosity levels are fairly low not to rule out the life after death possibility. Significant numbers either expressed believe in life after death or said they didn't know – Sweden, for example, at 39% and 15% respectively, Japan 32% and 38%, Russia 26% and 28%.

Some 58% said that they believe in heaven – just above the 50% who believe in hell.

- As with Canada, we would expect fairly high correlations to exist between service attendance and belief in God, life after death, and heaven.

- A statistical look at the relationships bears out those expectations (see details in notes).[17]

- But the fact the correlations are far from perfect points to these beliefs being fairly common among people not involved in religious groups.

- Further, the three beliefs are not necessarily closely tied to each other.

Table 8.10. Attendance, Belief in God, Life After Death and Heaven: Select Countries			
	Attend	God	LAD	Heaven
Nigeria	89%	99	86	99
India	73	99	59	66
Saudi Arabia	68	99	97	98
Philippines	64	99	81	95
Poland	62	96	70	70
Mexico	60	97	67	85
South Africa	57	99	66	87
Ireland	56	96	69	77
Pakistan	56	99	100	100
Iraq	53	99	95	98
Italy	49	83	61	50
Iran	45	99	95	94
United States	43	88	75	84
Turkey	42	98	89	93
Singapore	40	95	68	75
Spain	39	92	43	42
Japan	38	87	32	22
Chile	33	90	76	75
Germany	30	77	27	23
Greece	29	97	47	38
CANADA	**26**	**85**	**65**	**70**
Netherlands	26	74	47	36
Ukraine	23	85	29	29
Australia	23	83	53	56
France	20	80	38	28
United Kingdom	20	86	43	45
Sweden	17	70	39	28
Finland	12	91	45	50
Czech Republic	15	57	29	17
Russia	15	91	26	25

Sources: Attendance Gallup WorldView 2010;. God computed from World Religion Database in Smith 2009:284-287; LAD and heaven World Values Survey 2000. Australia LAD and heaven Nielsen 2009.

Reincarnation – the idea that our spirit or soul will return in another life form after we die - is, of course, particularly associated with Hinduism. Accordingly it has been widely held in countries like India.

The most recent information we have suggests that, to varying degrees, belief in reincarnation extends to countries throughout the world. For example:

- One in 2 Brazilians believe in the idea, as do about 1 in 3 people in countries such as Mexico, Argentina, and South Africa.

- About 1 in 4 Canadians say they believe in reincarnation, as do similar proportions of people in settings including Russia, France, and the United States.

- Just under 1 in 5 Scandinavians also indicate that they hold the belief, and are joined by similar percentages of many other European groups, including Brits, Belgians, Greeks, and Poles.

These findings on heaven, hell, and reincarnation illustrate the fact that people have highly divergent ideas concerning the nature of life after death. But what the majority of people on the planet have in common is a sense that we will continue to exist somewhere, in some form, after we die.

Table 8.11. Belief in Reincarnation by Select Countries

India	88%
Brazil	54
Mexico	37
Nigeria	36
Argentina	33
South Africa	30
Japan	29
Ukraine[1]	28
CANADA	**27**
Portugal[1]	27
Russia[1]	26
Ireland[1]	25
France[1]	22
Hungary[1]	22
United States[2]	21
Spain[1]	20
United Kingdom[3]	19
Finland[1]	18
Netherlands[1]	18
Belgium[1]	17
Denmark[1]	17
Sweden[4]	17
Germany[1]	16
Czech Republic[1]	15
Greece[1]	15
Italy[4]	17
Poland[1]	15

Sources: World Values Survey 1990; [1]European Value Surveys 2008; [2]Harris 2007; [3]Associated Press 2005. [4]World Values Survey 2000.

Some additional global findings further illustrate how extensive the belief in life after death actually is.

The responses to an item administered in the World Value Survey three decades ago are not necessarily indicative of what the levels might be today; until the item is repeated we won't know for sure. But it demonstrates something of the extent to which large numbers of people believe that relatives, friends, and others have not ceased to exist after they die.

The survey asked people a question about what many would think is a fairly unusual phenomenon: *"Have you ever felt as though you were really in touch with someone who had died?"*

- About 1 in 5 people (22%) said that they had – not exactly a small number of people.
- The levels ranged from around 4 in 10 in Iceland through 3 in 10 in the United States and what then was West Germany, to 2 in 10 in Britain and some 1 in ten people in the Netherlands, and the three Scandi-navian countries.
- The level in Canada: 25% – 1 in 4 people. Translate that into 1 in 4 people in a given

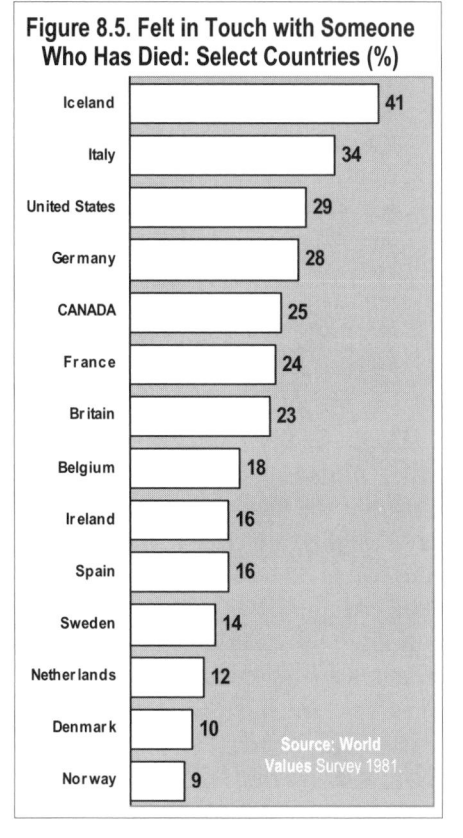

Figure 8.5. Felt in Touch with Someone Who Has Died: Select Countries (%)

Country	%
Iceland	41
Italy	34
United States	29
Germany	28
CANADA	25
France	24
Britain	23
Belgium	18
Ireland	16
Spain	16
Sweden	14
Netherlands	12
Denmark	10
Norway	9

Source: World Values Survey 1981.

mall or on a given highway or just about any-where and you get a sense of the magnitude of the claim.

If these reports have seemed like fodder for supermarket tabloids because they sound bizarre and extremely rare, we need to think again. The fact of the matter is that a lot of Canadians back in the early 80s were keeping such experiences to themselves. I suspect that sizable numbers of people these days are doing the same thing.

One of the reasons that belief in life after death appears to readily outdistance and outlive involvement in organized religion is because the belief that we have souls is so pervasive. I'm not exaggerating.

A World Values Survey item, administered in 33 countries as the new century began, asked the question, *"Do you believe that people have a soul?"*

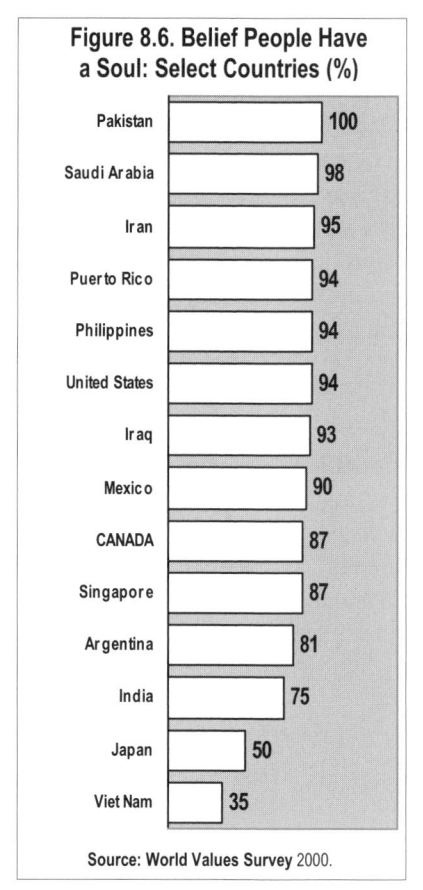

Figure 8.6. Belief People Have a Soul: Select Countries (%)

Country	%
Pakistan	100
Saudi Arabia	98
Iran	95
Puerto Rico	94
Philippines	94
United States	94
Iraq	93
Mexico	90
CANADA	87
Singapore	87
Argentina	81
India	75
Japan	50
Viet Nam	35

Source: World Values Survey 2000.

- Eighty-five percent said "Yes," 10% "No," and 5% indicated they didn't know.
- The levels range from highs of 100% or so in countries like Pakistan and Saudi Arabia, through 90-95% in places such as Iran, the United States, Iraq, and Mexico, to 75% in India, 50% in Japan and 35% in Viet Nam.
- Canada came in at 87%.

These diverse probes into the hereafter point to a very clear overall conclusion: the market for answers to the ongoing, universal question of what happens after we die remains extremely vast.

In his classic work, *The Future of an Illusion*, Freud acknowledged that everyone would like to be able to believe that there is life after death. Using the language of his day, Freud pointed out that the desire to live after death is a universal wish of all mankind.

The problem, he said, is that just because it is hoped for doesn't make it any more real. His expectation was that, in time, we would "learn to endure with resignation" such "great necessities of fate, against which there is no remedy."[18]

Through the present time, people worldwide have continued to defy Freud's prediction. To put things bluntly, his assumption that one day we would put such hopes behind us was wrong.

Survey after survey has demonstrated that the belief there is something "out there" after we die – as nebulous as views of what that "something" might be – simply persist.

It's axiomatic: as long as people die, most of us will contemplate what, if anything, happens next.

Actually, that's an understatement. The majority of people around the planet do more than simply contemplate.

Table 8.12. Belief Death is Not the End by Belief in God: 10 Select Countries		
"I don't believe death is the end"		
	Death Not the End	Believe in God
Nigeria	79%	99
Lebanon	75	92
United States	74	88
Indonesia	64	99
South Korea	57	98
Mexico	55	97
Russia	54	91
United Kingdom	54	86
India	51	99
Israel	50	95

Sources: Death is not the end - ICM poll conducted for the BBC Two program, "What the World Thinks of God." 2004; belief in God: God computed from Smith 2009:284-287.

They do not believe that death is the end.

Assessment

The age-old questions about meaning and purpose, suffering and purpose continue to be raised in our time.

Just this past week I received word that my best friend during the late 70s and early 80s, Mark Gibson, died. They said it was surprising. A student had to withdraw from my class. His beloved one-year-old son is undergoing life-threatening brain surgery. That was more than surprising.

Journalist Wente writes, "I envy people of faith. By all accounts, they are happier, healthier and more emotionally secure than the rest of us. They give away more money and do more good works. They are kinder, more generous and more community-minded." She wryly adds, "We secular humanists, by contrast, tend to be stingy, lonely folks" who are still in search of some larger purpose. "I wouldn't choose to be a nonbeliever if I could help it, but I can't."[19]

The purpose question can be set aside; the death question cannot. The emotions that are felt when loved ones die, as well as the awareness that we too will only live so long, awakens it over and over again in our lifetimes: "What happens when we die?"

With increasing religious polarization in Canada and around the world, we will not see a decrease in the inclination of people to ask the life-after-death question. Reflective people *have to* raise it – and not answer it prematurely. There is too much at stake.

However, our findings also make another conclusion clear: without religion, hope will be hard to find.

We are wary of people who seem to know too much – of titles such as, *What Happens When I Die?* [20] or *Everything You Ever Wanted to Know About Heaven.*[21] Yet we do want some solid, authoritative assurances.

At the end of his book, *Life After Death*, published in 1991, Tom Harpur hinted that he personally believed in life after death. Two decades later in 2011, his update appeared – with the title, *There Is Life After Death*.

The desire for increasing clarity on this critical issue is something most of us want. That widespread desire guarantees a permanent place for religion.

9 The Comeback

"Our souls are restless until they find their rest in Thee, O God"
-St. Augustine

PROPHECY is not exactly a social science virtue. We can do a reasonably good job of explaining what happened after the fact. But we haven't been known for our ability to accurately foresee economic slowdowns, the rearranging of nation-states, or the arrival of the Web with its transforming powers. For years I have taught students in Research Methods classes that the three great goals of social science are description, explanation, and prediction. To date we don't have much to show in the way of success in long-range social forecasting.

It's not that we never try. When it comes to religion, we have had a good share of would-be social prophets. People like Auguste Comte (1798-1857), Karl Marx (1818-1883), and Sigmund Freud (1856-1939) saw religion's disappearance as inevitable. Comte said scientific thought would replace religious thinking, Marx felt the resolving of social and economic inequities would eliminate the need for religion as a pain-killing drug, and Freud maintained that science and personal resolve would combine to allow us to abandon our child-like fantasies about a father-like God and a future existence in heaven.

There obviously is much data that point to the fact that such thinkers were too quick to write off religion. In settings where religion is currently flourishing, a measure of secularization undoubtedly will take place. The historical precedents of Europe and North America suggest such a trend will be closely associated with heightened levels of development.

But in other places where polarization is prominent, or where secularity is pronounced, comebacks are in the works.

Why It Can Be Expected

Not every social science prophet has declared that religion is doomed.

In 1912, French sociologist Emile Durkheim (1858-1917) offered many stimulating thoughts about the nature, functions, and future of religion in his classic work, *The Elementary Forms of the Religious Life*. Durkheim believed that, theoretically-speaking, science would one day answer all of our questions. However, he maintained that religion would continue to have an important speculative function because science "is fragmentary and incomplete; it advances but slowly and is never finished; but life cannot wait."[1] In the foreseeable future, religion would continue to exist.

Durkheim's point about religion's gap-filling role is important. However, the problem does not only lie with the speed with which science progresses. The problem also lies with the nature of science itself. Put bluntly, science is not equipped to say very much about many of religion's claims.

The reason is that scientific knowledge is based on verifiable observations. The problem with such an empirical method is that important questions about the existence of God and life after death cannot be addressed through observation. They consequently stand outside the grasp of science. This second limitation is not one of speed, but capability. Science simply cannot address everything.

Precisely because of such limitations, other meaning-makers have stepped forward to fill the market void. That's why religion and other such initiatives have been able to have a significant presence throughout the world in the past and present. That's also why they – and their market successors – will have a place in the future.

So it is that social scientists beyond the classic high-profile positivists have taken quite a different position on religion's future.[2]

For example, three prominent twentieth century Harvard sociologists offered some stimulating ideas about what happens to religion over time.

Sorokin, Davis, and Bell. One was Russian-born Pitirim Sorokin (1889-1968), who founded the Department of Sociology at Harvard. The second was Kingsley Davis (1908-1997), a student of Sorokin's, who spent most of his career at the University of California Berkeley. The third was Daniel Bell, (b. 1919) a renowned social forecaster at Harvard who wrote extensively on the emerging post-industrial world.[3]

Sorokin maintained that societies oscillate or swing between an emphasis on "rationality" and "irrationality," between a moving away from religion and a moving toward it. History more generally, he said, has consisted of pendulum-like fluctuations between "ideational" and "sensate" cultures. The ideational period is characterized by ideals and spiritual concerns, while the sensate period is a time when a society emphasizes material values.

Davis picked up on Sorokin's thinking in arguing that there is "a limit to the extent to which a society can be guided by illusion." But "there is also a limit to which a society can be guided by sheer rationality." Secularization, he wrote, will therefore "likely be terminated by religious revivals of one sort or another," complete with new sects. But religion is unlikely to be replaced by secular substitutes.[4]

In like manner, Bell saw people in post-industrial societies as experiencing the limits of modernism and alternatives to religion. He wrote that "a long era is coming to a close. The theme of Modernism was the world beyond.... We are now groping for a new vocabulary whose keyword seems to be limits."[5] Bell predicted that new religions will arise in response to the core questions of existence – death, tragedy, obligation, and love.

This "oscillation" argument became increasingly popular in the last two decades of the twentieth century. Social analyst Jeremy Rifkin, for example, claimed that it accounted for the emergence of the charismatic movement and the accelerated success of evangelical Christianity.[6]

Intentionally or not, American research in the late 1980s and early 90s suggesting that "Baby Boomers" were heading back to the churches fed the idea that the religious pendulum was swinging once again.[7] Even prominent futurist John Naisbitt proclaimed in 1990 that the world was on the verge of a massive return to spirituality.[8]

Parsons and Greeley. It needs to be pointed out that there were some observers – standing alone for the most part – who had been protesting that the notion that a major religious shift had taken place was a gross exaggeration.

Perhaps inadvertently taking their cues from the writer of Ecclesiastes who I have often cited over the years – that "there is nothing new under the sun" – they disputed the claim that religion's influence had been diminishing. Among the most prominent were still another Harvard sociologist, Talcott Parsons, along with American sociologist, priest and, more recently, best-selling novelist, Andrew Greeley.

In a very influential essay, Parsons (1963) maintained that it has been a mistake to equate either the decline of the church's authority over life, or the individualistic approach to religion, with a loss of religious influence. Christianity, said Parsons, has continued to have an important place in the western world, particularly in the United States. While there has been a decrease in religion's direct control in a number of societal spheres, its legacy nonetheless was being felt. Values emphasized by Christianity, such as tolerance and decency, Parsons claimed, have been institutionalized. He wrote, "I suggest that in a whole variety of respects, modern society is more in accord with Christian values than its forebears have been."

Parsons argued that the increasingly prevalent personal expressions of religion were consistent with both "the individualistic principle inherent in Christianity" and the emphasis on differentiation in modern societies. The result? Religion has become a highly "privatized," personal matter, differing from earlier expressions in being less overt and less tied to formal group involvement.

For Parsons, Christianity was not in a state of decline. Rather, it has been both institutionalized and privatized. Similar to the traditional family, Parsons wrote, religion "has lost many previous functions and has become increasingly a sphere of private sentiments." But, he insisted, "It is as important as ever to the maintenance of the main patterns of the society."

One might conclude from reading Parsons that all was well on the religious front. Individuals were still taking religion seriously, but were keeping their commitment to themselves. Religious groups had not lost influence. They were helping to shape cultural values and, if anything, were in a better position than ever before to concentrate on religion.

Andrew Greeley went even further than Parsons. He argued that secularization is a myth. Greeley acknowledged that religion was facing significant secular pressures and was not important to everyone. However, he insisted that such realities were not unique to our time.

Greeley explicitly addressed a number of common claims about the decline of religion. He maintained that:

1. faith was not being seriously eroded by science and education, religion was no less significant in daily life than in the alleged great ages of faith;
2. participation levels were not down relative to periods of time beyond the immediate past;
3. the impact of religion was continuing but in less obvious ways;
4. private commitment was having an impact on the public sphere; and
5. the sacred remained highly visible in everyday life.

According to Greeley, religion was continuing to flourish. Rumours of its decline and death simply were not warranted.

For quite some time, Greeley – always the unflappable individualist – stubbornly stood his ground. These days he does not lack for company.

Stark and Market Demand. As we saw earlier, since the late 1970s Rodney Stark has played a major role in championing the idea that secularization actually stimulates innovation. Ironically, the decline of existing religious forms actually triggers the appearance of new ones.

The process is not just something that will take place in the future. On the contrary, it always has been in place. The reason is that the demand for religion has been and continues to be constant. What has changed is not the demand for religion, but its "suppliers."

Such an argument clearly goes back at least as far as Durkheim. While he observed that Christianity in late nineteenth century Europe was in decline, he believed that religion more generally would persist because of its "gap-filling" role. Science and religion had co-existed since the birth of science, and would continue to do so. Religious explanations might be forced to retreat and reformulate, and give ground in the face of the steady advance of science.[9]

Table 9.1. Reflections on Meaning & Purpose and Prayer-Meditation: Select Countries

	Meaning & Purpose	Prayer/ Meditation
Ethiopia	93%	95
Jordan	89	99
Iran	88	95
Morocco	87	88
Zambia	84	86
Italy	88	78
South Africa	88	85
Korea, Republic of	88	47
Brazil	87	89
CANADA	**83**	**77**
Mexico	81	84
United States	80	84
Ukraine	75	62
Argentina	73	76
Poland	72	87
Malaysia	71	85
Chile	71	78
Germany	70	47
Finland	79	70
United Kingdom	75	50*
Norway	73	33
Sweden	70	47
India	67	80
Hong Kong	63	---
China	61	---

Items: "Do you think about *meaning & the purpose of life?*" Here: "often" or "sometimes"; "Do you take some moments for prayer, meditation, or contemplation, or something like that?" – "Yes"

Source: World Values Survey, 2005. Surveys span 2005-2007. *World Values Survey, 2000.

But, as Kingsley Davis noted in summing up Durkheim's point, "Religion retreats. But it never surrenders."[10]

Stark and his colleagues have maintained that religion is guaranteed an indispensable role when it comes to meaning. Only ideas that are grounded in the supernatural, they say, can provide plausible answers to the big, "ultimate questions" pertaining to the meaning of life and death.

As carriers of explanations based on such supernatural assumptions, religion plays a unique and irreplaceable role in human affairs.

Religious activity, they argue, is dynamic and ever-changing. Some religions and some groups are always losing ground. But because the market for religion persists, the activity only increases and the competition intensifies, as old groups and new groups struggle to gain, retain, and increase market shares.

The never-ending human quest for meaning ensures religion's viability.

Table 9.2. Importance of Religious Rites of Passage: Select European Countries

"Do you personally think it is important to hold a religious service for..."

	Birth	Marriage	Death
ALL	73%	73	82
Poland	96	95	96
Ireland	91	93	96
Portugal	90	89	92
Italy	89	85	89
Ukraine	86	69	85
Finland	84	83	90
Slovakia	83	80	85
Austria	81	76	85
Spain	78	75	80
Russia	75	54	79
Iceland	74	67	91
Belgium	70	70	74
Greece	67	83	87
Denmark	65	63	80
France	61	66	73
Sweden	60	62	78
United Kingdom	59	69	79
Germany	50	56	60
Czech Republic	42	40	50
Turkey	42	82	95
Netherlands	40	45	56

Source: World Values Survey 2000..

The Old or Something Else?

The good news that such thinking brings to religious groups is that religion's future is not in question. Ongoing needs guarantee that it will always have a place in the lives of large numbers of people in Canada and around the world. Note – not everyone, but very large numbers.

That said, the sobering news for groups everywhere is that their own specific futures are anything but guaranteed. Quite the opposite. To the extent that they can effectively address the needs of people relating to ultimacy – led by the question of life after death – they have a future. But the success of any given group – measured by size and sheer ongoing vitality – will depend on how well it performs.

As Stark and his associates have pointed out, the viability of religious groups over time in the United States, for example, has been determined by how well they have addressed the needs of Americans. They argue that the same pattern holds for the entire planet. The demand is universal; the question is which suppliers will emerge.

Stark and his associates maintain that sects and revival, cults and innovation, potentially contribute to lively religious marketplaces. But they typically face stiff competition from the existing, well-established groups that, to varying degrees, reinvent themselves in the light of social change and changing demographics. The Church of England did not disappear just because upstart groups such as Methodists and the Salvation Army came into being. Southern Baptists did not shrivel up just because Nazarenes and Pentecostal groups arrived on the American scene. Canadian Catholics are not going to limp to the sidelines just because Muslim franchises are springing up across the country. We would expect no less of Mainline Protestants.

Apart from performance, however, there are no guarantees as to which "religious companies" will thrive and which will, in effect, be headed toward insolvency. All we know for sure is that universal and national market demand means there will be both winners and losers.

The Canadian Situation

As we look at Canada, some general observations about the immediate future of some of the groups can be made with a high level of confidence.

Roman Catholics. Make no mistake about it – this is the big player in Canada. The 2001 census revealed that close to 13 million Canadians (43%) viewed themselves as Catholic – about 7 million outside Quebec (23%), 6 million in Quebec (20%). The median age of Catholics is 37.8, about the same as the Canadian population as a whole.

As the Roman Catholic Church goes, so goes organized religion in the nation. Other groups may get much of the ink. Some might even believe they are the key to the country's religious health. But at the end of the day, Catholics rule. Don't fear for their future. Besides, this is not just a big regional or national company. This is a vast and powerful multinational corporation.

Figure 9.1. Eight Fast Facts the Research Tells Us About Canadian Catholics
1. They have an enormous number of people.
2. They benefit immensely from immigration.
3. Their people are slow to defect.
4. Large numbers are enriched by their faith.
5. Many are open to greater involvement.
6. The less involved are looking for ministry.
7. The onus is on the Shepherds.
8. The Shepherds need the help of the Sheep.
Source: Presentations to Toronto Roman Catholic Archdiocesan priests, fall 2010.

Seen in such perspective, the Catholic Church in Quebec is "merely" a problem spot on the Catholic global map. Yes, the provincial government plays no religious favourites.[11] Yes, Catholics have become selective consumers. But the research to date is definitive: most people in the province remain Catholic and are not going anywhere. Lack of commitment understandably troubles leaders. But widespread defection is not on the horizon. Religion à la carte, Catholic-style, rules in Quebec.

Elsewhere, Catholicism's vitality is fuelled in part by new arrivals from other countries. But let's not minimize the importance of faith for earlier generations of people who were raised in Canadian Catholic homes.

The time has come to quit belittling the health of Canadian Catholicism. Large numbers may show up only occasionally for seasonal services, for rites of passage, or because they think they are overdue to share in a Mass. But they still show up. And they are still Catholic.

Large numbers also are open to greater involvement if they find it be worthwhile. The challenge lies with the supplier. If the Catholic Church comes through, who knows what could happen?

Mainline Protestants. As I look at the four primary "firms" in this grouping – the United, Anglican, Lutheran, and Presbyterians churches, I see far more than cold numbers. I see the faces of many people I have known who value faith and have been working hard to resuscitate their denominations. Minus their formal titles, they include people such as Lewis Garnsworthy, Ted Scott, Gord Turner, Ralph Milton, Muriel Duncan, Sandra Severs, Vince Alfano, Allan Saunders, Mardi Tindal, Tony Plomp, Wayne Holst, Michael Pryse, and Susan Johnson.

Yet, the research findings point to a reality that would not surprise any of them: it is difficult to see much hope for viable futures. The poetic line that Emile Durkheim used to describe the demise of Catholicism in nineteenth century Europe comes to mind: *"The old gods are growing old or are already dead."*

Such a prognosis set to poetry will result in some people dismissively declaring, "Bad News Bibby has been saying those things for years." My response is, "Yes, that's true. The problems have been evident for years."

Table 9.3. Mainline Identification: 1931 & 2001						
% of the Canadian Population						
	🍁	MLPROT	United	Anglican	Presbyterian	Lutheran
1931	**99%**	**48**	20	16	8	4
2001	**84**	**20**	10	7	1	2
Median Age	37.6	44.0	44.1	43.8	46.0	43.3
Source: Statistics Canada census data.						

Kenneth Bagnell, in a recent, astute article in *The Observer*, sees hope for the United Church. He is not clear, however, as to why.[12] We have seen that there is no secret as to why the Mainline Protestant groups have been declining numerically since the 1960s.

- Growth via their once-potent immigration pipelines has dropped off considerably from pre-60s levels.
- They have not been successful in retaining their children.
- They have not been inclined to emphasize and be engaged in very aggressive evangelism – the result being limited additions of "outsiders."

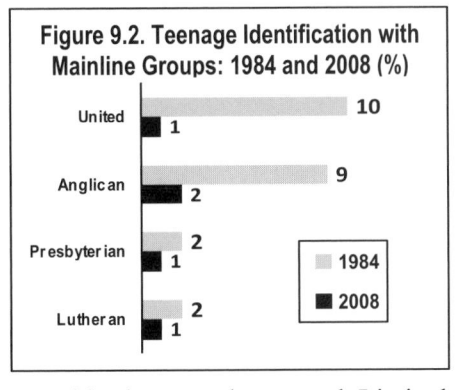

Figure 9.2. Teenage Identification with Mainline Groups: 1984 and 2008 (%)

In short, the demographics have not been good. Limited growth through immigration, migration, and birth, coupled with mortality, add up to an obvious result: zero or negative growth. Given their global nature, Anglicans have the potential to be helped considerably by immigration. But to date their potential global gains have been neutralized considerably by divisive homosexuality and gender issues.

There's an additional problem. To the extent Stark and others are right in maintaining people will be drawn to groups which address questions that "only the gods can answer," it's not clear that Mainline Protestants have particularly strong ultimate answer "product lines." Tom Harpur doesn't mince his words. In the case of life after death, he says that many groups simply "avoid the topic completely."[13] And he's not talking about the evangelicals.

Unlike Catholics, for example, who give a fair amount of attention to things like heaven and the importance of "last rites" so that people are ready for life after death, the United Church – for example – rightly or wrongly is seen by many as focusing almost exclusively on life. Perhaps Anglicans, Presbyterians, and Lutherans are different.[14]

Beyond tirelessly debating the reasons for the decline, the bottom line is that Mainline numbers are down, with significant resource implications: good ministry is all the more difficult to accomplish.[15] Still, Diana Butler Bass could be right: it may yet be possible for Mainline churches to be renewed "by weaving personal spiritual quests" with a primary strength – their "more traditional forms of religious life."[16] David Harris, editor of the *Presbyterian Record*, comments that "the church desperately needs to find a way to move forward." But he cautions that flexibility and creativity can be hard to come by. In the words of one former moderator, "Zacchaeus was not a Presbyterian."[17]

Conservative Protestants. The "evangelicals," as they are commonly known collectively, are characterized by considerable vitality. Their major demographic accomplishment has been their ability to sustain a market share of approximately 8% (7% Baptist) from the first census in 1871 through to the present day.

Religious intermarriage alone should have decimated the Conservative Protestants. Yet, because of factors that include immigration, their emphasis on tight-knit communities and strong youth and family ministries, they have been able to sustain their market share. The thesis of Mainline Protestant executive Dean Kelley, put forth in the early 1970s, also knows increasing support. In his book, *Why Conservative Churches Are Growing*, Kelly maintained that two key factors of central importance were (1) the demands that evangelicals placed on their members, in the form of expectations such as participation, tithing, and lifestyles and (2) the provision of answers to ultimate questions, including life after death.[18]

My examination of Calgary evangelical church growth dating back to the late-1960s shows that, contrary to popular myth, Conservative Protestants know only modest growth through the recruitment of outsiders. Their numerical stability and growth are tied primarily to their ability to retain their own people – their children and their geographically-mobile members.[19]

To the extent they add outsiders, the key factor is relationships: they tend to either befriend or marry them.

Table 9.4. Select Conservative Protestant Group Identification as Percentages of the Population: 1901-2001

	1901	1921	1941	1961	1981	2001	1000s	Median Age
1. Christian	*	*	*	*	*	2.6	780	30.2
2. Baptist	5.9	4.8	4.2	3.3	2.9	2.5	729	39.3
3. Pentecostal	.0	.8	.5	.8	1.4	1.2	369	33.5
4. Mennonite	.6	.7	1.0	.8	.8	.6	191	32.0
5. Salvation Army	*	*	.3	.3	.5	.5	88	39.3
6. Christian Reformed	*	*	*	.3	.3	.3	77	32.3
7. Evangelical Missionary	*	*	*	*	*	.2	67	35.2
8. Christian & Miss Alliance	*	.0	.0	.1	.1	.2	66	34.5
9. Adventist	*	.2	.2	.1	.2	.2	63	35.5
10. Non-denominational	*	*	*	*	*	.1	41	33.0
11. Brethren in Christ	*	*	*	.1	.1	.1	21	38.2
12. Church of Christ	*	.2	.2	.1	.1	.0	15	39.4[a]
13. Church of Nazarene	*	.0	.0	.0	.0	.0	14	39.1[a]
14. Free Methodist	*	*	.1	.1	.1	.0	14	36.5[a]

[a]Mean.

Source: Statistics Canada census data & Hiller 1976a:360-361.

Those demographic patterns are consistent with Kelley's argument. The emphasis on a religion that has value and addresses life's big questions helps to explain the vitality and significance that contribute to evangelicals' high level of retention.

Somewhat paradoxically, while Conservative Protestants tend to stay with their "Believers' Church" denominations, they move fairly freely between individual evangelical groups.[20] As a result, no single denomination in this "family" makes up even 3% of the Canadian population, nowhere near the 7% who identified themselves as "Baptist" when the first census was conducted in 1871. Many prefer to go simply by "Christian."[21]

Evangelicals, who typically are younger than Mainline Protestants, will continue to be a smaller player on the Canadian religious scene. But their steady market share of 8% is finally about to increase. Why? The explosive growth of evangelicals in many parts of the world will result in an increasingly robust immigration pipeline – and an increasingly multicultural church. More about this shortly.

Other Faith Entries. As people came to Canada from an array of countries, they brought other religions besides Christianity to Canada. At the time of Confederation, Jews made up about one-tenth of one percent of the population. With the arrival of increasing numbers of people from countries other than Europe and the United States, additional faiths also took root.

Through about 1981, the number of people identifying with faiths other than Christianity remained very small. Much of the difficulty such groups had, of course, was tied to the fact that they had difficulty holding on to their children: many married Protestants and Catholics.

The net result was that, by 1981, less than 3% of Canadians indicated they were either Jewish, Muslim, Buddhist, Hindu, or Sikh. Another 1% were either Jehovah's Witnesses or Mormons.

As we have seen, over the past three decades or so, immigration has seen the percentage of people who identify with the other major world religions double to about 6%. The largest of these is Islam at 2%.

The historical track records of a number of these faiths – Judaism, Buddhism, Hinduism, and Sikhism, along with the Latter Day Saints and Jehovah's Witnesses – suggest that they will continue to be part of the Canadian religious scene. But like the four Mainline Protestant groups, they will not be among the major religious firms.

Table 9.5. Identification with Other Religious as Percentages of the Population: 1921-2001							
	1921	1941	1961	1981	2001	1000s	Median Age
1. Muslim	*	*	*	.4	2.0	580	28.1
2. Jewish	1.4	1.5	1.4	1.2	1.1	330	41.5
3. Buddhist	.1	.1	.1	.2	1.0	300	38.0
4. Hindu	*	*	*	.3	1.0	297	31.9
5. Sikh	*	*	*	.3	.9	278	29.7
6. Jehovah's Witnesses	.1	.1	.4	.6	.5	155	38.7
7. Latter Day Saints	*	.2	.3	.4	.3	102	28.7

*Confucianism: .3% in 1921, .2% in 1941; smaller %'s since.

Source: Statistics Canada census data.

Islam is another story. There already are more Muslims in Canada than Presbyterians, Pentecostals, and Jews, for example. They may well be on the verge of attaining the proverbial "critical mass" – such as the evangelicals have experienced – where their numbers reach a point where they are able to cut down on losses through intermarriage. Moreover, Islam obviously is a very powerful multinational religion. In light of the diverse number of countries in which it is prominent, the immigration pipeline that has been such a critically important component of religious group growth over the years will continue to produce new people for some time to come.

In addition, a relatively high birth rate and an emphasis on the retention of children will further contribute to Islam's viability. It is worth noting that the median age of Muslims as of the 2001 census was 28.1. Some additions through proselytism – or what many social scientists call switching" – also can be expected.

Finally, the two traits that observers such as Kelley and Stark see as essential to success – an emphasis on demands and rewards, as well as the ability to speak to ultimate questions – are major features of Islam.

Table 9.6. Canada's 16 Largest Religious Groups			
	Numbers	%	Median Age
1. Roman Catholic	12,793,125	44	37.8
2. United Church	2,839,125	12	44.1
3. Anglican	2,035,500	8	43.8
4. Christian (unspecified)	780,450	3	30.2
5. Baptist	729,475	3	39.3
6. Eastern Orthodox	606,620	2	40.1
7. Lutheran	606,590	2	43.3
8. Muslim	579,640	2	28.1
9. Protestant (unspecified)	549,205	2	40.4
10. Presbyterian	409,830	1	46.0
11. Pentecostal	369,475	1	33.5
12. Jewish	329,995	1	41.5
13. Buddhist	300.345	1	38.0
14. Hindu	297,200	1	31.9
15. Sikh	278,410	<1	29.7
16. Greek Orthodox	215,175	<1	46.1
* No Religion	4,796,325	16	31.1

Source: Statistics Canada. 2001 Census.

In short, as we look to the future of religion in Canada, we can anticipate that the Roman Catholic Church will continue to be the dominant player. Other key market members will be the Conservative Protestants and Muslims. The marketplace will not lack for other players, both old and new. But those groups will have to work hard just to retain – let alone expand – their market shares.

The Global Situation

As with Canada, there are and will continue to be people all over the world who are not in the market for religion, old or new. But they will be in the minority.

At this point in history, some 6 billion of the planet's 7 billion people are identifying with a religion. They are led by Christians (2.1 billion), Muslims (1.5 billion) and Hindus (900 million).

Like the auto multi-ationals, including Toyota, GM, Volkswagen, Ford, and Hyundai, these religious powerhouses will continue to lead the way as the most prominent religious "suppliers" on earth.

To the extent that markets in any country become open to their presence and that of other smaller suppliers – in part because their existing clienteles simply move to new places – religions will make national inroads.

Table 9.7. The World's 16 Largest Religions	
1. Christianity	2.1 billion
2. Islam	1.5 billion
3. Hinduism	900 million
4. Chinese folk	395 million
5. Buddhism	375 million
6. Sikhism	23 million
7. Juche	19 million
8. Spiritism	15 million
9. Judaism	14 million
10. Falun Gong	10 million
11. Bahäi	7 million
12. Cao Dai	5 million
13. Confucianism	5 million
14. New Age	5 million
15. Jainism	4 million
16. Shinto	4 million
* No Religion, secular	1.1 billion

Sources: www.adherents.com 2010 and www.religionfacts.com 2010..

Collectively, the religious companies have been performing very well of late. In the words of Harvey Cox, "Instead of disappearing, religion is now exhibiting new vitality all around the world."[22]

Christianity's Growth. In recent years Christianity has experienced more worldwide growth than any religion. Such a reality of the faith's global health will come as news to many people. After all, as Philip Yancey noted recently, it's not making the headlines of CNN.[23] *Globe and Mail* columnist Neil Reynolds similarly wrote in early 2010, "You could call it the greatest story never told."[24]

Reynolds drew on two prominent observers of the global religious scene, U.S. political scientist Walter Russell Mead and British scholar Scott M. Thomas. Their thoughts are worth retrieving in detail.[25]

The flamboyant Mead has noted that Christianity is now "on its biggest roll" in its 2,000-year history.[26] It is both the world's largest faith and the world's fastest-growing faith. Its absolute numbers and market share are at all-time highs. In the last fifty years, Mead says, "It has surpassed Islam as the most popular religion in sub-Saharan Africa and as the leading Abrahamic religion in China." The Christian faith, he asserts, "claims almost twice as many adherents as Islam worldwide."[27] By 2050, the worldwide Christian population could top three billion.

- Roman Catholic commentator John Allen would note that, between 1950 and 2000, the number of Catholics worldwide grew from just under 500 million to over one billion. The Church suffered serious losses in the global North (Europe and North America), but grew dramatically in the global South (Africa, Asia, and Latin America).[28]
- In a country like Russia, Orthodox Christianity is enjoying a revival after seventy years of communist suppression.[29]
- But of particular significance, Pentecostals have experienced the fastest growth of any religious movement in history, says Mead, "from zero to something like half a billion members in the last 100 years." Growth has been pronounced in Africa, Asia, and Latin America.[30]

Thomas likewise maintains that "around the world, religion is on the rise, and notes that "the most dramatic religious explosion is the spread of evangelical Protestantism, led by Pentecostalism." After Catholics, he says, Pentecostals represent the largest single group of Christians worldwide.[31] It typically crosses class lines.

What perhaps is startling to learn is not only that evangelicals now number close to 700 million people worldwide; it's that they have achieved strategic masses in such places as China, Indonesia, India, Nigeria, the Philippines, South Africa, and Brazil.

For example, it is estimated that, by 2050, there could be 220 million Christians in China – about 15% of the population.[32]

In many instances, Thomas notes, Christianity is "returning to its roots by becoming a post-Western religion dominated by the peoples, cultures, and countries of the global South."[33] While having a strong personal focus, it also has become increasingly politically active, especially in Latin America.[34]

Table 9.8. Presence of Pentecostals and Charismatics in 10 Countries: 2006			
	Pente-costals	Charis-matics	Total
UNITED STATES	10%	18	28
LATIN AMERICA			
Guatemala	20	20	60
Brazil	15	34	49
Chile	9	21	30
AFRICA			
Kenya	33	23	56
Nigeria	18	8	26
South Africa	10	24	34
ASIA			
India	1	4	5
Philippines	4	40	44
South Korea	2	9	11

Source: PewResearchCener 2006.

These expansion patterns, of course, have not been without conflict. Thomas points out that "three countries with substantial Muslim communities – India, Indonesia, and Nigeria – also have large Pentecostal populations and sizable minorities of Christians more broadly." Tensions have been rising, resulting in violence such as the conflict in Nigeria in 2010 that left over 500 people dead.[35]

In addition, competition with Catholicism in various parts of the world is frequently intense. John Allen writes that as "Pentecostals march across the planet," they have been "siphoning off significant numbers of Catholics." He notes that "the Catholic Church is itself being 'Pentecostalized' through the Charismatic movement."[36]

A massive shift in population growth from the developed countries of the North to the developing countries of the global South will result in a changing global religious landscape. Thomas points out that the developed countries of the North accounted for 32% of the world's population in 1900 and 18% in 2000. By 2050, that figure will drop to just 10%.[37] "A new kind of world is in the making," he says, "and the people, states, and religious communities that compose the global South are making it."[38]

In the case of Roman Catholics, Allen notes that the Church was dominated in the last century by the global North. Today, two in three Catholics are found in Africa, Asia, and Latin America.[39] One obvious result? An unprecedented number of Catholic leaders are coming from all over the world[40] – often, in the Canadian instance, to a parish near you.

Table 9.9. World Religion Increases: Next 24 Hours	
Christians	69,000
Roman Catholics	*37,000*
Pentecostals	*30,000*
Muslims	68,000
Hindus	37,000
Chinese folk	10,700
Buddhists	10,600
Atheists	1,200
Sikhs	1,100
Jews	350
Source: Barrett et al. 2001:4.	

Mead and Thomas both draw attention to the fact that the rise in evangelical Christianity in particular can be expected to bring with it a concomitant increase in Protestant ideals, such as the work ethic, entrepreneurial aspirations, and personal freedom.[41] Thomas sees global Christianity as becoming more conservative than European Christianity, but more liberal than the Catholic model which, in some Latin American settings, will be replaced by evangelicalism. Sometimes it will be a hybrid with Catholicism, sometimes not.[42]

In addition, both Mead and Thomas maintain that the spread of evangelical Christianity will have important social consequences. Globally, "Evangelicals will be a major religious, social, and political force in the coming century," Thomas writes.[43] In China, for example, he maintains that the government tacitly allows the established religions of Christianity and neo-Confucianism "to operate relatively freely, believing that they can promote social harmony amid rapid social changes." He suggests that if Christianity achieves the culture permeation in China that it knows in South Korea – at around 25%– it could fundamentally alter China's political fabric."[44]

Islamic Growth. Observers maintain that Islam also is experiencing a revival that extends well beyond the more extreme Islamic fundamentalist movements. As we have seen with the global Gallup data, large proportions of people in predominantly Muslim countries are saying that religion is an important part of their daily lives. In reminding readers that Islamic renewal is extending far beyond the Arab world, Thomas writes that "more Muslim women are wearing the veil, more Muslim men are growing beards, and more Muslims are attending mosques more often."[45]

- Russia now has more Muslims than any other country in Europe.
- Northwestern China "is home to over 20 million Muslims and is now in the grip of an Islamic reawakening."[46] Many young Chinese Muslims are studying across the Middle East.
- Sheer numbers alone mean that Christian-Islam relations will, in John Allen's words, "be a major driver of world history in the twenty-first century."[47]

Table 9.10. Ten Largest Muslim Nations (Millions)	
1. Indonesia	202
2. Pakistan	160
3. India	151
4. Bangladesh	125
5. Egypt	72
6. Turkey	71
7. Nigeria	68
8. Iran	64
9. Morocco	33
10. Algeria	33

Source: CIA World Factbook; cited in Allen 2009:99.

One cannot underestimate the role that the Internet is playing in connecting Christians, Muslims, and people of many other faiths who, because of geographical separation, were isolated religious diasporas.

Yet, ironically, notes Thomas, globalization in general simultaneously contributes to "a more unified and yet more fragmented world."[48]

Assessment

Obviously the receptivity levels to religion vary considerably around the world. In Stark's parlance, settings are variously religiously "regulated" and "deregulated." They have open as well as closed markets, robust competition as well as long-standing monopolies.

But because of both (1) the ongoing demand and (2) the ongoing availability of global suppliers, one thing is clear: religion will persist as far as the social scientific eye can see, individually and organizationally.

The scope of the market for religion is so vast that, apart from the gods, entrepreneurial human beings would find its potential too great to ignore.

Religions, major and minor, well-established and freshly minted, will continue to be at work, attempting to increase their local, national, and global market shares.

Individuals will continue to explore the options, and will usually opt for one – or more. After all, for some, religion enriches life. For all, it offers market entries when it comes to death.

And as for the gods, if they actually exist and people ignore them for very long, they can be expected to shake things up from time to time.

It is, I think, significant that Scott Thomas would conclude his recent overview of global religious developments by underlining the importance that religion has for the vast majority of people around the world. Precisely because "faith informs the daily struggles of millions in confronting" life, he says, countries like the United States need to understand the worldwide religious resurgence. If they fail to do so, says Thomas, "the potential for religiously motivated violence across the globe may increase dramatically over the next century."[49]

At a time when the debate about God's existence has become something of a spectator sport, the scale of the resurgence of religion will affect the entire planet.

Did someone say that people are fiddling, while some parts of "Rome" are flourishing – and others are burning?

Conclusion

"When people believe that the future will be different,
it transforms the way they feel about the present."
-Harvey Cox

To look at the religious situation in Canada, all by itself, is to learn a fair amount about ourselves. We are characterized by religious polarization. That polarization seems to be increasing, particularly as growing numbers of people take a pass on organized religion.

When we ask the question, "So what?" we receive a number of reasonably clear-cut answers.

- With or without religion, the quality of *personal well-being* will probably not change very much.
- *Spiritual needs* will continue and, for the most part, they will also continue to be met, with and without religion.
- When it comes to *social well-being*, the loss of religion – to the extent that such a reality takes place – will be met with a societal loss of one important source of civility and compassion. It may be that the religious pathway to positive interpersonal life can be replaced. But in the interim, however long that might be, something will be lost.
- The one area that undoubtedly would suffer the most from the demise of organized religion is *death*. Despite the enormous market for meaning-makers in this area, our society is not showing signs of producing strong and viable alternatives to religion.

To the extent that we try for some perspective on our situation as Canadians, we typically ask, "How do we compare to the Americans?" That's not a bad strategy. But I think it is readily apparent that we can get a much better reading on our religious situation by expanding the comparisons to countries around the world.

I have no illusions that I have been comprehensive. As I have emphasized throughout the book, to try for cross-national comparisons is a daunting task. The complexities and nuances make it extremely difficult to identify clear and consistent patterns.

Nonetheless, these limitations acknowledged, I would suggest that we have some good, preliminary findings in the four "so what?" areas we have focused on in Canada. Globally-speaking:

1. Subjective *personal well-being* often is associated with high levels of religiousness. However, objective measures of personal well-being are typically associated with strong economies. Those economies in turn provide the varied physical, educational, and health resources that elevate a country's quality of life. Such strong economies are found disproportionately in countries where Christianity is or was prevalent.

2. *Spiritual needs* are highly pervasive throughout the world. They persist regardless of whether or not countries are characterized by religious monopolies, polarization, or secular monopolies. In the latter two situations, spiritual needs are addressed by both non-religious and religious means.

3. The importance of *social well-being* is emphasized by religious groups. In many if not most cases, their teachings include ethical components. Followers are expected to exhibit honesty and integrity, and to be respectful and compassionate in their dealings with other people. Accordingly, religiousness is associated with a somewhat greater tendency to value such traits. Behaviourally, indicators such as the lack of crime and global generosity do not point to clear national patterns. Some observers would argue that in highly secularized settings such as Europe, for example, something of religion's "shadow effect" is at work, but is not reflected well in measures of current religiousness. Maybe, maybe not.

4. The desire to address the question of *life after death*, and to believe that death is not the end, are both universal inclinations. There is little evidence to suggest such questions and beliefs will be set aside in the foreseeable future.

This last point brings us back to the central feature of most religions. They typically have clear multidimensional components. Christianity, for example, emphasizes God, self, and society – summed up in the so-called Great Commandment to "love God with all one's being and one's neighbour as oneself." But while religions have a number of key facets, the indispensable starting place is the gods.

Beyond the Gods...and Back

Are there dangers in being religious? Of course. Highly acclaimed American philosopher and novelist Rebecca Goldstein is among many humanists and atheists who express alarm about the destructive potential of religion. In an interview with the *Globe and Mail*'s Martin Levin in early 2010, she commented that it "is terrifying" to see the strength of mounting, primitive religious emotions."[1] That's true. But there are also significant losses when religion is abandoned.

In Canada and around the world, the majority of people do not live life beyond the gods. It is further worth noting that, for many who do, the experience is not life-long.

The reason is not that they are deprived or unintelligent or brainwashed. Rather, in the words of esteemed anthropologist, Clifford Geertz, it appears that "in all probability most [people] are unable...just to look at the stranger features of the world's landscape in dumb astonishment or bland apathy without trying to develop...some notions as to how such features might be reconciled with the more ordinary deliverances of experience."[2] Max Weber put things this way: religion is the product of an "inner compulsion to understand the world as a meaningful cosmos and take up a position toward it."[3] Charles Taylor argues that people continue to have a need for a sense of fullness that reflects transcendent reality. In his words, "Our age is very far from settling in to a comfortable unbelief."[4]

Apart from the role of reflection, personal experience seems to confirm for many that the gods exist. Consistent with some neuroscientists who go so far as to say we are "wired" to the gods,[5] I reminded readers in *Restless Gods* how sociologist Peter Berger has suggested that our sense of justice, order, hope, and even humour might be innate "signals of transcendence."[6]

For close to three centuries now, there have been prominent thinkers who have been telling us that religion is destined to become a thing of the past. The old Comtean formula was presumably law-like. Civilizations move through three dominant thought-form stages – from religion to metaphysics to science.

But Comte and his Enlightenment and post-Enlightenment colleagues were wrong. It's time for a mind-shift. Religion is still very much with us. The gods have not gone anywhere.

When we revisit polarization in Canada, what the data tell us is that we are polarized when it comes to organized religion, as seen in attendance, but far less so by belief.

The same pattern holds across the planet. It's evident that more than a few thinkers have been taking notice.

In a new book, *God Is Back*, John Micklethwait and Adrian Wooldridge, editor in chief and Washington bureau chief respectively of *The Economist*, have agreed that religion is making a major comeback. Their analysis seems consistent with much of what Rodney Stark has been saying now for some time. There is a market for religion; the question is, what suppliers will come through?

Micklethwait and Wooldridge, like other observers we have noted, maintain that the resurgence can readily be seen in such diverse places as Africa, China, Southeast Asia, Brazil, and Europe, as well as the United States. Central to much of the new life, they argue, is an American-style emphasis on marketing and choice. The emphases and styles of the U.S. megachurches are being exported around the world, with considerable success.

"Those things that seemingly were going to destroy religion," they write, "democracy and markets, technology and reason – are combining to make it stronger." They optimistically conclude that the global rise of faith, despite frequently being associated with violence and instability, can eventually be channelled away from volatility.[7]

Their argument is consistent with the research findings of Stark and his associates as they carried out research around the world, including Canada, back in the late 1970s and 1980s. Regardless of the national setting, they said, the demand persists for religions that address questions that only the gods can answer. When religious groups address those demands, people will respond.

The problem with living without the gods is that there are times when we are forced to deal with the mysteries of life and death. There are experiences of ecstasy and euphoria, perplexion and despair, suffering and tragedy that sometimes seem to call out for something beyond us.

Yancey has written that in his extensive travels, "I have found certain themes to be universal. The question, 'What good is God?' occurs in some form to every person who experiences pain or death or poverty or unfairness – in other words, to everyone." Yancey clearly believes that there is a God that "can wrest permanent good out of this flawed planet."[8]

If there is nothing there – if, in the graphic words of Helmut Thielicke, we look to the heavens for the eye of God and see only an empty socket – so be it.[9] But if there *is* Something....

During those "deep times" in life, there are many who find significant resources in believing that back of all of creation there is a Presence that brought everything into being, is sustaining it, and will be there at the end of history to greet it.[10] This is not merely Something to rely on when we die. It is Something that is an unmatched resource when we live...resulting in lines like this being penned years ago:

> *The Lord is my shepherd, I shall not want...*
> *He restores my soul...I will fear no evil.*
> *And I will dwell in the house of the Lord forever.*[11]

Rolheiser sums things up this way: "Given that we live under a smiling, relaxed, all-forgiving and all-powerful God, we too should relax and smile, at least once in a while, because irrespective of anything that has ever happened or will ever happen, in the end, 'all shall be well'."[12]

Because of what we experience in our lifetimes and because we are exposed to the possibility of such a Presence, it is not precarious to conclude that most of us will choose to live life beyond the gods for only so long.

That said, don't get me wrong. People are not yearning for churches and their counterparts. No one should trivialize what twenty-first century Canadians want by naively assuming that the findings tell us that most will "come back to church." I've been reminding everyone for some time now that we *have never found* anything in our research that points to the uninvolved being in the market for churches.

What we *have found* is that, to the extent that people "come back" to organized religion, it is because they have discovered there are some things taking place that resonate with their desire to know the presence and the resources of the gods.

For example, large numbers of teens say they will want that presence in the future when they experience some of life's "big events" – things like marriage, the birth of a child, or the death of a parent. Moreover, as we have seen, when Canadians speak of spiritual needs, very often they have something in the way of transcendence in mind.

They consequently are open to groups that are in touch with and can respond to their spiritual, personal, and relational needs.

Table C1. Desire for Religious Rites of Passage in the Future: 1987-2008 (%)

	1987	2000	2008
Wedding ceremony	94	89	84
Funeral	93	86	83
Birth-related	85	70	65

Sources: Project Teen Canada Surveys, 1987, 2000, 2008.

Table C2. Teenage Openness to Greater Involvement

"I'd be open to more involvement with religious groups if I found it to be worthwhile"

	< Monthly	Monthly+
Nationally	**38%**	**65**
Catholic: Outside Quebec	55	67
Catholic: Quebec	30	65
Orthodox Christian	56	63
Christian: unspecified	39	59
Conservative Protestant	35	65
Mainline Protestant	47	62
Other Faiths	51	69
Buddhism	56	60
Islam	54	72
Judaism	47	62
Aboriginal spirituality	49	**
Hinduism	30	74
Sikhism	**	63
No Religion	28	53

**N's insufficient to permit accurate and stable percentaging.
Source: Project Teen Canada 2008.

People who are inclined to give religion a serious look can be expected to *start* with the traditions with which they have some kind of affinity – notably the religions of parents and, partners. These are the same groups to which many of them, on occasion at least, already are turning.

Here, an organization like the Roman Catholic Church in Quebec, for now at least, has a unique opportunity and huge "market advantage." The research suggests that, ironically, the only religion most Quebeckers are willing to seriously entertain in the foreseeable future is Catholicism. Seasonal services and unique events – such as the October 2010 mass for the province's newest saint, Brother Andre, which brought more than 30,000 people to the Olympic Stadium – serve as reminders that the Catholic faith has not vanished.[13]

Yet, unless the Church responds to the latent demand, journalist Konrad Yakabuski probably is right: the parish steps where their forefathers assiduously greeted the curé each Sunday may, for young Quebeckers, be nothing more than a good place to skateboard."[14]

Beyond only Quebec and even beyond Canada, John Allen explicitly warns Catholic leaders that, in the twenty-first century, what they will need above all else is imagination. "They'll need the capacity to reconsider how they think about the Church and what they do with their faith," he says. Otherwise, instead of rising to the occasion and responding to important new challenges, the Church will "be steamrolled by them."[15]

On paper, groups such as the United and Anglican churches also are not yet out of the running in Canada, given the size of their affiliate pools. But time is not on the side of either denomination. They have to move quickly. Their problems are exacerbated by a sharp decline in human and financial resources. As we have seen, both have nothing less than a mega-crisis, for example, with respect to their young people. Yet national staff cutbacks for both denominations in 2010 included the United Church laying off its youth and young adult coordinator.[16]

A basic problem is that many and perhaps most people who identify with Catholic and Protestant traditions have no particular reason to associate what they want and need with what those groups are doing.

That has to change. People have to know that groups are addressing the life and death questions that they are asking, and are capable of having a positive impact on their lives and the people and issues they care about.

Religious groups that can do those kinds of things have futures. Those that can't or won't are going to fade away.

Over the past four decades, Harvey Cox has been carefully studying the religious times. His work has spanned the era when the secularization argument was pervasive (*The Secular City* 1965), through the explosion of pentecostalism (*Fire from Heaven* 1995). In 2009, the year he retired from Harvard Divinity School, he offered his thoughts about where religion is headed (*The Future of Faith*). He has some important things to say.

Cox maintains that modern science and traditional religion, after three centuries of slugging it out for the privilege of being the ultimate source of meaning and value, have – like two tired boxers – reached an exhausted stalemate. He says that "people are still willing to rely on science for the limited things it has proven it can do, but they no longer believe it will answer their deepest questions. People remain vaguely intrigued with the traditional religions, but not with conventional churches."

His conclusion? "Increasing numbers of people appear ready to move on, and are on the lookout for a more promising map."[17] But most are not looking for creeds and hierarchies. They want personal faith. "The experience of the divine is displacing theories about it," says Cox.[18]

What is less clear is *where* they can experience faith.

In the conclusion of their landmark work, *American Piety*, in which they documented the state of religion in the United States at the end of the 1960s, Rodney Stark and Charles Glock wrote that "the institutional shape of the religion of the future is as difficult to predict as its theological content."[19] Their last two lines were borrowed from poet William Butler Yeats:

> *And what rough beast, its hour come round at last,*
> *Slouches toward Bethlehem to be born?*[20]

Similarly, there's value in recalling the rest of that "old gods" thought of Durkheim's that I mentioned in discussing the future of Canada's Mainline Protestants. The words were penned a century or so ago as he reflected on religion in Europe:

> *The old gods are growing old or are already dead, and others are not yet born. There are no gospels which are immortal, but neither is there any reason for believing that humanity is incapable of inventing new ones*[21].

It may well be that, in the course of reaching out for answers to those questions "that only the gods can satisfy," large numbers of people in Canada and elsewhere are going to bypass the existing groups altogether, and opt for some "new ones" that are "not yet born."

What is certain is that the needs that call for the gods will persist. Until the responses that are required appear, we will have the paradoxical situation where many groups are going broke precisely at a time when many people are going hungry.[22]

The gods potentially can contribute to life in a number of ways. They can elevate personal and social well-being. They can make us happy, contribute to justice, satisfy our spiritual needs, and make us better stewards of the planet.

So can everyone else.

But in addition to speaking to all of life, and adding to all of life, the gods are unique in that they alone can also speak to death. What's more, they have some encouraging things to say.

As the people around us, and we ourselves, approach that inevitable and mysterious ending of life, the gods may be our best hope...in fact, they may be our only hope.

Some people will choose to go it alone. Yet, it's hard to escape the conclusion that there's really no need for us to experience life and death alone.

That's why, in the long run, many people may say goodbye to any number of forms of organized religion.

Few of us will say goodbye to the gods.

Appendix

The Project Canada Survey Series Methodology

Since the mid-1970s, I have been carrying out a series of national surveys from the University of Lethbridge that have provided considerable data on social trends, including religion. Seven "Project Canada" surveys of adults were conducted every five years from 1975 through 2005, while four complementary "Project Teen Canada" surveys were completed in 1984, 1992, 2000, and 2008. Another adult survey is on the drawing board for 2015.

With respect to religion, the surveys have generated comprehensive information on attitudes, beliefs, values, and behaviour. The adult samples have averaged about 1,500 people who are 18 and over, and have been highly representative of the adult population. The youth samples have been comprised of teenagers between the ages of 15 and 19 who are still in high schools/secondary schools or their equivalents (e.g., CEGEPs in Quebec). These highly representative samples have been comprised of an average of about 3,800 cases. The sample of 5,564 in 2008 was our largest ever, and included an important oversample of 818 teens attending Aboriginal schools.

Full methodological details for the surveys can be found in three books: *The Emerging Millennials* 2009:214-219, *The Boomer Factor* 2006:225-226, and *Restless Gods* 2002:249-254.

A Methodological Note for the Statistically-Minded: Correlates of the Three Religiosity Measures

Some readers – including many quantitatively minded social scientists – undoubtedly will be inclined to view the three religiosity measures of attendance, identification, and belief in God as three variables, whose individual impact on various values needs to be "flushed out" using statistical techniques like regression analysis. The assumption is that other factors besides attendance, identification, and belief *per se* could be accounting at least in part for the differences. Such factors might include family structures, race and ethnicity, education, and the religiosity of family members and friends. Age and education, of course, are already controlled for in the case of teenagers. Gender is frequently isolated in the table presentations.

Such analyses, of course, can readily be carried out.

But appropriate statistics are determined by the task at hand. They are merely tools to be drawn upon as required in the course of testing clear and good ideas.

What I am assuming is that all three religion measures – attendance, identification, and belief – are not so much important in and of themselves, but rather as indices of the broader personal settings in which people live.

For example, I am not so naïve as to think that a teenager's attending a church every week is, all by itself, shaping the young person's values. Rather, regular attendance presumably is associated with other key learning variables, such as pro-religious parents and friends, and the personal importance of faith. I have little interest in pontificating about the sole influence of attendance and then comparing its impact with these other related variables that, frankly, make it noteworthy.

The same is true of the other two religiosity variables I am using – identification and belief in God. They are potentially helpful as two additional indices of religious and non-religious social environments, and not primarily as measures of only identification and belief as such.

Measures of association, however, that sum up the broad relationships between religious environments and the dependent variables being examined are, in my mind, statistics that in both table and correlation coefficient form are very useful and important in summarizing the data. Many are offered.

A Memo to Neuroscientists, Evolutionary Biologists, and Other Scientists Who Are Increasingly Focusing on Religion

The burgeoning amount of work that is being done on religion by people other than social scientists is potentially extremely valuable. As I indicated in the preface, the experience I have had in trying to understand my young daughter's development has given me an overdue appreciation for what neuroscience, for example, can tell us about so many things. The University of Lethbridge is home to the Canadian Centre of Behavioural Neuroscience, with three colleagues among the top neuroscientists in the world – Ian Whishaw, Bryan Kolb, and Rob Sutherland. They are a reminder of the field's importance.

I am not in a position at this point to be able to adequately and appropriately critique such work. But I do want to acknowledge it and, for starters, argue that a comprehensive understanding of religion will require drawing on the contributions of both the physical and social sciences. In my next life, I plan to do a Ph.D. in social neuroscience.

Notes

Introduction

[1] See, for example, Thiessen and Dawson 2009 and my response, Bibby 2009, as well as a critical *United Church Observer* piece by Wright, 2009.

1 The Days of God's Dominion

[1] Grant 1988:1.
[2] Grant 1988:8.
[3] Bramadat and Seljak (eds.) 2008 and 2009.
[4] Grant 1988:65.
[5] Beyer, 1997:276-277.
[6] CBC, 1973.
[7] Grant, 1988:161.
[8] The sources for table 1.1: *Yearbook of American and Canadian Churches, 1916-1966*; United, Anglican, Baptist, Pentecostal, Lutheran, and Presbyterian yearbooks; McLeod, 1982; Beyer, 1997; Stats Canada, *The Daily*, June 1, 1993.
[9] Beaucage and LaRoque 1983:31.
[10] CBC documentary, *The Quieter Revolution*, 1976,
[11] Noll 2007:18.
[12] Kristofferson, "Sunday Morning Coming Down," 1969.

2 The Boomer Bust

[1] Noll 2007:36-37. For a valuable set of responses to Noll, see *Church and Faith Trends* 2008.
[2] Foote, 1996:1.
[3] Yakabuski 2009.
[4] Bibby 1990:9.
[5] Hordern 1966:46.
[6] Quote below taken from Bibby 2006:67.
[7] Smith 2008. Also discussed by Harris 2008.
[8] Taylor 2007:580.
[9] Taylor 2007:588.
[10] Putnam 2000:195.
[11] Some of these ideas, accompanied by data, are described in more detail in Bibby 2005.
[12] Statistics Canada catalogue 96F0030XIE2001015, p. 6.
[13] Taken from the Toronto Archdiocese website, http://www.archtoronto.org, December 2010.

[14] For a summary of the key findings regarding Aboriginals, see Bibby with Fox and Penner, 2010.

[15] Valpy 2010.

[16] Dueck 2010. A take on the debate is offered by Scrivener 2010a.

3 The New Polarization

[1] Valpy and Friesen, December 11, 2010.

[2] Dobbelaere 1981, 2002.

[3] Berger, 1961.

[4] See Luckmann, 1960 and Berger 1961.

[5] Berger, 1961.

[6] See, for example, Cox 1995:xv-xvi and Berger 1999:2.

[7] Specifically, the 1990 General Social Survey and the Survey of Giving, Volunteering, and Participating, 2000. For details, see Bibby 2002:75-76.

[8] Bibby 2002:73. The table accidentally omitted the "Other Faiths" data line.

[9] Bibby 2002:90.

[10] See, for example, his work with Bainbridge (1985), Finke (1992 and 2000), and Iannaconne (1992ff).

[11] Stark and Bainbridge 1985:7.

[12] Stark and Bainbridge 1985:2.

[13] Stark and Bainbridge 1985:529-530.

[14] Finke and Stark 1992:238,250.

[15] Finke and Stark 1992:252-255.

[16] Stark and Bainbridge 1985.

[17] Bibby, 2002:62ff.

[18] The "no religion" figure was 4% in 1971, 7% in 1981, and 12% in 1991.

[19] This argument is developed in detail in Bibby 2002:66ff.

[20] Stark and Finke, 2000:259-274.

[21] Bibby, 2002:68.

[22] Bibby 1993:282.

[23] Gregg 2005:21-22.

[24] See, for example, Dawkins 2006, Hitchens 2007, Harris 2006.

[25] Hiller 1976b.

[26] See the WVS website at http://www.worldvaluessurvey.org.

[27] See, http://www.gallup.com and backgrounder document, http://media.gallup.com/dataviz/www/WP_QuestionsWHITE.pdf.

[28] See http://pewglobal.org.

[29] For a background sketch see http://experts.uchicago.edu/experts.php?id=174.

[30] Data included in Smith 2009:88.

[31] See, for example, Winseman 2002, describing how Gallup measures "spiritual commitment." The article views commitment in highly traditional religious terms.

[32] Smith 2009:15-16.

[33] For a sampling of information on resource issues, see Sumner (2010), and Williams 2010a and 2010b (Anglicans); Shepherd 2010 (Lutherans), Kouwenberg 2010 (Presbyterians), Johnson 2009 (Lutherans).

[34] Peritz 2010.

[35] For an excellent article summing up this paradox, see Yakabuski 2009.

4 Polarization & Pluralism

[1] Bibby 1990:9.

[2] Bibby 1990:9.

[3] *Globe and Mail*, October 8, 2010. See also the *Globe and Mail* articles by Peritz and Friesen, 2010 and Friesen and Martin, 2010.

[4] McDonald 2010. The correlational data are from PC2005. For a very good response from the Conservative Protestant side, see Koop 2010.

[5] Bibby 1990:92.

[6] See, for example, de Souza, 2010.

[7] Martinuk 2011.

[8] Murphy 2009.

[9] Park and Burgess 1921.

[10] Bibby 1990:24.

[11] Bibby 1990:24.

[12] Bibby 1990:48.

[13] Bibby 1990:48.

[14] Cited in Bibby 1990:25-26; Palmer, 1988:1741.

[15] Cited in Bibby 1990:28; Palmer, 1988:1742.

[16] In contrast to the past; see Bibby 1990:32.

[17] Bibby 1990:19.

[18] Bibby 1990:19.

[19] Bibby 1990:21.

[20] Bibby 1990:20-21.

[21] Cited in Bibby 1990:54; Boyd 1984:1.

[22] Cited in Bibby 1990:50. Christiano 1990:19-20.

[23] Giuliano 2009: http://www.united-hurch.ca/communications/news/moderator/ 090130.

[24] Howard 2009: http://www.emergingspirit.ca/wondercafe joins the dialogue on atheist ads. Posted January 30.

[25] Quoted in Mackey 2009.

[26] Quoted in Morton 2009.

[27] Quoted in Mackey 2009.

[28] Drake 2010.

[29] Quoted in Chai 2010.

[30] Centre for Inquiry website, http://cficanada.ca, accessed December 5, 2010.

[31] Peters 2010.

[32] Allemang 2010.

[33] Chase, 2010.

[34] Quoted in Breen 2010.

[35] Hitchens 2007:153.

[36] Hitchens in Hart House, 2006.

[37] Breen 2010.

[38] Mackey 2009.

[39] The following summary draws on *The Catholic Herald* 2010.

[40] Flaccus 2010.

[41] D'Emilio 2010.

[42] Schmidt 2010.

[43] Baetz 2010.

[44] D'Emilio 2010.

[45] CBC 2010.

[46] Thanh Ha 2010.

[47] CCCB, 2010.

[48] For a succinct summary of the controversy and mixed reactions surrounding his visit, see Winfield 2010.

[49] Beckford 2010.

[50] This was my interpretation then and remains my take now; see Bibby, *Unknown Gods* 1993:68-75.

[51] Saad 2009.

[52] Gallup, April 9, 2009.

[53] Persichilli 2010.

[54] This item was taken from Glock and Stark's survey of church members in the San Francisco Bay area in the early 1960s. See Stark and Glock 1968:1-10.

[55] Grossman 2008.

[56] Bibby 2009:158.

[57] Valpy and Friesen 2010.

[58] PewCenter report on Islamic terrorism, August 14, 2005.

[59] The item wording: "If your party nominated a generally well-qualified man/person for president who happened to be....an atheist, would you vote for that person/him?"

[60] Jones 2007.

[61] Lewis 2010a..

[62] Reid 2010.

[63] Mani 2010.

[64] Lewis 2010b.

[65] See the website, www.charterforcompassion.org.

[66] Interview, *Bill Moyers Journal*, March 13, 2009.

[67] Blair in *Globe and Mail*, Geiger November 29, 2010.

[68] Valpy and Friesen 2010.

5 Polarization & Personal Well-Being

[1] Dawkins 2006:281, 308.

[2] Hitchens, 2007:13.

[3] Harris 2004:236, 79.

[4] An interview in Gruending 1996.

[5] Collins, 2010.

[6] Quoted in Wallace 2010.

[7] Helpful reviews of the first three are offered by Kolbert 2010. For a review of happiness research in economics through 2005, see Frey and Stuzer 2005. A journalist's comment on scientific efforts to explore joy is offered by Scrivener 2010b.

[8] Samuel 2009.

[9] Vandore 2008.

[10] See Castle 2010; also Watson and Coates 2010.

[11] Putnam and Lim 2010. For a brief synopsis, see the Harvard press release, Brockmeyer 2010. A good journalistic take on the study is offered by the *Globe and Mail*'s Sarah Hampson 2010. General information on social capital material is available at http:www.socialcapital. wordpress. com.

[12] Drawn from Southard 1961.

[13] Hampson 2010.

[14] For gender breakdowns, see Bibby 2009:70.

[15] See Bibby 2006:115.

[16] Bibby 2009:66.

[17] Bibby 2009:31.

[18] Newport 2007.

[19] Newport, Agrawal and Witters 2010.

[20] Miller 2000.

[21] Specific quotes from Miller 2000

[22] Stokes 2007.

[23] Pelham and Nyiri 2008.

[24] See, for example, Crabtree 2010:2.

[25] Stratton, 2010.

[26] Social Capital Blog, October 27, 2010.

6 Polarization & Spirituality

[1] Rolheiser 1999.

[2] Rolheiser 1999:6-7.

[3] Rolheiser 1999:7-11.

[4] Taken from the website, "SBNR.org", January 2, 2011.

[5] Taylor 2007:506.

[6] Roof 2001.

[7] Nouwen 1999, Tickle 2008, Young 2008, McLaren 2011. Explicit spirituality titles for the other religions mentioned can readily be found with a simple scan of sites such as Amazon or Chapters.

[8] *The Secret* Byrne 2006; Aboriginal, Friesen 2000; Celtic, Davies 2002; Mormon Davies 1987; Wicca Saunders 2002.

[9] *God Without God*, Hampson 2008; *Little Book* Comte-Sponville 2007; *Spirituality Without God*, de la Rouvière 2005; *The Christian Atheist*, Blake 2003; *The Homemade Atheist*, Brogaard 2010.

[10] http://www.ehow.com/how_4728678_be-spiritual-atheist.html.

[11] http://www.naturalism.org/spiritual.htm.

[12] http://centreculturelchretiendemontreal.org. See "program 2010, "The spiritual quest: with or without God."

[13] Rigler, 2008.

[14] Allemang 2010.

[15] Miller 2010.

[16] The sample was non-probability in nature and was selected using purposive and "geometric" sampling, through a wide-range of contacts throughout the province. With minor weighting, the sample is highly representative of Albertans with respect to age, gender, and religious identification.

[17] Roof 1999:91.

[18] Roof 1999:9.

[19] Wuthnow 2007:134.

[20] Smith 2009:

[21] Smith 2009:15. See, for example, Davie 2006, Gill 2004.

[22] Luckmann 1967.

[23] See, for example, Bailey 2006.

[24] The pearson correlation coefficient (r) is .418.

[25] Todd 2009a and 2010a. The quotes that follow are from Todd 2010a.

[26] See, for example, Todd 2008, 2009b, and 2010b; an example of an academic take on hockey is Sinclair-Faulkner 1977, American football French 2001.

[27] McCaig 2010.

[28] Cited in Cogley 1968:171.

[29] Crabtree and Pelham 2008.

7 Polarization & Social Well-Being

[1] Edge Conference 2010.

[2] http://www.edge.org/3rd_culture/morality10.

[3] Hauser 2006.

[4] An insightful interview with Hauser is found in Ross 2006.

[5] Quoted in Ross 2006.

[6] Website: http://moral.wjh.harvard.edu/index2.html.

[7] See, for example, Highfield 2010.

[8] *USA Today* August 20, 2010.

[9] Harris 2010. For two informative reviews, see Appiah 2010 in the *New York Times* and Horgan 2010 in the *Globe and Mail*.

[10] http://www.edge.org/3rd culture/morality10/morality.harris.html

[11] An excellent video of Harris' views on science and morality is available via YouTube – "Sam Harris: Science can answer moral questions," posted by Tedtalks. (www.ted.com).

[12] Adler 2006.

[13] For expositions of the emerging field, see, for example, Cacioppo et al. 2002 and Todorov, Fiske and Prentice 2011.

[14] Quoted in Babington and Superville 2010.

[15] Ferguson 2010.

[16] Wood 2010.

[17] None of the correlation coefficients for these values and adult age cohort even reach .100.

[18] For reasons explained in detail in Appendix A, my interest is in the cumulative effect of religion – including other related variables such as age, gender, family characteristics and so on. That is why I am using measures that examine correlations – rather than regression measures that explore the unique impact of a single variable, such as attendance, controlling for these other variables.

[19] This item appeared in both the teen and adult surveys in 2000; it did not appear in the Project Canada 2005 survey. That is why we do not have recent comparable adult data.

[20] A number of these same items were included in the 2000 national adult and youth surveys. For items and findings, see Bibby 2001, pp. 17 & 233.

[21] Smith and Stark 2004:4.

[22] Pelham and Crabtree 2008:3.

[23] Smith and Stark 2009:2.

[24] Mead 2010:3.

[25] Noll 2007:56.

[26] Goar 2006.

[27] Pennings and Van Pelt 2009. The entire policy paper, "A Canadian Culture of Generosity" is available via the Cardus website, www.cardus.ca/Generous Culture.
[28] Hall et al. 2009:6, 41. Frank Jones (2002) the 1997 and 2000 data sets, examines these correlations in considerable details, including looking at religious groups differences.
[29] *Maclean's* 2010.
[30] Harris, 2008:vii.
[31] Lewis 2007.

8 Polarization & Death

[1] Harpur 1991:16. See also his updated volume 2011.
[2] Coren 2005.
[3] Line from Randy Newman, "Old Man on the Farm," 1977; *Little Criminals* album, Warner Bros.
[4] Wente 2009.
[5] Freud 1927.
[6] Richler 2010:18.
[7] For expositions of the positions various religions take on life after death, see, for example, Harpur 1997 and 2011.
[8] Bibby 2002:133-136.
[9] The pearson correlation coefficient r's for the three religiosity measures and belief in life after death are .437, .316, and .664 respectively for adults, and .363, .311, and .612 for teenagers.
[10] The r's for belief in God and belief in life after death is .654 for adults and .440 for teens.
[11] The pearson correlation coefficient r's are as follows: heaven-hell .790; LAD heaven .728, LAD hell .657.
[12] Rigler 2008.
[13] Pausch 2008:191-192.
[14] Apostle Paul , Philippians 1.23-25.
[15] *Lethbridge Herald*, September 25 and following.
[16] World Values Survey 2000.
[17] The pearson r's: attendance and God .270, LAD .232, heaven .303; God and LAD .411, heaven .531; LAD and heaven .639.
[18] Freud 1957:89.
[19] Wente 2009.
[20] Stiller 2001.
[21] Kreeft 1990.

9 The Comeback

[1] Durkheim 1965:477-479.

[2] An earlier version of some of the following material appeared in my chapter in Hewitt 1993.

[3] See, for example, Sorokin 1957, Davis 1949, and Bell 1977.

[4] Davis 1949:542-544.

[5] Bell 1977.

[6] Rifkin 1980.

[7] See, for example, again Roozen et. al 1990, Brady 1991, Koop 1991.

[8] Naisbitt and Aburdene 1990.

[9] Durkheim 1965:477-479.

[10] Davis 1949.

[11] See, for example, de Souza 2010 re: the government's apparent commitment to secularism.

[12] Bagnell 2011.

[13] Harpur 1991:15.

[14] For some forthright thoughts about life after death from an Anglican priest, see Nicolosi 2010.

[15] Bagnell (2010) offers an excellent, brief overview of the United Church's numerical decline, its current resources problems, and hopes for the future.

[16] Butler Bass 2006:45; this is her central thesis.

[17] Harris 2009.

[18] Kelley, 1972.

[19] See, for example, Bibby and Brinkerhoff 1973 and Bibby 2003.

[20] See Bibby and Brinkerhoff 1973ff and Bibby 2003.

[21] For a helpful analysis of "Christian," see Clarke and Macdonald, 2007.

[22] Cox 2009:1.

[23] Yancey 2010:4.

[24] Reynolds 2011.

[25] See Mead 2010 and Reynolds 2010.

[26] Mead 2010:2.

[27] Mead 2010:2.

[28] Allen 2009:20.

[29] Thomas 2010:96.

[30] Mead 2010:2-3.

[31] Thomas 2010:94

[32] Thomas 2010:95.

[33] Thomas 2010:93.

[34] Thomas 2010:94-95.

[35] Thomas 2010:94.

[36] Allen 2009:3.

[37] Thomas 2010:95.

[38] Thomas 2010:101.

[39] Allen 2009:2.

[40] Allen 2009:2.

[41] Mead 2010:3.

[42] For research that includes examples of hybrid and non-hybrid possibilities and remains relevant see Brinkerhoff and Bibby 1985.

[43] Thomas 2010:95.

[44] Thomas 2010:95.

[45] Thomas 2010:95.

[46] Thomas 2010:95.

[47] Allen 2009:98.

[48] Thomas 2010:97.

[49] Thomas 2010:101.

Conclusion

[1] Levin 2010.

[2] Geertz 1968.

[3] Weber 1963.

[4] Taylor 2007:727.

[5] See, for example Wade 2009 and Tiger and McGuire 2010, and Brian Bethune's interview with Tiger in *Maclean's* 2010.

[6] Bibby 2002:165-182; Berger 1963.

[7] Micklethwait and Wooldridge 2009. For excellent informative and provocative reviews, see Goldstein 2009 and Rosin 2009.

[8] Yancey 2010:7.

[9] Thielike 1960.

[10] Thielike 1960.

[11] Psalm 23; combination of KJV and NRSV.

[12] Rolheiser 1990:241.

[13] For an account of the Olympic Stadium mass, see, for example, Sutherland 2010.

[14] Yakabuski 2009.

[15] Allen 2009:1.

[16] Milne 2010.

[17] Cox 1995:299.

[18] Cox 2009:19-20.

[19] Stark and Glock 1968:223-224.

[20] Cited in Stark and Glock 1968:224.

[21] Durkheim 1965:475.

[22] Bibby 1993:181.

References

Adler, Jerry. (2006). "The new naysayers." *Newsweek*, September 11. http://www.msnbc.msn.com/id/14638243/site/newsweek.

Allen, John L., Jr. (2009). *The future church*. New York: Doubleday.

Allemang, John. (2010, November 6). "A tournament of atheists, then and now." *Globe and Mail*.

Appiah, Kwame Anthony. (2010, October 1). "Science knows best." A review of Harris' *The Moral Landscape* in the *New York Times*.

Armstrong, Karen. (1994). *A history of God*. New York: Ballantine Books.

Armstrong, Karen. (2010a). *The case for God*. New York: Random House.

Armstrong, Karen. (2010b). *Twelve steps to a compassionate life*. New York: Random House.

Babington, Charles and Darlene Superville. (2010, September 28). "Obama opens up about his faith." Associated Press.

Baetz, Juergen. (2010, April 2). "Bishops condemn 'appalling crimes', call for urgent 'renewal.'" AP. *Globe and Mail*, April 2.

Bagnell, Kenneth. (2011). "Secular shift." *The United Church Observer*. January.

Bailey, Edward I. (2006). *Implicit religion in contemporary society*. Leuven: Peeters.

Barrett, David B., George T. Kurian, and Todd M. Johnson. (Eds.). (2001). *World Christian encyclopedia*. New York: Oxford University Press.

Baum, Gregory. (2000) "Catholicism and secularization in Quebec." In David Lyon and Marguerite Van Die. (Eds.). *Rethinking church, state and modernity*. Toronto: University of Toronto Press. Pp. 249-165.

Beaman, Lori G. (2008). *Defining harm: religious freedom and the limits of the law*. Vancouver: UBC Press.

Beckford, Martin. (2010, September 21). "Pope visit declared 'overwhelming success' by Lord Patten." *The Telegraph*.

Berard, John, James Penner, and Rick Bartlett. (2010). *Consuming youth: Leading teens through consumer culture*. Grand Rapids: Zondervan.

Berger, Peter L. (1961). *The Noise of Solemn Assemblies*. Garden City, NY: Doubleday.

Berger, Peter L. Berger. (1974). "Some Second Thoughts on Substantive Versus Functional Definitions of Religion." *Journal for the Scientific Study of Religion* 13:125-133.

Berger, Peter L. (Ed.). (1999). *The Desecularization of the world: Resurgent religion and world politics.* Washington: Ethics and Public Policy Center/Grand Rapids: Eerdmans.

Bethune, Brian. (2007: April 16). "Is God Poison?" *Maclean's*, 39-44.

Bethune, Brian. (2010: March 4). "Interview: Lionel Tiger." *Maclean's*

Beyer, Peter. (2006). *Religions in global society.* New York: Routledge.

Beyer, Peter and Lori Beaman. (Eds.). (2007). *Religion, globalization and culture.* Leiden: Brill.

Bibby, Reginald W. (1987). *Fragmented gods: The poverty and potential of religion in Canada.* Toronto: Irwin.

Bibby, Reginald W. (1990). *Mosaic madness: Pluralism without a cause.* Toronto: Stoddart.

Bibby, Reginald W. (1993). *Unknown gods: The ongoing story of religion in Canada.* Toronto: Stoddart.

Bibby, Reginald W. (1995). *The Bibby report: Social trends Canadian style.* Toronto: Stoddart.

Bibby, Reginald W. (2001). *Canada's teens: Today, yesterday, and tomorrow.* Toronto: Stoddart.

Bibby, Reginald W. (2002). *Restless gods: The renaissance of religion in Canada.* Toronto: Stoddart Softcover 2004, Ottawa:Novalis.

Bibby, Reginald W. (2004a). *Restless churches: How Canada's churches can contribute to the emerging religious renaissance.* Ottawa: Novalis.

Bibby, Reginald W. (2004b). *The future families project: A survey of Canadian hopes and dreams.* Ottawa: Vanier Institute of the Family.

Bibby, Reginald W. (2006a). *The boomer factor: What Canada's most famous generation is leaving behind.* Toronto: Bastian Books.

Bibby, Reginald W. (2006b). "Why bother with organized religion? The views of insiders, marginals, and outsiders." Presented at the annual meeting of the Pacific Sociological Association, Los Angeles, April.

Bibby, Reginald W. (2008). "The perils of pioneering and prophecy: A response to Thiessen and Dawson." *Studies in Religion* 37:417-425.

Bibby, Reginald W. (2009). *The emerging millennials: How Canada's newest generation is responding to change and choice.* Lethbridge: Project Canada Books.

Bibby, Reginald W. (2009). "Canada's data-less debate about religion: The precarious role of research in identifying implicit and explicit religion." *Implicit Religion* 12:251-270.

Bibby, Reginald W. and James Penner. (2009). *10 Things we all need to know about today's teens: That is, IF we care about them.* Lethbridge: Project Canada Books.

Bibby, Reginald W., Terri-Lynn Fox, and James Penner. (2010). *Canada's emerging Aboriginal millennials: A national survey reading of Aboriginal teens & other teens.* Lethbridge: Project Canada Books.

Blake, John. (2010). "Are there dangers in being 'spiritual but not religious'?" *CNN Living*, June 3.

Blake, Robert R. (2003). *The Christian Atheist.* Bloomington, IN: AuthorHouse.

Bowen, Kurt. (2004). *Christians in a secular world: The Canadian experience.* Montreal: McGill-Queen's University Press.

Bramadat, Paul and David Seljak. (Eds.). 2008. *Christianity and ethnicity in Canada.* Toronto: University of Toronto Press.

Bramadat, Paul and David Seljak. (Eds.). 2009. *Religion and ethnicity in Canada.* Toronto: University of Toronto Press.

Breen, Joseph. (2010). "Hitchens, Dawkins try for Pope's arrest during U.K. visit." *National Post*, April 12.

Brierley, Peter. (2006). *Pulling Out of the Nosedive: A contemporary picture of churchgoing.* London: Christian Outreach.

Brinerhoff, Merlin B. and Reginald W. Bibby. (1985). "Circulation of the saints in South America." *Journal for the Scientific Study of Religion* 24:253-262.

Brockmeyer, Meghan M. (2010, December 15). "Religious networks promote happiness." *The Harvard Crimson.*

Brogaard, Betty. (2010). *The homemade atheist: A former evangelical woman's freethought journey to happiness.* Berkeley: Ulysses Press.

Brown, Callum. (2009). *The death of Christian Britain: Understanding secularisation, 1800-2000.* London: Routledge.

Bruce, Steve. (2002). *God is Dead: Secularization in the West.* Oxford: Blackwell.

Bruce, Steve. (2011). *Secularization: In defense of an unfashionable theory.* Oxford: Oxford University Press.

Butler Bass, Diana. (2006). *Christianity for the rest of us.* New York: HarperOne.

Byrne, Rhonda. (2007). *The secret*. New York: Atria Books.

Cacioppo, John T. et al. (Eds.). (2002). *Foundations in social neuroscience*. Cambridge, MA: MIT Press.

CBC. (2010). "Clergy must report sex abuse: Vatican." April 12. http://www.cbc.ca/world/story/2010/04/12/vatican-abuse-guidelines.html.

Canadian Conference of Catholic Bishops. (2010, April 9). "Statement by the Canadian Conference of Catholic Bishops in response to an article published on 9 April 2010 by the *Globe and Mail*." http://www.cccb.ca/site/eng/media-room.

Castle, Tim. (2010, , November 25.). "U.K. to measure happiness alongside GDP." *Globe and Mail*

Chase, Steven. (2010, March 23). "Ann Coulter's speech in Ottawa cancelled." *Globe and Mail*.

Chai, Carmen. (2010, December 1). "Atheist group hopes its ads spark debate." *National Post*.

Church and Faith Trends. (2008). "What happened to Christian Canada?" A panel response to Mark Noll with a reply by Noll. October, Volume 2, Issue 1.

Clarke, Brian and Stuart Macdonald. (2007). "Simply Christian: Canada's newest major religious denomination." *Toronto Journal of Theology* 23:109-126.

Clifton, Jim. (2010). *"Global migration patterns and job creation."* Washington: Gallup.

Cogley, John. (1968). *Religion in a secular age*. New York: New American Library.

Collins, Archbishop Thomas. (2010). Easter Sunday homily. Podcast. Toronto: Roman Catholic Archdiocese.

Comte-Sponville. (2007). *The little book of atheist spirituality*. New York: Viking.

Coren, Michael. (2005, April 1). "Dignity in death comes with confidence in God." *Presbyterian Record*.

Coward, Harold and Kelly Stajduhar (Eds,). (2011). *Religious understandings of a 'good death' in hospice palliative care* Albany: NY, SUNY Press.

Cox, Harvey. (1995). *Fire from heaven: The rise of Pentecostal spirituality and the reshaping of religion in the twenty-first century*. Reading, MA: Perseus Books.

Cox, Harvey. (2009). *The future of faith*. New York: HarperOne.

Crabtree, Steve and Prett Pelham. (2008, December 24). "The complex relationship between religion and purpose." Washington, DC: Gallup.

Crabtree, Steve. (2010, August 31). "Religiosity highest in world's poorest nations." Washington, DC: Gallup.

Crabtree, Steve and Prett Pelham. (2009 February 9). "What Alabamians and Iranians have in common." Washington, DC: Gallup,.

Davie, Grace. (1994). *Religion in Britain since 1945*. Oxford: Blackwell.

Davies, Douglas James. (1987). *Mormon spirituality: Latter Day Saints in Wales and Zion*. Nottingham: University of Nottingham.

Davies, O. (2002). *Celtic spirituality*. Ottawa: Novalis.

Dawkins, Richard. (2006). *The God Delusion*. New York: Houghton Mifflin.

Dawson, Lorne. (2004). *Religion online: Finding faith on the Internet*. London: Routledge.

Dawson, Lorne L. (2006). *Comprehending cults: The sociology of new religious movements*. Second edition. Toronto: Oxford University Press.

Deaton, Angus. (2008, February 27). "Worldwide, residents of richer nations more satisfied." Washington, DC: Gallup.

de la Rouvière, Möller. (2005). *Spirituality Without God*. Tamarac, FL: Llumina Press.

D'Emilio, Frances. (2010, April 2). "Pope's preacher likens sex-abuse allegations to violence against Jews." AP. *Globe and Mail*.

de Souza, Father Raymond J .(2010, December 30). "Quebec worships the idol of secularism." *National Post*.

Dentsu Communications Institute. (2006). Research Center.

Dobbelaere, Karel. (1981) "Secularization: A Multi-Dimensional Concept." *Current Sociology* 19:201-216.

Dobbelaere, Karel. (2002). *Secularization: An Analysis at Three Levels*." Oxford: Oxford University Press.

Drake, Tim. (2010). "The war over Christmas is in full swing." *National Catholic Register*, December 2, 2010.

Dueck, Lorna. (2010). "Blair v. Hitchens: What you believe to be true matters." *Globe and Mail*, November 25.

Durkheim, Emile. (1965). *The Elementary Forms of the Religious Life*. New York: The Free Press. Originally published in 1912.

Edge (2010). *The New Science of Morality*. An Edge Conference. http://www.edge.org/3rd_culture/morality10/morality10_index.html.

Epstein, Greg. (2010). *Good without God: What a billion nonreligious people do believe*. New York: Harper.

Feierman, Jay R. (2009). (Ed.). *The biology of religioius behavior: The evolutionary origins of faith and religion*. New York: Praeger.

Ferguson, Eva. (2010, January 24). "Online program pushed to bring respect to the rink." *Calgary Herald*.

Finke, Roger L. and Rodney Stark. (1992). *The Churching of America, 1776-1990*. New Brunswick, NJ: Rutgers University Press.

Flaccus, Gillian. (2010, April 9). "Letter shows future Pope Benedict resisted defrocking molester priest." AP. *Globe and Mail*.

Foote, David. (1996). *Boom, bust, & echo*. Toronto: Macfarlane, Walter, and Ross.

French, Hal W. (2001). "Religion and football." In Edward I. Bailey (ed.). *The secular quest for meaning in life: Denton papers in implicit religion*. Lampeter, Wales: Edwin Mellen Press.

Freud, Sigmund. (1957). *The future of an illusion*. Garden City, NY: Doubleday. Originally published in 1927.

Frey, Bruno S. and Alois Stuzer. (2005). Happiness research: State and prospects. *Review of Social Economy*, June.

Friesen, Joe and Sandra Martin. (2010 October 5). "Canada's changing faith." *Globe and Mail*.

Friesen, John W. (2000). *Aboriginal spirituality and Biblical theology: Closer than you think*. Calgary: Detselig Enterprises.

Friesen, Milton. (2011 January 21). Review of Elaine Howard Ecklund's What scientists really think. *Comment*.

Gallup, Inc. (2009). *The Gallup Coexist Index 2009: A Global study of interfaith relations*. Washington, DC: Gallup.

Gallup, Inc. (2010). *Gallup Global Wellbeing: The Behavioral economics of GDP growth*. Washington, DC: Gallup.

Giuliano, The Very Rev. David. (2010)"WonderCafe Joins the Dialogue on Atheist Ad Campaign." http://www.united-church.ca/communications/news/moderator/090130.

Globe and Mail. (2010, June 17.). Editorial. "For the killers of Aqsa Parvez, 'culture' is no defence."

Globe and Mail. (2010, October 8.). Editorial. "Strike multiculturalism from the national vocabulary."

Globe and Mail. (2010, November 29). "Interview: Tony Blair, on his faith and religious ideology." Interview with John Geiger.

Globe and Mail. (2010, November 29). "Interview: Christopher Hitchens, on not believing. Interview with John Geiger.

Globe and Mail. (2010, December 11). "The state of religion in Canada today: By the numbers."

Globe and Mail. (2010), December 13. "Faith Exchange: The future of religion in Canada."

Goar, Carol. (2006, May 5). "Loss of faith imperils charities." *Toronto Star*.

Goldstein, Yoni. (2009, May 4). The return of God." *National Post*.

Grant, George Webster. (1988). *The church in the Canadian era.* Expanded edition. Burlington, ON: Welch.

Gregg, Allan. (2005). "The Christian Comeback." *Saturday Night*, November: 21-22.

Grossman, Cathy Lynn. (2008, January 9). "Survey: Non-attendees find faith outside church." *USA Today*.

Gruending, Dennis. (1996). *Revival: Canada's Christian churches.* Video. Ottawa: Carleton University.

Habermas, Jurgen. (2010). *An awareness of what is missing: Faith and reason in a post-secular age.* Cambridge: Polity Books.

Hall, Douglas John. (1989). *The future of the church.* Toronto: United Church Publishing House.

Hall, Michael, David Lasby, Steven Ayer, and William David Gibbons. (2009). *Caring Canadians, involved Canadians: Highlights from the 2007 Canada survey of giving, volunteering and participating.* Catalogue no. 71-542-XPE. Ottawa: Statistics Canada.

Hampson, Michael. (2008). *God without God: Western spirituality without the wrathful king.* Berkeley: O Books/Small Press Distribution.

Hampson, Sara. (2010, December 13). "Happiness and the God spot." *Globe and Mail*.

Harpur, Tom. (1991). *Life after death.* Toronto: McClelland and Stewart.

Harpur, Tom. (2011). *There is life after death.* Toronto: Thomas Allen.

Harris, David. (2009, October 1). "Start something unthinkable: The church needs to be flexible." *Presbyterian Record*.

Harris, Sam. (2004). *The end of faith: Religion, terror, and the future of reason.* New York: Norton.

Harris, Sam. (2006). *Letter to a Christian Nation.* New York: Knopf. Vintage Book edition 2008.

Harris, Sam (2010). *The moral landscape: How science can determine human values.* New York: Free Press

Hart House. (2006). Video. Christopher Hitchens on Free Speech and Freedom of Expression. A debate at Hart House, University of Toronto. http://video.google.com/videoplay?

Harvey, Bob. 2000. *The future of religion: Interviews with Christians on the brink.* Ottawa: Novalis.

Hauser, Marc. (2006). *Moral Minds: How nature designed our universal sense of right and wrong.* New York: Harper Collins.

Hewitt, W.E. (1993). (Ed.). *The sociology of religion: A Canadian focus.* Toronto: Butterworths.

Higgins, Michael W. and Douglas R. Letson. (2002). *Power and peril: The Catholic Church at the crossroads.* Toronto: Harper Collins.

Highfield, Roger. (2010, August 31). "Marc Hauser: Monkeying with the truth." *The Telegraph.*

Hiller, Harry H. (1976a). "The sociology of religion in the Canadian context." In G.N. Ramu and Stuart D. Johnson (eds.). *Introduction to Canadian Society.* Toronto: Macmillan, 349-400.

Hiller, Harry H. (1976b). "Alberta and the Bible belt stereotype." In Stewart Crysdale and Les Wheatcroft (eds.). *Religion in Canadian society.* Pp. 372-383. Toronto: Macmillan.

Hitchens, Chrisopher. *God is not great.* Toronto: Emblem.

Horgan, John. (2010, October 9). "The acid test for doing the right thing." A review of Harris' *The Moral Landscape* in the *Globe and Mail.*

Ingleheart, Ronald. (2004). "Subjective well-being rankings of 82 societies." A summary of World Values Survey data on happiness and life satisfaction scores. WVS publication #488. http://www.worldvaluessurvey.org/wvs/articles/folderpublished/publication_488.

Johnson, Susan. (2009). "Financial reality check." *Canada Lutheran,* March.

Jones, Jeffrey M. (2007, February 20). "Some Americans reluctant to vote for Mormon, 72-year old Presidential candidates." Washington, DC: Gallup News Service.

Jones, Frank. (2002). "How is volunteering associated with religious commitment?" Religious Commitment Report 02-09. Ottawa: The Christian Commitment Research Institute.

Jones, Tony and Phyllis Tickle. (2005). *The sacred way: Spiritual practices for everyday life.* Grand Rapids: Zondervan.

Kelley, Dean. (1972). *Why conservative churches are growing.* New York: Harper and Row.

Kolb, Bryan and Ian Q. Whishsaw. (2009*). Fundamentals of human neuropsychology.* New York: Worth.

Kolbert, Elizabeth. (2010, March 22). "Everybody have fun." *The New Yorker,*

Koop, Doug. (2010, June 18). "A shiver runs through it: The Armageddon Factor misconstrues a subculture." *Christian Week.* June 18.

Kouwenberg, Hans. (2010, December 1). "A shift in the wind: Where is the Life and Mission Agency taking us?" *Presbyterian Record.*

Kreeft, Peter. (1990). Everything you ever wanted to know about heaven. San Francisco: Ignatius Press.

Leger Marketing. (2007, May 15). "Profession Barometer." OmniCan Report.

Levin, Martin. (2010, February 20). "Atheist with a soul." *Globe and Mail.*

Lewis, Charles. (2007, October 11). "Social virtues linked to faith." *The National Post.*

Lewis, Charles. (2010a, December 5). "Dear atheists: most of us don't care what you think." *National Post.* HolyPost.

Lewis, Charles. (2010b, December 16). "Dear atheists: can't we all just get along or whatever?" *National Post.* HolyPost.

Lim, Chaeyoon and Robert D. Putnam. (2010). "Religion, social networks, and life satisfaction." *American Sociological Review,* December 75:914-933.

Lyon, David and Marguerite Van Die. (Eds.). (2000). *Rethinking church, state and modernity.* Toronto: University of Toronto Press.

Luckmann, Thomas. (1967). *The invisible religion.* New York: Macmillan.

Mackey, Lloyd. (2009, February). "Canadian Christians welcome atheist 'competition' on buses. *Canadian Chrisitianity.com.*

Maclean's.ca. (2010, May 6). "Do atheists care less?" http://www2.macleans.ca/2010/05/06/do-atheists-care-less.

Mahoney, Jill (2010, November 26). "Blair v. Hitchens: Is religion a force for good or ill?" *Globe and Mail*

Manji, Irshad. (2010, December 10). "Elevating the God discussion." *Globe and Mail.*

Martin, David. (2000). "Canada in comparative perspective" In David Lyon and Marguerite Van Die. (Eds.). *Rethinking church, state and modernity*. Toronto: University of Toronto Press. Pp. 23-33.

Martinuk, Susan. (2011, January 14). "Told you gay rights would trump religion." *Calgary Herald*.

McCaig, Sam. (2010, February 6). "Death of Brian Burke's son reinforces what's really important." *The Hockey News*: Sam McCaig's Blog: THN.com.

McDonald, Marci. (2010). *The Armageddon factor: The rise of Christian nationalism in Canada*. Toronto: Random House.

McLaren, Brian D. (2011). *Naked Spirituality: A life with God in 12 simple words*. New York: HarperOne.

Mead, Walter Russell. (2010, May 28). "Pentecostal power." A blog in *The American Interest*.

Micklethwait, John and Adrian Wooldridge. (2009). *God Is Back: How the Global Revival of Faith Is Changing the World*. New York: Penguin Press.

Miller, Geoffrey. (2000). "Social policy implications of the new happiness research." The Third Culture. http://www.edge.org/l 3rd_culture/story/86.html .

Miller, Lisa. (2010, October 18). "Sam Harris believes in God." *Newsweek*.

Milne, Mike. (2010, September). "General Council lays off 16 staff: Youth and young adults portfolio is among the positions cut." *United Church Observer*.

Morton, Graeme. (2009, January 28). "Calgary next for atheist bus ads, activist group says." *Calgary Herald*.

Murphy, Rex. (2009, November 6). "Crucifix out, warming in." *Globe and Mail*.

Naisbitt, John. (1982). *Megatrends*. New York: Warner Books.

Naisbitt, John and Patricia Aburdene. (1991). *Megatrends 2000*. New York Avon Books.

Nason-Clark, Nancy and Catherine Clark Kroeger. (2006). *Refuge from abuse: Healing and hope for abused Christian women*. Downers Grove, IL: InterVarsity Press.

Newport, Frank. (2007, April 6). "Just why do Americans attend church?" Washington, DC: Gallup.

Newport, Frank, Sangeeta Agrawal, and Dan Witters. (2010, October 28). "Religious Americans enjoy higher wellbeing." Washington, DC: Gallup.

Nicolosi, Gary. (2010, November 1). "Guest reflection: What happens when we die?" *AnglicanJournal.Com.*

Nielsen Survey Report. (2009, December 16). "Special Nielsen poll: Faith in Australia 2009." Sydney: Nielsen.

Noll, Mark A. (2007). *What happened to Christian Canada?* Vancouver: Regent College Publishing. Originally published in *Church History* 75, June 2006:245-273.

Nouwen, Henri J.M. (1998). *Reaching out.* Grand Rapids: Zondervan.

Organisation for Economic Co-operation and Development "Development aid rose in 2009 and most donors will meet 2010 aid targets." Table 1. http://www.oecd.org.

Overholt, L. David and James A. Penner. (2005). *Soul searching the millennial generation.* Ottawa: Novalis.

Park, Robert Ezra and Ernest W, Burgess. (1966). *Introduction to the science of sociology.* Third edition. Chicago: University of Chicago Press. First published in 1921.

Pausch, Randy (2008). *The last lecture.* New York: Hyperion.

Pelham, Brett and Zsolt Nyiri (2008, July 3). "In more religious countries, lower suicide rates." Washington, DC: Gallup.

Pennings, Ray and Michael Van Pelt. (2009). "The Canadian culture of generosity." *Policy in Public*, Winter. http://www.cardus.ca/policy/article/2155.

Peritz, Ingrid. (2010, December 14). "As churches crumble, communities fear loss of heritage." *Globe and Mail.*

Peritz, Ingrid and Joe Friesen (2010, October 1). "When multiculturalism doesn't work." *Globe and Mail.*

Persichilli, Angelo. (2010, April 4). "Resilient church will overcome latest scandal." *Toronto Star.*

Peters, Ted. (2010). "Evangelical atheism today: A response to Richard Dawkins." Counterbalance. http://www.counterbalance.org/bio/ted-frame.html

Pew Research Center. (2004, May 13). "Global gender gaps." Pew Global Attitudes Project. http://pewglobal.org/2004/05/13.

Pew Research Center. (2005, July 14). "Islamic extremism: Common concern for Muslim and Western publics." Pew Global Attitudes Project. http://pewglobal.org/2005/07/14.

Pew Forum on Religion and Public Life. (2006). "Spirit and power: A 10-country survey of Pentecostals." October 5. http://pewforum.org/Christian/Evangelical-Protestant-Churches/Spirit-and-Power.aspx.

Pew Research Center. (2007). "A rising tide lifts mood in the developing world." Pew Global Attitudes Project. July 24. http://pewglobal.org/2007/07/24.

Pew Forum on Religion and Public Life. (2009, December 10). "Many Americans not dogmatic about religion." http://pewresearch.org/pubs/1434/multiple-religious practices-reincarnation-astrology-psychic.

Posterksi, Donald C. and Irwin Barker. (1993). *Where's a good church?* Winfield, BC: Wood Lake Books.

Pyles, Franklin. (2003). "Cathedrals of the new century." *Christian Week* Spring 1-2.

Redfield, James. (1993). *The celestine prophecy.* New York: Warner Books.

Reid, Gary. (2010, December 17). "A secularist responds to Charles Lewis." *National Post.* Holy Post.

Reimer, Sam. (2003). *Evangelicals and the continental divide.* Montreal: McGill-Queen's University Press.

Reynolds, Neil. (2011, Janaury 10). "The globalization of God in the 21st century." *Globe and Mail.*

Richler, Noah. (2010, December 27). "Author Christopher Hitchens in conversation with Noah Richler. *Maclean's,* 16-18.

Rigler, Sara Yocheved. (2008). "Spirituality without God." November. http://www.aish.com/sp/ph/48962441.html.

Rolheiser, Ron. (1999). *The holy longing: The search for a Christian spirituality.* New York: Doubleday.

Roof, Wade Clark. (1999). *Spiritual marketplace: Baby boomers and the remaking of American religion.* Princeton, NJ: Princeton University Press.

Rosin, Hanna. (2009, April 24). "Religious revival." A review of Micklethwait and Wooldridge's book, "God is Back." *New York Times.*

Ross, Greg. (2006). "An interview with Marc Hauser." *American Scientist.* http://www.americanscientist.org/bookshelf/pub/marc-hauser.

Saad, Lydia. (2009, April 9). "Churchgoing among U.S. Catholics slides to tie Protestants." Washington, DC: Gallup Poll.

Samuel, Henry. (2009, September 14). "Nicolas Sarkozy wants to measure economic success in 'happiness'." *The Telegraph.*

Sartison, Telmor. (1998). *The voice of one: A continuing journey in faith.* Winnipeg: Evangelical Lutheran church in Canada.

Saunders, Kevin. (2002). *Wiccan Spirituality*. Somerset, UK: Green Magic Publishing.

Schmidt, Ted. (2010). April 4. "The Roman Catholic tragedy." *Toronto Star*.

Scrivener, Leslie. (2010a, November 27). "Feisty chat for Blair, Hitchens." *Toronto Star*.

Scrivener, Leslie. (2010b, December 20). "Blindfolded by science." *Toronto Star*.

Shantz, Douglas H. (2009, March 16). "The place of religion in a secular age: Charles Taylor's explanation of the rise and significance of secularism in the west." *The Iwaasa Lecture on Urban Theology*, Foothill Alliance Church, Calgary.

Shepherd, Harvey. (2010,October 26). "Lutheran and Anglican bishops brainstorm solutions to common problems." *AnglicanJournal.Com*.

Sinclair, Donna and Christopher White. (2003). *Emmaus Road: Churches making their way forward*. Kelowna: Wood Lake Books.

Sinclair-Faulkner, Tom. (1977). "A puckish look at hockey in Canada." In Peter Slater (ed.). *Religion and culture in Canada*. Toronto: Canadian Corporation for Studies in Religion, 383-405.

Smith, Buster G. and Rodney Stark. (2009, September 4). "Religious attendance relates to generosity worldwide." Washington, DC: Gallup.

Smith, Tom W. (2009). *Religious change around the world*. Report prepared for the Templeton Foundation. http://news.uchicago.edu/files/religionsurvey_20091023.pdf.

Social Capital Blog. (2010, October 27). "Summary of recent happiness research." http://socialcapital.wordpress.com.

Southard, Samuel. (1961). *Pastoral Evangelism*. Nashville: Abingdon.

Stackhouse, John G. Jr. (1998). *Canadian evangelicalism in the twentieth century: An introduction to its character*. Vancouver: Regent College Publishing.

Stark, Rodney. (1999). "Secularization, R.I.P." *Sociology of Religion* 60:249-273.

Stark, Rodney. (2007). *Discovering God: The origins of the great religions and the evolution of belief*. New York: HarperOne.

Stark, Rodney and William Sims Bainbridge. (1985). *The Future of religion*. Berkeley: University of California Press.

Stark, Rodney and Charles Y. Glock. (1968). *American piety*. Berkeley: University of California Press.

Stark, Rodney and Roger Finke. (2000). *Acts of faith: Explaining the human side of religion*. Berkeley: University of California Press.

Steinfels, Peter. (2009, October 24). "Globally, religion defies easily identified patterns." *New York Times*.

Stiller, Brian C. (2001). *What happens when I die?* Toronto HarperCollins.

Stokes, Bruce. (2007). "Happiness is increasing in many countries – but why?" Pew Global Attitudes Project, July 24. http://pewglobal.org/ 2007/07/24/happiness-is-increasing-in-many- countries-but-why.

Stratton. Allegra. (2010, November 14). "Happiness index to gauge Britain's national mood." *The Guardian*.

Stueck, Wendy. (2010, December 13). "'Highway to heaven's many paths to salvation." *Globe and Mail*.

Sumner, Geroge. (2010, September 27). "Guest opinion: Thoughts on the quiet crisis." *AnglicanJournal.Com*.

Sutherland, Anne. (2010, October 30). "Quebecers celebrate St. Brother Andre." *The National Post*. Holy Post.

Swenson, Donald S. (2009). *Society, spirituality, and the sacred*. Second edition. Toronto: University of Toronto Press.

Taylor, Charles. (2007). *The secular age*. New York: Belknap Press.

Thanh Ha, Tu. (2010, April 9). "Vatican, Canadian church officials tried to keep sex scandal secret." *Globe and Mail*.

The Catholic Herald. (2010, April 2). "The Pope and the abuse scandal: A guide for perplexed Catholics."

Thiessen, Joel and Lorne L. Dawson. (2008). "Is there a 'renaissance' of religion in Canada? A critical look at Bibby and beyond." *Studies in Religion* 37:389-415.

Thomas, Scott M. (2010). "A globalized god." Foreign Affairs, November/December 89:93-101.

Tiger, Lionel and Michael McGuire. (2010). *God's Brain*. New York: Promotheus Books.

Tickle, Phyllis. (2008). *The great emergence: How Christianity is changing and why*. Ada, MI: Baker Books.

Todd, Douglas. (1994). *The soul-searchers guide to the galaxy*. Vancouver: Self-Counsel Press.

Todd, Douglas. (1996). *Brave souls*. Toronto: Stoddart.

Todd, Douglas. (2008, December 22). "Are Trevor Linden and Mats Sundin bigger than Jesus?" *Vancouver Sun*.

Todd, Douglas. (2009a, January 2). "Five spiritual trends to watch for in 2009." *Vancouver Sun*.

Todd, Douglas. (2009b). "Hallelulah! Canucks unite British Columbians with religious zeal." *Vancouver Sun*, April 14.

Todd, Douglas. (2010a). "Five spiritual trends for '10s." *Vancouver Sun*, January 9.

Todd, Douglas. (2010b). "The new US cliché: Hockey is Canada's 'religion'." *Vancouver Sun*, March 1.

Todorov, Alexander, Susan T. Fiske, Deborah Prentice (Eds.) (2011). *Social neuroscience: Toward understanding the underpinnings of the social mind*. New York: Oxford.

United Nations. (2009). *Human Development Report 2009 –HDI rankings*. http://hdr.undp.org/en/media/HDR_2009_EN_HDI.pdf.

United Nations Office on Drugs and Crime. (2010). "Global homicide rates stable or decreasing, new UNODC report says." February 16. Homicide Statistics.

USA Today. (2010, August 20). "Updated: Harvard says Marc Hauser guilty of science misconduct."

Valpy, Michael. (2010, December 15). "Young Canadians increasingly shunning religious institutions." *Globe and Mail*.

Valpy, Michael and Joe Friesen. (2010, December 11). "Canada marching from religion to secularization." *Globe and Mail*.

Vandore, Emma. (2008, April 2). "French use happiness as economic measure." AP. *USA Today*.

von Heyking, John. (2010). "The persistence of civil religion in modern Canada." 2010 Hill Lecture. *Policy in Public*, fall. www.cardus.ca/policy/article/2273.

Vosper, Gretta. (2008). *With or without God*. Toronto: Harper Collins

Wade, Nicholas. (2009). *The faith instinct*. New York: Penguin.

Wallace, Kenyon. (2010, November 28). "Q & A: Canada leads in happiness research." A discussion with Chris Barrington-Leigh." *The National Post*.

Watson, Roland and Sam Coates. (2010, November 25). "Happiness" index to be compiled by Office for National Statistics." *The Times*.

Wente, Margaret. (2009, December 18). "When in doubt: an atheist's Christmas." *Globe and Mail*.

Wente, Margaret. (2010, June 17). "The immigration debate we don't want to have." *Globe and Mail*.

Wike, Richard and Kathleen Holzwart. (2008). "Where trust is high, crime and corruption are low." Pew Global Attitudes Project, April15. http://pewresearch.org/pubs/799/global-social-trust-crime-corruption.

Wilkinson, Michael. (Ed.). (2009). *Canadian Pentecostalism: Transition and Transformation*. Montreal: Institute for Research on Public Policy.

Williams, Leigh Anne. (2010a, November 21). "Council of General Synod approves balanced budget for 2010 – but treasurer warns of difficulty years ahead." *AnglicanJournal.Com*.

Williams, Leigh Anne. (20101b, November 22). "Council of General Synod backs nationwide fundraising initiative." *AnglicanJournal.Com*.

Wilson, Bryan. (1966). *Religion in Secular Society*. London: CA Watts.

Wilson, Bryan (1982). *Religion in Sociological Perspective*. Oxford: Oxford University Press.

Winfield, Nicole. (2010, September 16). "Pope acknowledges church failures in abuse scandal at start of U.K. visit." AP. *Globe and Mail*.

Winseman, Albert L. (2002). "How to measure spiritual commitment." Washington, DC: Gallup.

Wood, Michael. (2010, October 24). "Hockey Calgary scores win over disrespect." *Calgary Sun*.

Wright, Richard. (2009, November). "The fence-sitters: How real is the hope?" *United Church Observer*.

Wuthnow, Robert. (2007). *After the baby boomers: How twenty-and thirty-somethings are shaping the future of American religion.* Princeton, NJ: Princeton University Press.

Yakabuski, Konrad. (2009, August 14). "Neither practising nor believing, but Catholic even so." *Globe and Mail*.

Yancey, Philip. (2010). *What good is God?* New York: FaithWords/Hatchett Book Group.

Young, William Paul. (2008). *The shack*. Newbury Park: CA, Windblown Media.

Index

Buddhism
    growth in, 6, 131
    helping behaviours and, 156
Burgess, Ernest, 63
Burke, Brendan, 134
Burke, Brian, 134

C

Cameron, David, 101
Cameron, James, 132
Campbell, Kim, 67
Canada
    belief in reincarnation, 181
    belief in soul, 183
    helping behaviour in, 155
    largest religious groups in,
    200
    more religious than U.S., 13
    thoughts about death in, 179
    trust & crime rates in, 158,
    159
Canadian Centre of Behavioural
    Neuroscience, 217
Canadian Council of Catholic
    Bishops, 81
Canadian Secular Alliance, 96
Cardus, 161
Catholic Church, Roman. *See*
    Catholicism; Catholicism in
    Quebec
Catholicism
    abuse scandals, 79-83
    arrival of Irish Catholics, 7
    attacks against, 75
    attendance changes, 4, 5-6, 10,
    11, 16, 19, 28-29, 36-37
    beliefs, 54, 55, 176-78
    civility/compassion and, 154
    durability, 41
    end of deference to
    Church 19-25
    future of, 193, 194-95, 201,
    212-13
    growth in global South, 202-04
    historical place in Canadian
    life, 5, 8-12, 39
    identification re, 32-33, 39,

47, 48
    immigration and, 14, 30-32,
    194
    importance of rites of passage,
    212
    receptivity of youth, 212
    what faith adds, 108
    See also Catholicism in
    Quebec; Charismatic
    Movement
Catholicism in Quebec
    beliefs, 54, 176-78
    changes, 5, 10, 11, 19,22, 28,
    29, 37, 54, 55, 61
    Boomer impact on, 17
    changes in, 13, 15, 32-33, 36
    future of, 193, 194-95, 212-13
    history of, 7, 12
    identification and, 53, 61
    secularization and, 5-6
Cavanaugh, Perry, 143
Centre for Inquiry, 73-74
Centre of Naturalism, 121
charismatic movement, 188, 203
charitable sector, 161-62
Charter of Compassion, 97
China
    Christianity and neo-
    Confucianism, 204-5
    Muslims in, 205
Chi Tzi movement, 131
Christian and Missionary Alliance
    198
Christian Cultural Center of
    Montreal, 121
Christianity
    beliefs of, 208
    in China, 204-5
    early monopoly by, 8
    Golden Rule and, 97
    growth of, 202-5
    legacy of, 161, 189-90
    See also specific faiths
Christian Reformed, 198
Christian unspecified, 47, 198,
    200